Fictional Space
in the Modernist and
Postmodernist
American Novel

Fictional Space in the Modernist and Postmodernist American Novel

Carl Darryl Malmgren

Lewisburg
Bucknell University Press
London and Toronto: Associated University Presses

Associated University Presses
440 Forsgate Drive
Cranbury, NJ 08512

Associated University Presses
25 Sicilian Avenue
London WC1A 2QH, England

Associated University Presses
2133 Royal Windsor Drive
Unit 1
Mississauga, Ontario
Canada L5J 1K5

Library of Congress Cataloging in Publication Data

Malmgren, Carl Darryl, 1948–
    Fictional space in the modernist and postmodernist
American novel.

    Bibliography: p.
    Includes index.
    1. American fiction—20th century—History and
criticism.   2. Fiction.   3. Semiotics and literature.
I. Title.
PS379.M29   1985   813'.5'09   83-73236
ISBN 0-8387-5067-2

Printed in the United States of America

Contents

Fictional Space
in the Modernist and
Postmodernist
American Novel

Acknowledgments

In writing this manuscript I have benefited from the insights and assistance of many. I would first like to thank Mas'ud Zavarzadeh, who encouraged me to undertake a project of this scope and helped to draft the shape of the study. I am also grateful to William Strange, Don Taylor, Anthony Franzese, Susan Hawkins, Terry Ross, David Lodge, J. Hillis Miller, and especially Raymond Federman for their written definitions of "fictional space." Conversations with Loren Minnick and Tom Vishanoff helped me to sharpen my ideas and approach. And I would like to thank Clark Griffith, Francoise Calin, Kingsley Weatherhead, and Joseph Hynes for the close reading they gave the manuscript and for their feedback on matters of tone and style.

Portions of chapters 2 and 3 appeared in slightly revised form in *The Henry James Review* and *The Review of Contemporary Fiction*. I wish to express my gratitude to the editors of these journals for permission to reprint these materials. The lines of poetry from Nabokov's *Pale Fire* are reprinted by permission of G. P. Putnam's Sons from *Pale Fire* by Vladimir Nabokov, copyright © 1962 by G. P. Putnam's Sons. Katharine Turok and Beth Gianfagna at Associated University Presses helped me immensely with the editing process, and Donna Balderstone and Julia Anderson patiently and accurately typed different versions of the book.

Finally I would like to thank my wife Kristin for her logistical help and moral support. And I would like to dedicate the book to Carl and Ascia, who encouraged me to read and to keep an open mind.

Part I

Once upon a time a member of the tribe began to declaim a sequence of words. This was not done in order to elicit the more or less obvious response from others in his tribe. The real purpose was to see how far words could be linked up, to test their reciprocal fertility.
Italo Calvino, *"Notes Toward a Definition of Narrative Form as a Combinatory Process"*

Actually, the very existence of narrative fiction, whatever its content, is an indictment of history on esthetic and moral grounds.
Robert Champigny, Ontology of Narrative

The observer external to all earthly cultures would probably experience considerable difficulty in explaining the existence of the enormous number of texts relating events which are known not to have taken place. The number of works of this kind contradicts any essential social function which we might ascribe to them.
Jurij Lotman, "The Origin of Plot in the Light of Topology"

Pretext: The Relation of Fiction and Reality

The two semiotic functions, autonomous and informational, coexisting in the representational arts, constitute together one of the essential dialectical antinomies of the evolution of these arts; their duality makes its effect, over the course of evolution, in constant oscillations of the relationship to reality.
                    Jan Mukarovsky, "Art as Semiotic Fact"

A major problem area in the theory of fiction has been definition of the relationship between fiction and reality, a more specific case of the question of the relation between Art and Life. The debate generally polarizes around the two basic semiotic functions of language; one critical camp stresses the mimetic and communicative function of fiction whereas the other emphasizes its autotelic and autonomous function. Throughout much of the history of Western critical discourse dealing with fiction, Aristotle's prescription of mimesis has prevailed: Art Imitates Life, or in its application to fictional artifacts, fiction imitates reality. Mimesis should be understood here not only in its etymological sense of "truth to life," or the "mirror held up to nature," but also in its higher sense of a unified ethical vision connected in some way with the way we live now. Proponents of the mimetic school of course recognize the existence of nonmimetic narratives; but they valorize those fictions which adopt as a basic narrative world one that is essentially congruent with the real world.[1] This conception of the proper ontological status for fiction has dominated critical thought until quite recently, despite the fact that it was challenged as early as the 1920s by Continental critics like Ortega y Gasset and Victor Shklovsky, not to mention the aesthetic assumptions and techniques of modernist fictionists like Joyce, Faulkner, Woolf, Gide, and others. Ortega y Gasset begins *The Dehumanization of Art* with the "illiberal" notion that the human response and the aesthetic response to respective stimuli are of two different orders; therefore, to demand of any aesthetic artifact that it provide the unmediated kind of experience that life gives is to destroy the aesthetic experience, which is based upon distance and contemplation; "life is one thing, art is another . . . the poet begins where the man ends."[2] Whereas Ortega's remarks are aimed at the aesthetic act in general, Shklovsky's are directed at fiction in particular; in his now-familiar essay on *Tristram Shandy* he argues, "the forms of art are explainable by the laws of art; they are not justified by their realism. . . . The assertion that *Tristram Shandy* is not a novel is common; . . . *Tristram Shandy* is the most typical novel in world literature."[3] Of course Shklovsky's ideas were not made known to the Anglo-American community of critics until Wellek and Warren's *Theory of Literature* appeared in 1949, and Ortega y Gasset's views could well be seen as applicable only to modernist poetry. In any case, these particular counterformulations did not earn a great deal of critical acceptance in the Western arena until they were taken up again by an imposing field of critics and fictionists, spurred on by the gradual ascendance of the modernist aesthetic in various artistic realms as well as by certain implications of the literary perspective formulated and hypostatized by the New Criticism. This countervailing aesthetic stresses the autonomous and autotelic nature of fiction; it accepts and exalts the artifice of fictional artifacts, emphasizing the language, structure, or point of view of a fiction. This countermovement culminates in any number of polemical assertions by contemporary fictionists about the nature of fictional worlds. For example, Raymond Federman defines a new species of fiction—surfiction—as follows:

> To write is to produce meaning and not to re-produce a pre-existing meaning. . . . As such fiction can no longer be reality, or a representation of reality, or an imitation, or even a re-creation of reality; it can only be A REALITY—an autonomous reality whose only relation to the real world is to improve the world. To create fiction is, in fact, a way to abolish reality, and especially to abolish the notion that reality is truth.[4]

John Fowles has said that the primary motivation of the novelist is to create worlds other than, but as real as, the real one.[5] William Gass has argued that fictions are not ways of viewing reality but rather are additions to it.[6] Ronald Sukenick has similarly asserted that fiction adds itself to the world, "creating a meaningful 'reality' that did not previously exist."[7] And John Barth has particularly abdicated the responsibilities of realistic literature, claiming in a rather disarming manner that he doesn't "know much about Reality."[8] For the time being proponents of fiction as an autonomous, rather than mimetic, discourse seem to dominate the critical arena, to the extent that proponents of realism or a higher mimesis feel compelled to speak out against the prevailing trend in the climate of narrative, one recent example being John Gardner's *On Moral Fiction*.

The debate goes on; every anthology, every essay dealing with fiction and its theory, implicitly or explicitly endorses the mimetic or the "formalist" (Harvey uses the term "autonomous") position, and some critics have suggested that the issue is irreconcilable. Robert Davis, for example, utilizes formalist versus mimetic approaches to fiction as a kind of shaping principle for his selection of essays on the novel and makes this comment in one of his summary remarks: "However much they borrow each other's methods, the formalist and mimetic approaches remain fundamentally distinct. It might be argued— as recent theorists seem increasingly inclined to do—that different kinds of literature, even different kinds of novels, demand different approaches, and that theoretical statements should be used as explanations rather than as slogans in a critical holy war."[9] The polarization infects even criticism that attempts to redefine the "experience" of literature, as can be seen in the East German Marxist critique of the fashionable and influential German school of the aesthetics of reception. Peter Hohendahl argues, for example, that the phenomenological reception aesthetics of Jauss and others reduces the dialectical relationship of production and consumption of texts to an intraliterary phenomenon, that with its emphasis upon the literary horizon of expectations it overlooks the fact that the reader is a living member of a real material society that "determines in many ways his scope of consciousness and action," that it "transfers the concept of the reader entirely into the text."[10] The focus here shifts from text to reader and the terminology is somewhat different, but the issues are fundamentally the same. It is to this sort of impasse that the problem seems inevitably to bring critics. And, to circumvent the impasse, critics suggest that fiction constitutes a special case for poetics; that fiction is an intransigent genre; that the essential quality of fiction is its tendency to break rules, to defy conventions, to explode neat prescriptions about theoretical matters like the relation of Art to Life; that theorists must substitute for a global theory of narrative various local theories especially adapted to the terrain they seek to map. This has been the case for fiction ever since one of its first theorists, Clara Reeve, felt that it was necessary to distinguish between Novel and Romance and thus divided prose narrative into reciprocal genres. The critical "holy war" continues, as is witnessed by the polemical nature of the essays in Federman's *Surfiction*. One solution to the controversy would be generalized narratology or theory of narrative that would avoid the problem by transcending it.

One of the sources of the problem in the ongoing debate rests in the definition of terms, particularly the word *reality*.[11] To clarify this issue, I should like to propose some alternative terms. I shall use the term *empirical world* (W_e) to refer to the contingent world as it presents itself in prosaic events, commonplace objects, and ordinary people. Every fiction creates a *fictional world* (W_f), which conflates elements drawn from the empirical world and elements that have been invented. These elements are given a unique configuration by the transforming imagination of the fictionist, a configuration that gives this world its narrative identity. This is to say that any and all fictions incorporate both autonomic and mimetic elements, that the world that a fiction creates is both added to the empirical world and at the same time related in some way to that world. Each fictionist is free to order or "privilege" these elements in ways or relations that accord with his or her intentions. W. J. Harvey's metaphor of the mimetic angle graphically demonstrates this idea.[12] Harvey argues that all fictions create a fictional world (W_f) that intersects the real world (W_e) at some angle of mimesis (θ):

Diagram 1

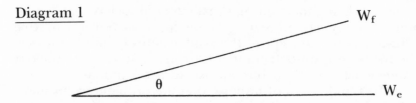

If the angle of mimesis is small, then the fiction is more mimetic; if the angle is large, then the fiction is more autonomous, more self-contained. With the aid of the diagram, we can imagine a continuum of fictional forms generated by the sweep of the mimetic angle ($O<\theta<90$). Mimetic fictions, those whose θ is acute, will be characterized by certain authorial assumptions, some of which are (1) that the most important "reality" exists prior to the fiction; (2) that the text comes into existence primarily to *re*-present that reality; (3) that this *re*-presentation will order that external world into a coherent and significant whole; and finally, (4) that the reader's exposure to this world should enable him or her to perceive and comprehend the real world more sharply and sensitively. To enact these assumptions and effect these ends, the author usually relies on language that is essentially transparent—language that does not call attention to itself as language and that therefore acts as a window on the world. The reader looks through the language to the world represented. In addition the author attempts to create characters who are like "real people," who demonstrate the variety and unpredictability of human beings. This type of fiction, often generically identified as the NOVEL, has been called by Harvey "the distinct art form of liberalism," embodying as it does a state of mind that has as its center "the acknowledgment of the plentitude, diversity, and individuality of human beings in society, together with the belief that such characteristics are good as ends in themselves."[13]

More autonomous fictions, on the other hand, fictions whose angle of mimesis is relatively large (Harvey cites as a representative example *Alice in Wonderland*), are characterized by a constitutive discourse, one that begets itself as it proceeds, so as to "discover reality" or "invent reality" according to Robbe-Grillet; by an emphasis upon the aesthetic response of the reader, wherein *aesthetic* is understood in Ortega's sense, as the attainment of a degree of remoteness that makes possible "pure observation";[14] by language that is deliberately opaque and/or highly foregrounded;[15] and by characters who are two-, one-, or zero-dimensional, a simple locus of semes or an empty counter (a countercharacter). This type of fiction, which has been given any number of labels, occupies one extreme of the continuum of fictional forms postulated by Harvey's mimetic angle.

Let us return for a moment to Diagram 1 and turn our attention from its usefulness as a metaphor for the problematic status of fictional worlds to its potential as a heuristic tool, one that can clarify the "bias" of a particular critical methodology.

Critics who prefer the mimetic theory of fiction, who privilege the representative function of fictional worlds, constantly project downward from the fictional world toward the empirical world.

Diagram 2

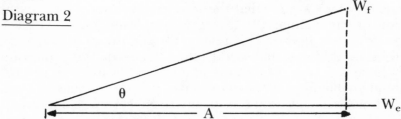

The critics try to define dimension *A*, where *A* is equivalent to what Harvey calls the "truth value" of the fiction. *A* is a measurement of the relationship of the fiction to life. One might notice in passing that all of Harvey's essential parameters of fiction, the four "constitutive categories"—Time, Identity, Causality, and Freedom—are taken from life. Harvey thus elevates one dimension of the fictional world at the expense of others. His concerns are echoed by numerous other humanistic critics like George Lukács, who sees the "attenuation of reality" in modern fiction as a source of real concern,[16] and like Stephen Marcus, who complains, "One thing that seems clear is that the novel has nearly ceased to give us what we need: an adequate notion of what it is like to be alive today, why we are the way we are, and what might be done to remedy our bad situation."[17] Marcus's gloomy assessment of the state of contemporary fiction might be contrasted with the insouciance and nonchalance (and perhaps irresponsibility) of a contemporary fictionist's view: "To predict where writing is going is like begging the question. I believe, for example, that the world is going to blow itself up sometime between 1980 and 1990, and the question of writing will become academic. Hopeless. So I don't think about it. If we don't blow ourselves up or starve ourselves to death, we will probably be saved by some kind of new technological development. . . . Consequently I find myself bored and morally petrified by the present, and I desire an escape. Fiction is my escape. I believe in it, I think of it as a conspiratorial act, and one of these days I'm going to blow it up."[18]

We have noted above that fictions in general take advantage of (at least) both dimensions of the fictional world/empirical world axes, that a fiction will employ both autonomous and mimetic elements. But it is clear that the same may not be said of critical approaches to fiction. It seems (as yet) that a critical methodology presupposes allegiance to one or the other of the axes, that some sort of stance on the mimesis/autonomy issue is an unavoidable concomitant of a critical approach. Most "solutions" to the fiction/reality polarity in critical practice consist in deliberate evasions of the problem. There is, for example, Clara Reeve's distinction between narrative genres:[19] the Novel adheres to a mimetic poetics whereas the Romance (and its numerous successors) enacts an autonomous poetics; in terms of intention the former aims to instruct while the latter is content to delight. Lukács adopts a similar tactic in his analysis of the modernist attack upon realism, except that he divides his fictional modes according to a historical, rather than generic, model. He asserts that there are two modes of fiction, based upon two very different views of the world: realistic fiction, whose episteme conceives the world as dynamic and developmental (mimetic poetics); and modern fiction, which portrays the world as static and sensational (autonomous poetics). A Marxist, Lukács obviously prefers the fiction of realism; hinting that modern fiction is unhealthy in that it ignores the fact that people are social animals, he prescribes fictions in which the characters' ontological being "cannot be distinguished from their social and historical environment."[20] The alternatives offered by Reeve and Lukács sidestep the issue; they concede from the beginning that fiction is a many-headed beast, and they propose separate descriptions for each of those heads. These local descriptions fail especially at one particular point, from the standpoint of narratology. They fail to provide a model that can describe the way in which fiction evolves from a Dos Passos to a Federman, that can explain how fiction gets from Dos Passos's actual incorporation of a historical personage into a fictional narrative for the purposes of mimetic density (in his *U.S.A.*) to the typographic legerdemain of Federman's *Take It or Leave it*—his "spatial displacement of words." Any comprehensive theory of fiction should supply a lexicon and syntax whereby phenomena like these could be described and explained.

As the situation stands today, critics must choose between fiction and reality, and in the long run reality will have out. As Murray Krieger has correctly pointed out:

> The critical tradition has always resisted . . . any theory that took
> the literary work away from "reality," whatever that may mean, and
> kept it away too long. The tradition has sought, in the end, to
> return fiction to the mundane truths about us. . . . The scholar-
> critic has traditionally justified his interest in literature by returning
> again and again to his claim that the literary work must affect that
> world that precedes and follows it; he must always see in that work,
> the product of human skills and invention, a model of that world, if
> not a model *for* it.[21]

As Krieger notes, there is considerable pressure upon fictionists
and critics alike (especially the latter, given their double
superfluity) to justify their life work by demonstrating its inti-
mate connection with the real world. It is not really surprising,
in the light of this pressure, that the most "experimental" writer
will attempt to validate his or her work by bespeaking its relation to the real. Thus Federman, in the course of his assault
upon realistic fiction, suggests that "surfiction" is closer to the
reader's experience of reality than traditional fiction, and that
its primary function is to improve that reality.[22] By a similar
argument, Ronald Sukenick attempts to demonstrate how the
new tradition of fiction obeys this primary dictum: "I presume
that the movement of fiction should always be in the direction
of what we sense as real."[23]

Federman's and Sukenick's arguments constitute yet another
way to explain the differences between traditional fiction and
modern and contemporary fiction. One of the more plausible
explanations for the irrealism[24] of modernist fiction is that reality itself has undergone drastic transformations in the past dec-
ades, and that the bizarre shapes and weird situations in new
fiction merely reflect those transformations. Reality has become
fantastic or surreal or fabulous, and the new tradition in fiction
registers this experiential change as faithfully as it can; if one
lives in a fabulous land, one writes fabulous fictions. Lukács is
one of the first to suggest that literary experimentation is a
consequence of conditions that prevail in the empirical world.
Recent explorations in "culturology" have adduced convincing
evidence that fiction is indeed "cooked" in the sociocultural
environment in which it is conceived, that the experimentation
of the modernist novel and its offspring evolves from a general
epistemological crisis occurring in many disciplines in the twentieth century.[25] But to argue that fiction is cooked in reality is
not to specify the exact nature of its relation to that reality;

frequently this argument further obfuscates an already murky issue. For example, Federman and Sukenick seem to argue in one breath that fiction adds itself to the world, creating a reality that did not previously exist, and in the next breath to insist that their inchoate fictions are in fact faithful transcriptions of contemporary experiential reality. Now these two assertions are not mutually exclusive (in fact, they can be reconciled once we understand that the definition of reality, as well as the implicit notion of mimesis, has shifted from one statement to the next), but they certainly cause confusion.

This kind of confusion, combined with the polarization of critical thought, clearly indicates that the fiction/reality dichotomy constitutes a state that must be transcended in whatever way is possible. One logical way would be to make the leap from state to metastate, to make the bipolarity of the state one of the terms in a critical metalanguage. Barth employs an operation very similar to this for fictional discourse in his well-known essay, "The Literature of Exhaustion."[26] In the essay he demonstrates how a metafictional operation can transform a reality of exhaustion into a fiction of inexhaustibility. The act of dwelling on the state can thrust the discourse beyond state to metastate, can turn a constrictive reality into a liberating fiction. Mas'ud Zavarzadeh makes a similar shift from language to metalanguage in his examination of the use of fact in fiction. Rejecting the restrictive division of narrative into "factual" and "fictional" categories, Zavarzadeh makes the tension between the fictive and the real the subject of his discourse. He establishes two categories of his own that transcend the factual/fictional polarity: *monoreferential* and *bireferential.* The former mode utilizes only a single field of reference, either the *in*-referential world of the fiction or the *out*-referential world of facts; the latter mode, a product of the "fictuality" of contemporary experience, merges the once-separate realms of factuality and fictionality into a hybrid "zone of experience." By making the oft-noted tension between the factual and the fictional part of his discourse, by coining neologisms like "fictual," Zavarzadeh escapes the pitfalls of the fiction/reality debate and generates a partial grammar of nonfictional narrative.[27]

In similar fashion a comprehensive theory of narrative, a "narratology," needs to develop a metalanguage raised to a level of generality such that local problems, like the polarization of fictional and nonfictional discourse, are subsumed under a larger perspective. Given the problems that this pretext has discussed, what would seem to suffice is a theory of narrative that would accommodate a number of problem areas. It would take into account the fact that narratives of all types respond to the pressures of the experiential reality in which they are created; it would deal with the very real problem of narrative semantics, with the fact that narratives have meanings; it would describe the various signifying systems of a narrative as *systems;* and it could be adapted to historiological purposes, could, for example, chart a coherent history for American fiction in the twentieth century. In generating such a theory, I hope to free the imagination of the constraints of genres, of periods, of local applicability, as well as of Gordian knots such as the relation of fiction and reality. To accomplish these ends, I propose a theory of "fictional space."

1

A Theory of Fictional Space

A theory is a connected set of propositions which are divided into two groups. One group consists of statements about some collection of ideas which are characteristic of the theory; the other group consists of statements of the relation between these ideas and some other ideas of a different nature. The first group will be termed collectively the "hypothesis" of the theory; the second group the "dictionary." The hypothesis is so called . . . because the propositions composing it are incapable of proof or disproof by themselves; they must be significant, but, taken apart from the dictionary, they appear arbitrary assumptions.

Norman Campbell, Foundations of Science

The literary work itself is not studied but rather the potentialities of literary discourse which have made the work possible: in this way, literary studies can become a science of literature.

Tzvetan Todorov, in Bersani, "Is There a Science of Literature?"

In order to write, in order to inscribe language into fiction, I need to invent a space within which to move my chess pieces. I have to invent a playground, if you wish. We now come to the double meaning of the play: first, to play a game; second, to move freely in the invented space (freely in the sense of loosely). So the idea of playfulness for me is to create a playground into which I can project myself in order to start writing.

Raymond Federman, "Tri(y)Log"

I

At the beginning of *The Scarlet Letter,* in the sketch of the custom house that he uses to ground the romance that is to follow, Nathaniel Hawthorne speaks of the conditions in which a fiction comes into existence. Although his description is particularly aimed at the imaginative processes of the writer of romances, it can throw light on the originary imaginative proc-

ess of fictionists in general. Hawthorne suggests that the sol-
itude that prevails in the evening hours in the writer's den
provides the most propitious circumstance for the play of the
fictive imagination. Moonlight and firelight cast upon the familiar surroundings a kind of spiritual illumination, endowing the
most trivial objects with a mystery of their own, and creating "a
medium the most suitable for a romance writer to get ac-
quainted with his illusive guests." In this ethereal atmosphere,
this intervening space between wakefulness and sleep, the entire room is "now invested with a quality of strangeness and
remoteness." A remarkable transformation has occurred: "the
floor of our familiar room has become a neutral territory, somewhere between the real world and fairy-land, where the Actual
and the Imaginary may meet, and each imbue itself with the
nature of the other."[1] In this region created by the play of
circumstance, the firm and constrictive grasp of actuality is at-
tenuated, and the fictive imagination is granted the degree of
latitude necessary to real-ize its "tribe of unrealities." Hawthorne is arguing, in effect, that art needs a domain of its
own—a neutral territory located in some foothold between the
purely imaginary and the concretely actual. The creatures of an
artist's fancy are actualized in this twilight zone between the
noon of actuality and the midnight of dream. Hawthorne
specifies that this region is neither one or the other, that it
partakes of both the Actual and the Imaginary; the fictive becomes real as the real becomes fictive; the two interpenetrate
and become something "other."

Terence Martin, in his analysis of Hawthorne's poetics of
fiction, notes that Hawthorne consistently describes the area in
which the imagination operates in spatial terms—it is a "territory," a "kingdom," a "region," or a "precinct." Martin points
out that this tendency indicates a desire to "materialize" a
metaphor, to give to an imaginal construct the kind of quiddity
and thereness that pertains to geographic locales. Another aspect of Hawthorne's metaphor that might be emphasized is the
liberating quality of his "neutral territory." Time and again in
"The Custom-House" Hawthorne speaks of the exigencies and
constrictions of everyday existence; he stresses the need to escape "the Present, the Immediate, the Actual," which oppresses
him and invariably "murders" the creatures of his fancy. Because of a need to have access to a "kingdom of possibilities," he
conceives of the realm of fiction as having its existence in some

neutral territory, free of the exigencies of everyday existence. Although Hawthorne's remarks are intended to characterize the procedure of romance-writers in particular, they might well serve, in somewhat modified form, to characterize the practice of creators of narrative in general. All narratives create some kind of imaginative expanse that is at a remove from the "real world," and a fictionist inscribes this space in part to escape the tyranny of the real. As Hawthorne says, "It is only through the medium of the imagination, that we can lessen those iron fetters, which we call truth and reality, and make ourselves even partially sensible what prisoners we are."[2]

In somewhat more theoretical fashion, one might say that in the process of relating, composing, or fabricating a narrative discourse, an author responds to a certain psychological need for freedom and control. The author reacts to that psychological pressure by "inventing" an area or expanse whose dimensions serve to satisfy that need for freedom and control. The narrative form bestows upon the author the opportunity to construct a verbal space endowed with psychological, ideational, and aesthetic dimensions that liberate him or her from the constrictions of the ordinary time/space matrix of "reality." By retreating to the neutral territory fashioned by the imagination, the author enjoys a measure of freedom that was not previously available. In this "kingdom of possibilities" he fabricates a verbal space with aesthetic contours. This verbal space is, moreover, permanent (in a manner of speaking) and therefore satisfies the "mortal desire for immortality" (John Barth's phrase in *Chimera*). I thus postulate a permanent verbal space as a common characteristic of all narrative discourse. The metaphoric term *space* (which I intend to make less figurative in what follows) is suggested by and predicated upon twin intuitions about narrative discourse: that fictional configurations simultaneously create and inhabit a hybrid zone or interface generated by the conflation of the Real and the Imaginary; and that inscribing a world itself represents an essentially spatial act.

This second point merits amplification. Inscribing a narrative text constitutes a spatial act in at least three senses. As Butor, Genette, and others have emphasized, a text occupies a material space, the space of textuality. A text displaces so much physical space, consists of so many pages, which in turn are *filled up* with sentences, which are composed of words that occupy their gramatically prescribed *places*. The book has an existence as a *total object* (the phrase is Genette's). Second, there is the imaginal space projected by the unfolding fictional world, the terrain "excavated" by the representative function of fictional signs. This is the space that the reader must "concretize" or "actualize" in the process of decoding the text. And, third, the fictional world itself evokes an interpretive space as its signifieds become second-level signifiers of a totalized reading of (extratextual) reality. The reader works from the fictional world to "fill" the space of meaning and rewrite a narrative metatext (of which more later). All these aspects of space inhere in the inscription of a fictional text. As Genette has said of literary spatiality, "the manifest spatiality of writing may be taken as a symbol for the profound spatiality of language."[3]

It should be emphasized that the metaphor of narrative space has as its two essential parameters the axiological notions of freedom and control. Within the boundaries of his narrative space the author simultaneously frees himself of contingency and establishes an expanse over which he wields a measure of authority. Adam Smith, in his somewhat cursory examination of popular psychological strategies and "games," mentions a rather interesting game entitled "Create a Space." The game has proved to be particularly effective in enabling prisoners to deal with the pressures and anxieties attendant upon a life of confinement. Prisoners are encouraged to expend imaginative energy in the creation of a comfortable private space that they may figuratively "put on" and go about in, thus suspending some of the harsher social pressures. As one prisoner expresses the strategy, "I wear my space and the guard don't bother me no more."[4] The same situation obtains for creators of narrative, particularly narrative fiction. They create their space and then reality "don't bother them no more"; they, like the prisoner, achieve a degree of autonomy that is not available to them in their experiential world.

It seems clear, however, that not all narratives have the same amount or kind of space. Certainly a *New York Times* report on the Middle East peace negotiations has not the space—in the sense of narrative and/or verbal freedom—of a short story like John Gardner's "Queen Louisa," in which the titular heroine is a frog. Among the several limitations operating upon the former is belief in, acceptance of, and respect for "factuality." The former would not intentionally misrepresent the "facts" of the case. The amount of space available to the writer is a product of a complex set of conventions adhering to the particular nature of the chosen narrative form. We might assert as a law of narrative that the amount of narrative space is related to the nature of the discourse: a factual news report has less space (in terms of aesthetic freedom) than a factual and yet shaped biography, which has less space than an autobiography or certain products of the "new journalism," which have less space than a "realistic" novel, which has less space than a science fiction "thought experiment" (the phrase is Ursula K. LeGuin's), which has less space than a "pure" fantasy, and so on. If we can enumerate the signifying systems that constitute any and all narrative spaces and demonstrate the ways in which various genres of narrative utilize space, we might construct a continuum of textual spaces in which the various species of fiction occupy the bands at one end.

It might be useful at this point to return to the fiction/reality polarity in order to distinguish between fictional and nonfictional narrative. A prose narrative is composed of various sign-vehicles, which have two possible modes of reference, factual or fictional. A sign-vehicle with a factual referent ($+$FACT) designates an entity with some sort of verifiable extratextual existence (person, place, thing, event, idea); sign-vehicles with a fictional referent ($+$FICTION) refer to "nonexistent states of affairs (events, objects) with truth value only in imaginative representation." They are "modally counterfactual and pragmatically intended as such by a speaker not denying the counterfactualness."[5] Sign-vehicles strung together in a narrative create a semantic continuum or "frame of reference" *(fr)*. According to whether the sign-vehicles are factual or counterfactual, that frame of reference is considered either factually "true" or fictionally justified. At the macrotextual level a prose narrative organizes its various *frs* into Fields of Reference *(FRs)*. A prose narrative thus consists of mutually intersecting Fields of Reference, and these Fields (depending on their constituent frames of reference) can be either out-referential (if its frames can be verified and validated by-comparison with the "originals" outside the text) or in-referential (if its frames create an internally consistent and self-contained fictional microcosm). In any prose narrative, if out-referential *FRs* constitute (or dominate or preponderate)[6] the narrative world, then that narrative can be said to be modally factual. If, however, out-referential *FRs* are subordinated to and integrated within in-referential

FRs, the resulting narrative is modally fictional. There is, however, a third alternative, a prose narrative that neutralizes the relation between out-referential and in-referential *FRs,* either by keeping them separate but equal or by confusing the difference between them. The resulting bi-referential narratives (examples might be the nonfiction novel and postmodern pseudo-autobiography) are anomalous and cause no end of problems for the narrative typologist.

A fictional narrative then, dominated as it is by in-referential *FRs,* offers the narratist considerable creative latitude. It should be noted, however, that fictionists do not have total license, that they too suffer limitations of narrative space. At different times in its history, fiction has been taken to task by readers responding to consideration of logic, verisimilitude, probability, sequentiality, coherence, or relevance. One of the basic sets of constraints affecting the fictionist derives from the medium he or she uses:

> Novelistic design and its execution are made in the medium of language, and a language is the property of a social community, impregnated with the values and thought patterns of that community. Selecting the linguistic structures that are available to him for his work of representation, the novelist loses some degree of personal control—the culture's values (including expectations about types of implied author) seep through, infiltrate his utterance, so that personal expression is necessarily qualified by the social meanings which attach to the expressions he chooses.[7]

Not only is his narrative circumscribed at that microcosmic level by the values that adhere to language in its particularity; it also is circumscribed at the macrocosmic level by generic conventions, by content limitations, by consideration of marketability, and so forth. As numerous commentators have noticed, fiction has, throughout its history, iconoclastically struggled against the limitations imposed by the public consensus of what fiction is and what it might legitimately do.

And just what is it that a fiction does? At an elementary level, it proposes and inscribes a "world" somewhere within our everyday world. This proposed world is not empirical, but imaginal and projectional; that is, the proposed world is not "solid"—it does not have "length," "width," or "height"—rather, it is a process. This process is initiated by a culture-specific author, enacted in *real*-ized text, and *re*-created by a *response*-ible reader. It conforms to the operational norms of the empirical world upon which the proposed world is inscribed. These operational norms constitute the culture in which the narrative comes into existence. To map this process of the creation of a proposed world, we must find a binding concept, a concept developed to a higher level of generality so as to embrace all the constituents of the process. This concept I shall call *fictional space,* by which I mean the imaginal expanse created by fictional discourse, a fictional field which, though ultimately self-referential and self-validating, necessarily exists in ascertainable relation with the "real world" outside the text. The dimensions of this space are not unlimited, but are predicated upon shared cultural assumptions as to what the author might do; in a sense authors share their space with their readers. This is to say that fiction and its space are inextricably bound up in the sociocultural and literary matrix.

The concept *fictional space* potentially encompasses all three centers of the act and experience of literature—the author, the reader, and the literary object itself—and thus avoids the inevitable shortcomings of partial approaches to narrative. Furthermore, the concept admits of an approach to fiction that may be alternately synchronic or diachronic (as I shall attempt to show in later chapters). Finally, this concept can contribute to a clarification of the generic identity of fictional discourse within the spectrum of prose narrative. In general, *fictional space* has great heuristic value.

I intend in the remainder of this chapter to describe the signifying systems that constitute a fictional space. Operating on the assumption that the field of fiction is composed of signs governed by various codes whose basic function is representation, I shall attempt to map the sign systems operating within that field. In attempting this, I shall often have recourse to linguistic terms and linguistic models. It must be stressed at the outset that such models are employed paramorphically rather than homeomorphically; that is to say that the use of linguistic models does not necessarily mean that a fiction signifies in exactly the same fashion as a language signifies, but only that linguistic models can shed light upon a heteromorphic subject matter. Linguistics is only a tool here, not an originary paradigm.

Before beginning the theoretical discussion, I must make two further comments about the central postulate. First, by the term *fictional space* I by no means refer to the particular school of criticism that speaks of particular (especially modern) novels as spatial constructs, to be apprehended instantaneously through the juxtaposition of fragments or episodes into some sort of *Gestalt,* much like a lyric poem. Joseph Frank, Sharon Spencer, and others designate as a subgenre of fiction those novels which elevate formal design (or "spatial form" or "archetectonics") above consideration of character and event. In this framework the concept of space is restricted to its denotative value within the time/space dimensional matrix; a novel attempts to achieve spatial form in order to overcome the entropy implicit in temporality and linearity. This kind of approach tends to ignore a fundamental aspect of fiction's generic identity, its progressive unfolding over a period of time and across a series of pages. In the present discussion, *fictional space* will be something more than an alternative to temporality.

Nor will fictional space refer to the "physical" locale in which the events take place, the geography of the fictional world, like Hardy's Wessex or Faulkner's Yoknapatawpha County. Although both of these definitions will find a place in this elaboration of fictional space, they should not be confused with the totality of the theoretical postulate.

II

In the "human sciences" one often finds an "ideological fallacy" common to many scientific approaches, which consists in believing that one's own approach is not ideological because it succeeds in being "objective" and "neutral." For my own part, I share the same skeptical opinion that all inquiry is "motivated." Theoretical research is a form of social practice. Everybody who wants to know something wants to know it in order to do something. . . . I think that it is more "scientific" not to conceal my own motivations, so as to spare my readers any "scientific delusions."

Umberto Eco, A Theory of Semiotics

Physical theories provide patterns within which data appear intelligible. They constitute a "conceptual gestalt." A theory is not pieced together from observed phenomena; it is rather what makes it possible to observe phenomena as being of a certain sort, and as related to other phenomena. Theories put phenomena into systems.

N. R. Hanson, in Mooij, "The Nature and Function of Literary Theories"

A postulate has no need of proofs; but its effectiveness can be measured by the results we reach by accepting it.

Tzvetan Todorov, The Fantastic: A Structural Approach to Literary Genre

An act of semiosis is characterized by the presence of a sign and the absence of the object to which the sign refers. That is to say that the sign in some way and for some purpose replaces, substitutes for, or "stands for" the absent entity, the empirical or ideal signified. Following Eco, I shall call the totality of the relation between a sign and its referent a "sign-function."[8] In linguistic semiosis a sign-function exists between the pair, language and "reality"; the relationship between a pair is signification. As Eco has pointed out, every time there is a sign-function, there is the possibility of lying. A sign-function can easily signify something to which no real state of things corresponds. Eco defines the "referential fallacy" as the tendency to assume that the "meaning" of a sign-vehicle has a basis of fact with respect to the object or situation designated.[9]

Any prose narrative is composed of a system of signs. A narrative establishes a sign-function between its sign-vehicles (the words that make up the narrative) and the narrative world that they designate. In fictional discourse the signs are twice removed from reality. They not only re-present a certain experience, they accept as their originary catalyst the notion that there need be no actual state of affairs that corresponds to the experience. This is to say that a fictional world is substantially other than the real world in which it is inscribed. The relationship between the fictional world and the real world is a matter of a system of explicit or implicit cultural conventions, "codes" that govern the signifying process. For example, realism is one narrative code that because of certain of its features has achieved a kind of formal and institutional status in Western literary aesthetics. Two of the features that lend to this code its particular force and popularity are verisimilitude, the conviction that there need be a direct correspondence between empirical reality and literary reality, and humanism, the idea that this correspondence can and should have some kind of impact on the way in which humanity conceives and orders its affairs. Both of these features of the code of realism serve to justify an imaginative enterprise that a purely utilitarian sensibility might condemn; both features emphasize the pragmatic value of literature.

We can say, then, that any fiction signifies by means of a complex and intricate culturological process that establishes conventions that describe, prescribe, and/or circumscribe fictive signification. These conventions define rules and delineate boundaries for fictional space. Fictional space (S_F) consists of signifying systems that we can enumerate and elaborate.

As numerous critics of fiction have noted, the quintessential feature of narrative is that it is mediated, that a narrative presupposes a speaker to narrate its events. Drama presents its characters and events directly to its audiences. Poetry renders an experiential moment in all its immediacy and instantaneity; poetry is speech that is "overheard." Fiction alone necessarily presents an experience that has been "cooked" or "digested"; someone stands between the reader and the fictional characters and events. And this is the case, as Wayne Booth has so convincingly shown,[10] whether the author resorts to showing or telling, to pictorial or dramatic modes of presentation, to personal or impersonal narration. The fact of mediation imparts to fiction the basis of its generic distinctiveness, and any theory of narrative might well begin with this fundamental characteristic.

The fact of mediation leads to an important quality of fiction, its preoccupation with interpretation. Drama seems primarily concerned with "real" actions and their inexorable consequences; characteristically, drama evokes from its audience some sort of normative response—we are moved to evaluate the behavior of the characters we watch. Poetry, on the other hand, elicits an empathetic response from its readers; it asks that we recapture the moment of intense emotion or rapture that the author has captured in the verses—the experience of poetry is aesthetic in the full etymological sense of that word. A fiction, however, is "filled" with interpretation; a fiction necessarily presents the reader with a world to be interpreted and at least a partial degree of interpretation, the operation of the speaker. The human instinct to extract some sort of significance from experience is at one and the same time fiction's *sine qua non,* its *raison d'être,* its subject matter, and the response that it seeks to elicit from its readers. Some critics have tried to define the novel generically as having as its subject matter the notion of the learning experience.[11] This oversimplification results from the emphasis that the fact of mediation inevitably puts upon one aspect of the mediator—his or her innate tendency to make sense of the experience being related and ultimately to learn from it. The very fact that the story merits telling implies that the teller (authorial persona, character, zone of consciousness, or whatever) sees in the tale some significance, some import; he or she has implicitly or explicitly performed on the raw material of the tale one degree of interpretation. Ralph Freedman has argued that a theory of the novel might be constructed around the distance and tension inherent between a self that encounters and a reality that is encountered, that the novel is fashioned by a *hermeneutic space* (the phrase is mine) that exists between consciousness and its objects.[12] Freedman's argument, while it does not lay the groundwork for a comprehensive narrative theory, does underscore the instrumentality of the hermeneutic activity in the narrative process. Fiction does enact a confrontation between a world to be experienced and an experiencing (and interpreting) self.

The fact of mediation provides for my theory of fictional space the basic areas of signification; the signifying systems can be derived deductively from the basic predicates of any notion of mediation. The act of narration presupposes three basic entities, each of which generates its own fictional space: a narrator, a narrated world, and a "narratee." In terms of fictional discourse, these three terms can be translated as speaker (and this may be either the implied author or a character/narrator like Nick Carroway in *The Great Gatsby*), fictional world, and reader (who "consists" of semiotic activities to be described later). These are the entities that create, compose, occupy, or fill up a total fictional space, In formulaic terms, fictional space can be rewritten as follows:

$$S_F = S_w + S_s + S_r$$

where S_w is the space of the fictional world; S_s the space of the speaker; and S_r the space of the reader. The first two systems of spaces, the subspaces of the fictional world and the speaker, exist concretely in the semantic and aesthetic dimensions of the world and pages and order of the text and thus constitute the TEXT SPACE of the fiction. The space of the reader, however, often consists in just those gaps which the TEXT SPACE refuses to fill or to complete; the space of the reader consists in a kind of PARASPACE that exists "next to" the TEXT SPACE of the fiction. The formula of fictional space can thus be rewritten as follows:

$$S_F = \text{TEXT SPACE} + \text{PARASPACE}$$

In articulating the components of a fiction's space(s), it will be to our methodological advantage to consider TEXT SPACE and

PARASPACE separately. One should not conclude that this procedure implies relationships of chronology or cause-and-effect; the various spaces of a fiction exist simultaneously and in a condition of continuous dynamic. In the sections that follow, I shall attempt to describe a set of partial grammars for the space(s) of a fiction. It should be obvious that these grammars remain to be articulated, elaborated, refined, revised, and otherwise improved upon; they offer a rudimentary system with which to achieve a purchase on the nature of fictional narrative.

III

Any fiction is by definition characterized by the inevitable presence of a teller and a tale. A speaker, in a discursive speech act, composes or fabricates a particular fictional world. This world is not to be confused with quotidian reality, but it does bear some relation to that reality, a relation prescribed by the narrative conventions to which it adheres. The TEXT SPACE of a fiction can thus be divided into two reciprocal subspaces: the space of the fictional world, which I shall term NARRATIVAL SPACE (generated as it is by the events recounted in the narrative); and NARRATIONAL SPACE (predicated upon the act of narration).

NARRATIVAL SPACE may be further divided into two reciprocal subspaces, roughly equivalent to the lexicon and syntax of a natural language—a WORLD and a STORY. By WORLD I intend the total stock of possible fictional entities; that is, the people, places, and things that "occupy" the imaginal space of the fiction. They constitute a fictionist's repertoire. When discussing aspects of WORLD, critics have generally used terms like *people, character, hero, setting, milieu, locale,* and the like. These terms are not completely satisfactory in that they derive from an implicit assumption that the fictional world being described is "realistic" or verisimilar. For the characters who populate fictional universes I shall use the term *actant;* for the locale or domain in which actants have their existence I shall use the term *topos.*[13] By this term I intend not only the geographical domain and local setting (*To the Lighthouse,* for example, takes place in the house and grounds of a large estate on one of the islands in the Hebrides), but also the implicit or explicit cultural milieu and its norms (the action in *Emma* adheres to an etiquette prescribed by the mores of drawing-room society) *and* the natural laws that govern that domain. For example, many science fiction stories unfold in a WORLD in which one or more natural laws (in time-travel stories, the conservation of momentum) do not obtain. As a matter of fact, any fantasy world may be described as a fictional world in which one or more natural laws are suspended.

As Chatman and others have noted,[14] there is a dearth of systematic or structural analysis of actants (or characters) *per se.* Structural analysis has found it much more fruitful to discuss characters as the products of plots, as "functions" or pairs of relationships (hero/villain, seeker/object, etc.) rather than as individuated essences or "wholes." For present purposes a typology of actants grounded in a "grammar" of stories remains an attractive theoretical possibility, but one outside the scope of my description of fictional space. It is sufficient to remark that fictional space is necessarily occupied in part by actants who exist in ascertainable relations, both to each other and to the "real world" outside the fiction. It should be emphasized that an actant exists not as an autonomous and individuated whole (an assumption that can lead to questions like "How many children had Lady MacBeth?"), but as the collocation of a number of attributes or "semes," even if "the proper name [of a character in fiction] enables the person to exist outside the semes, whose sum nonetheless constitutes it entirely."[15]

One should note, finally, that the WORLD of NARRATIVAL SPACE is particularly subject to demands of verisimilitude and relevance. That is, readers often demand of a WORLD that it bear a strong resemblance to their experiential reality, and that its characters be sympathetic, believable, or at least human.

By the STORY of NARRATIVAL SPACE I mean the concatenation of events and actions that take place within the space of the WORLD, regardless of their magnitude, plausiblility, or interconnectedness. At an abstract level, STORY organizes or collects elements of WORLD (actants and topoi) into basic narrative units, or *motifs.* The motifs are then linked, connected, or combined, according a system of narrative rules (equivalent to the syntax of a "natural" language). The combinatory rules of narrative syntax have yet to be codified, but it is intuitively clear that they exercise considerable control over narrative choices. "The working out of plot (or at least some plots)," Chatman argues, "is a process of declining or narrowing possibility. The choices become more and more limited and the final choice seems not a choice at all, but an inevitability."[16]

Sidestepping the issue of a grammar of stories,[17] I would like simply to differentiate between two possible ways in which narrative motifs may be linked—hypotaxis and parataxis. A narrative arrayed hypotactically links its successive motifs according to (explicit or implicit) relations of chronology, dependency, or subordination; it encodes causal/chronological connections between narremes. The French critic Claude Bremond argues that "without succession there is no narrative,"[18] but there nonetheless exist certain (especially contemporary) fictions that employ a different principle of arrangement. In paratactic fictions, narrative motifs are deployed side by side, without the benefit of specifying or subordinating connectives. Motifs are presented as separate, discrete, equal. The text itself is discontinuous, and traditional notions like teleology and irreversibility are subverted. The paratactic text clearly demands from its readers activities other than the "reading" of plot, which depends upon a conception of narrative as a series of states between which are inserted codifiable transformations. The paratactic fiction distributes its motifs (instead of developing them) and further implicates the reader in its narrative management.

In traditional (hypotactic) fiction, STORY serves as the skeleton, which the fictionist "fleshes" out. In terms of scope, a STORY might be built upon the perfectly ordinary, like the quotidian actions of a typical day (as is the case in *Ulysses*). In terms of presentation, a STORY need not abide by chronology; the distinction made by the Russian Formalists between *fabula* and *sujet* is crucial here. The *fabula* consists in the events that constitute the armature of the narrative in their proper chronological order; the *sujet,* on the other hand, consists in the way in which these events are presented to the narrative audience, in the narrative ordering.[19] The use of *analepse* (Genette's term for narrative "flashback"), for example, would mark a reworking of the fabula into sujet for aesthetic purposes. As Shklovsky has noted, the transformation of fabula into sujet particularly foregrounds the presence of the storyteller; it is the storyteller who arranges and edits the raw materials of the narrative to achieve a particular end. Most reworking of fabula into sujet serves as direct or indirect evidence of a speaker's presence.

There has been a considerable amount of interesting semiological work on the element of STORY as a basis for a narrative grammar, especially in the areas of "functional" or modal analysis.[20] This would seem to be so both because of the instrumentality of plot for any narrative and because of its susceptibility to abstraction or formalization. In terms of my own theory of fictional space, the component of plot, or STORY as I have chosen to call it, assumes its importance as that glue which gives to the larger space continuity, coherence, and teleology. Roland Barthes has noted that the components of STORY, which he subdivides into two codes, the proairetic and the hermeneutic, endow the classic (traditional) text with its readability by making the text unidirectional and thereby reducing the plurality of its meanings (its "polysemy").[21] STORY gives the narrative a certain density (a novel without events is often panned as "thin"), ascertainable boundaries (the story begins with this event and culminates with that), a gratifying inevitability (given event A, then necessarily reaction B, resulting in event C), and a sense of movement (we have progressed from state A to state B). Because of these very important cultural functions, STORY is often considered the *sine qua non* of narrative. This fact is reflected in the popularity of fiction that is particularly plot-oriented, which emphasizes the question "what happened," like detective fiction or science fiction or romance or melodrama. It should be noted that in serving these cultural functions, the very notion of plot embodies a certain number of cultural assumptions; the articulations of STORY are derived from cultural models, and willful departure from these models might well be interpreted as a kind of "ungrammatical" behavior. A STORY that abruptly stopped in the middle of its articulation would be considered not only "bad art" but a deliberate violation of the narrative contract. The cultural constraints bearing upon STORY act as a very forceful element of prescription, both normative and aesthetic, for the fictionist.

Some critics, accepting in some form the distinction between WORLD and STORY, go on to argue that these separate components create disparate responses in the reader. Kieran Egan, for example, suggests that the component of STORY is particularly responsible for affective response in the reader; the satisfactions of plot, he says, determine the reader's emotional satisfactions. Robert Scholes similarly attributes to plot the responsibility for "sublimative" gratification, but adds that it is

WORLD that particularly serves cognitive ends; by comparing carefully the similarities and differences between real and fictional worlds, the reader comes to understand the former better. Although these insights may oversimplify an admittedly complex interplay, systematic analysis of WORLD and STORY should help to explain fiction's cognitive and affective satisfactions.[22]

I have argued that the TEXT SPACE of fictional space may be divided into the space of the fictional world and the space of the speaker. The space of the fictional world may be diagrammed as follows:

Before moving on to the description of the other major component of TEXT SPACE, I should make some general comments about the nature of S_W. STORY and WORLD in any narrative tend to carry the weight of the referential function of the message because they constitute the bulk of the semantic space of the fiction. In Roland Barthes's phrase, they submit to the "law of the Signified," a fact that results in certain consequences. The world that the sign vehicles signify, their field of signifieds, is particularly subject to the constrictions of rules and expectations. Thus it is that the convention of realism, with its concern for the relation between the fictional world and the real world, will first of all emphasize these aspects of fictional space (often to the neglect of other components) and will attempt to impose certain constraints upon the lexicon and syntax of S_W. Proponents of realism sometimes confuse signification, which is a property of all sign systems, with communication of information, which is a property of certain sign systems. They seek to govern the kinds of signification generated by the fictional world in ways such that the fiction communicates information to its readers, enables them to apprehend and comprehend their own experiential reality. Fictions whose fictional worlds offer substantial disjunction from the real world are, according to this aesthetic, labeled as irrelevant, obscurantist, inconsequential, or "escapist." These kinds of fictions do not offer substantial insight into the way we live now, nor do they inform us "what might be done to remedy our bad situation."[23] What these critics overlook is the fact that fiction serves ends other than cognition and, more important, that for cognition to be effected there need not be a relation of resemblance between real and fictional worlds.

The second major component of a fictional space pertains to the necessary existence of a speaker within a fiction, a speaker who may be either foregrounded or backgrounded, who may either advertise his or her presence or attempt to erase any evidence of his or her existence. To the space of the speaker I shall assign the term NARRATIONAL SPACE, in that it is generated by the fact of narration. NARRATIONAL SPACE itself can be divided into two major subspaces: the space generated by the fact that the narrative rests on a speech act, and the space involved in the fact that this speech act must be recorded on some sort of physical medium; these two textual subspaces I shall call DISCURSIVE and ICONIC SPACE, respectively.

The idea that discourse constitutes an essential aspect of any narrative act has been a fruitful insight for students of narrative ever since Benveniste elaborated it in his *Problèmes de linguistique générale.* Benveniste distinguishes between two complementary systems operating within every narrative, that of story, by which he intends pretty much what I have referred to as fictional world, and that of discourse, by which he means any and all references to the speaker or the speech act. Todorov and others have applied Beneviste's ideas to literary narrative with some success.[24] It should be noted that Beneviste's two systems roughly correspond with the notions of NARRATIVAL and NARRATIONAL space, if we make the qualification that the notion of story is not elaborated, and that the notion of discourse constitutes but an aspect of our notion of the space of the speaker.

By DISCURSIVE SPACE I intend those aspects of the narrative which make reference to, or call attention to, the circumstance of the act of speech, or what I shall call the enunciation. And by enunciation I understand the fact that someone is speaking, that someone chooses to recite a story; that the speaker is "situated," that the speaker has a point of view that serves perceptual, aesthetic, and ideological functions; and that that speaker projects a personal configuration, a personality, which creates a certain mood or tone by which the narrative might be characterized. In its largest sense, discourse includes the most basic operations that a storyteller chooses to perform upon a narrative situation, those of ordering and selection. From the storehouse of detail and articulation that envelopes the narrative germ, the storyteller selects those elements which contribute to the effect he or she is striving for and presents them in an order that best accomplishes that effect. As was noted above, any discrepancy between the *fabula* and the *sujet* serves to foreground the presence of the storyteller and therefore to emphasize the enunciative act. In many instances, however, the storyteller attempts to "naturalize" the acts of ordering and selection, by providing smooth and familiar transitions for out-of-sequence material (i.e., a character fills in her history for another character) and by suggesting that nothing of any consequence has been left out. As Barthes has said of the "readerly" or classic text, "everything holds together."[25] *Discourse,* in this book, should be understood as speech acts that deliberately draw attention to the enunciation and therefore tend to foreground the presence of the speaker in the story. In my own terms these devices create a substantial DISCURSIVE SPACE attendant upon the fact that any narrative requires the presence of a speaker if it is to be communicated.

The manifestations of discourse in any narrative are manifold and frequently subtle. For example, most narratives are marked by the presence of deictics like adverbs of place or time *(last summer, here, now),* which indirectly locate the circumstance of the enunciation and therefore constitute part of the discursive matrix. The most important deictics for prose narrative are the personal pronouns, *I* and its explicit or implicit correlative, *you.* A first-person narrative systematically creates and exploits a substantial DISCURSIVE SPACE in that it emphasizes the location, importance, and motivation of the speaking subject; consequently discourse (in first-person prose fiction) becomes a significant field for potential imaginative exploration and experimentation. It is not at all surprising that the first "experimental" novel—*Tristram Shandy*—is a first-person narrative; one might argue that it had to be.

Another lexical manifestation of discourse involves presence of words that underscore the fact that an operation of interpretation has been performed upon the narrative fact. Speakers occasionally express a certain degree of reserve or tentativeness about their narrative worlds; for example, they might fall back upon phrases of speculation like *it seems* or *it appears* or *one would think;* or they might rely on certain words that denote hesitation or uncertainty like *perhaps* or *apparently* or *as if;* or they might express a lack of definite knowledge with phrases like *a sort of* or *some.* All of these linguistic features impart to the discourse a degree of distance from the events being narrated and thus indicate the presence of a speaking subject. Boris Uspensky refers to features of this kind as "words of estrangement."[26] Words of estrangement function in a dual capacity for a discourse. Like deictics, they indicate the existence of a speaker, but they also contribute to the characterization of that speaker. A narrative that is diacritically marked by a great many words of estrangement is a narrative whose speaker, be he overtly or covertly present, presents himself as diffident, circumspect, innocent, uninvolved, or simply ignorant.

A third type of discursive feature manifesting itself at the microlinguistic level is what we might call the pattern of diction. As Booth has tellingly demonstrated throughout *The Rhetoric of Fiction,* even the most impersonal narration must employ language that is impregnated with a personal and evaluational burden. The use of any adjectives of relation (i.e., *great, old, large*) implicitly suggests an act of judgment on the part of the speaker, and the ascription of qualities to any actant ("a kindly old man") presupposes an ethical position from which such evaluations can be made. The pattern of diction not only acts as an index for a particular narrational situation, but it also contributes extensively to characterization of the speaker and the "mood" of the text. The respective speakers in Kafka's impersonal narrations and those of Hemingway might well be distinguished by their patterns of diction (which systematically create the tone of the narrative). Studies of an author's "style" frequently dwell on the speaker's dictional pattern when attempting to describe a distinctive idiolect.

For present concerns, a more important manifestation of speaker involves discursive statements, or "commentaries," which serve to define the point of view of the speaker. These types of statements can be divided into three main groups: perceptual, ideological, and metalingual (roughly corresponding to statements of self, society, and literature). In the course of relating a narrative, a speaker occasionally feels justified or compelled or qualified to make general comments about the actants, events, topoi, or fictionality of the fictional world, comments of a descriptive or normative nature. Perceptual comments make reference to the speaker's own opinions, sets of beliefs, judgments, or thought processes concerning matters related to the fictional WORLD. In the opening pages of *Middlemarch,* the narrator describes Dorothea Brooke as follows: "Her mind was theoretic, and yearned by its nature after some lofty conception of the world which might frankly include the parish of Tipton and her own rule of conduct there; she was enamoured of intensity and greatness, and rash in whatever seemed to her to have those aspects; likely to seek martyrdom, to make retractions, and then to incur martyrdom after all in a quarter where she had not sought it." This magisterial assessment of character channels or circumscribes the reader's response to Dorothea. When the "authorial" speaker of *Tess of the D'Urbervilles* closes the final chapter with the Olympian pronouncement that " 'justice' was done, and the President of the Immortals, in Aeschylean phrase, had ended his sport with Tess," he interjects a normative discursive statement into the narrative, a personal evaluation of the course of events. In similar fashion, the speakers within many of Hawthorne's fictions interrupt their narratives to draw morals about the proceedings, or a narrator like Tristram Shandy can halt his story to launch an extended digression about the way in which his mind works. These kinds of comment contribute to the characterization of the speaker and establish his or her relation to the world being created. We gather from them clues as to the speaker's and the characters' thought processes, personal attitudes and beliefs, and ethical persuasion. The speaker is situated and "humanized" while at the same time the fictional WORLD is channeled or interpreted for the reader.

The second major system of discursive statements can be referred to as ideological because their presence presupposes the existence of a reading community that shares the value system, ideational matrix, or cultural milieu in which they are rooted. Jane Austen possesses enough sociocultural assurance to begin *Pride and Prejudice* with the categorical assertion that "it is a truth universally acknowledged, that a single man in possession of a good fortune, must be in want of a wife." Austen intends the statement to be received ironically, but, irony or no, the comment indicates an awareness on the part of the speaker of a cultural community for which such statements will have validity. Roland Barthes assigns all such statements to their own narrative code, which he calls the referential code,[27] composed of discursive assertions whose basis lies in scientific or moral authority of the originary culture. Barthes suggests that a systematic examination of the referential code of a single text or group of texts can reveal a "deep" ideology, which Barthes characteristically describes as a "monster" that seeks to govern its creator. His point, of course, is that acceptance of or adherence to any "Book" of cultural wisdom acts as a constricting influence upon narrative energies, channeling them into the acceptable, the conventional, the sanctioned. The presence of perceptual and ideological statements characterizes texts in which the speaker is said to be intrusive, classic or readerly texts in which the speakers feel that they possess the *author*-ity to speak from and for their culture. Extensive utilization of both the perceptual and ideological components of DISCURSIVE SPACE implies a degree of epistemological and ethical assurance on the speaker's part; he or she "occupies" a major component of DISCURSIVE SPACE. One of the distinguishing characteristics of modern texts is the evacuation of this portion of space; culturological circumstances and consequent epistemological crises result in a retreat from DISCURSIVE SPACE. The author becomes more and more circumspect; the whole notion of *author*-ity becomes suspect. Henry James initiates this retreat from interpretive and evaluative responsibility in the deliberate ambiguities of his later fictions; the problematics of interpretation become the narrative dominant for his fictions.

A third form of discursive statements, which I have designated *metalingual,* consists in explicit comments on, or reference to, the narrative act. For any number of reasons, the speaker chooses to address the how, what, where, or when of his or her composition (or those by others), and thus exposes or explores the enabling codes of fiction. After introducing a minor character in "The Overcoat," Gogol's intrusive narrator adds, "Of this tailor I ought not, of course, to say much, but since it is now the rule that the character of every person in a novel must be completely drawn, well, there is no help for it, here is Petrovich too." Metalingual interpolations like this destroy the fictional illusion, which is one reason why James chastised Trollope for using them. But contemporary fictionists like Barth, Barthelme, Fowles, and others tend to rely more and more on metalingual S_D to liberate themselves from constraints and expectations inherent in the fiction-making act itself.

As noted above, certain theorists of fiction have singled out the inevitable distance that exists between speaker and what is spoken, between the enunciation and the fictional world, as the distinguishing characteristic of prose narrative. I should emphasize that there *does* exist the potential for a considerable "interspace" between the space of the fictional world (S_W) and the space of the enunciation (S_D); the fictionist may either dilate or contract this intertextual space in accordance with his or her aesthetic ends. The distance between S_W and S_D can be both temporal and spatial. This distance is signaled temporally by the convention of the epic preterit as the controlling verb for prose fiction. The systematic use of the past tense creates a perspective that implies that the world being presented has been consumed and digested. Extraneous or irrelevant material has been eliminated; the speaker gives to his or her audience a world that is managed, finished, pregnant with significance. Traditional fiction characteristically keeps the distance between the speaker and the world as great as possible so as to verify the logic and sequentiality of the tale and, more important, to guarantee its significance. The recounted experience merits telling because it is complete and meaningful. The distance between S_W and S_D has also, especially in traditional fiction, a spatial dimension. In what might be termed "authorial" narration, the speaker's space exists in a position of privilege "above" the space of the world, enabling the speaker to move freely through that world, to penetrate its walls, to observe and pass judgment on its significant events. The amount of "commentary" in authorial narration (its occupation of DIS-CURSIVE SPACE) is predicated upon the speaker's awareness of this distance and the authority it bestows. In many modernist fictions this spatial dimension is eliminated; the time of the world becomes the time of the discourse, the story of the world becoming the story of the discourse (see chapter 4). The story does not exist prior to its articulation in written language; the fiction concerns itself with the time proper to the enunciation itself. Barthes describes this project as follows:

> The meaning or goal of this effort is to substitute the instance of discourse for the instance of reality (or of the referent), which has been, and still is a mythical "alibi" dominating the idea of literature. The field of the writer is nothing but writing itself, not as the pure "form" conceived by an aesthetic of art for art's sake, but, much more radically, as the only area [*espace*] for the one who writes.[28]

Reducing the distance between the instance of discourse and narrated world serves to liberate the narrative imagination from its subservience to an a priori "reality," or so Barthes would argue.

Prose narrative involves more than a fictional world and a narrative situation; it also involves the inscription of that narrative upon some material substance; a prose narrative in so many words, in such an order, on so many pages. Holquist and Reed point out that "in poetry and drama, the presence of the printed text is a secondary feature, subordinate to the phenomenon of voice or scene; this is true even if voice or scene are only perceived in the mind's ear or the mind's eye. Novels constitute a literature of the printed book and the peculiarities that this medium entails. . . . The novel was the first kind of literary work historically to experience the transition from 'work of art' to 'text.' "[29] The fact that any prose narrative has a material (as well as imaginal) existence creates another component of its NARRATIONAL SPACE, the ICONIC SPACE of the fiction. In semiological usage, an icon is a member of that class of signs for which there is a correspondence of resemblance between the signifier and the signified. For example, a photographic portait constitutes an iconic sign of the person portrayed. In iconic signs, the relationship between signifier and signified is established by physical resemblance and not convention. In adopting the term ICONIC SPACE, I mean to describe those aspects of a prose narrative in which there is a palpable correspondence between the signifying and the signified reality and which therefore draw the reader's attention to the materiality of the fictional discourse. ICONIC SPACE consists in deployment of the sign vehicles of fiction in such a way that the signifying practice either resembles or becomes part of the signified reality. The means by which the fiction is mediated—the materiality of the narrative medium—is foregrounded when the potential of ICONIC SPACE is exploited.

As noted above, a prose narrative consists of a certain number of words that are formed by the concatenation of certain groups of letters. These words are strung out across a certain number of pages that are meant to read in a certain order. Each of these aspects of prose fiction contributes to its potential ICONIC SPACE. That is to say, we may distinguish four levels of ICONIC SPACE, each corresponding to one aspect of the text's materiality: ALPHABETIC, LEXICAL, PAGINAL, and COMPOSI-

TIONAL. Before exploring and elaborating these various levels, I should note that most realistic fiction, because of its desire to represent an a priori external reality, attempts to make its readers forget about or ignore its materiality. It hopes to compel readers to look through its transparent language, as they look through a window, to the "real life" that it presents. This type of writing maintains strict compliance with certain "natural" conventions of writing and reading (linear presentation, left-to-right order, a single authorized reading direction, chapters in a specified order) because it wishes to naturalize the reading process and maintain the fictional illusion. Obviously these texts make minimal use of ICONIC SPACE. On the other hand, fictions that capitalize on the materiality of the discourse, by exploring aspects of textuality, violate some of the strongest and most honored textual conventions and are often dismissed as "gimmicky." What may be overlooked from this perspective is the fact that experimentation with ICONIC SPACE has as much validity as experimentation with other aspects of discourse and constitutes an attempt to multiply the types of space available for signification.

Any prose fiction is composed of individual words that can be further divided into so many letters drawn from the limited set enumerated by the alphabet. If words constitute the atoms of a literary molecule, then the letters of the alphabet constitute the subatomic particles and, as such, can be considered the "building blocks" of any and all discursive universes. To extend the metaphor, any narrative physicist may choose to limit his investigation of the stuff of narrative to the atomic level (the words of the fiction), or he may choose to expand his horizons to include the subatomic level. In Umberto Eco's terms, he extends the range of his exploration to incorporate the hyposemiotic stuff.[30] Any systematic exploration or manipulation of the hyposemiotic stuff of fiction generates an area of signification that I shall call the ALPHABETIC SPACE of the fiction. The discrete matter of the sign-vehicle is particularized in such a way as to create within the fiction a subsystem of signification that makes its own contribution to the aesthetic experience. One of the most elementary appropriations of ALPHABETIC SPACE is the anagram (Enos Enoch in John Barth's *Giles Goat-Boy* is an anagram for Chosen One). Anagrams and palindromes and the like might well be seen as a trivial subliterary trick, but what then does one make of Walter Abish's systematic use of

ALPHABETIC SPACE as simultaneously an ordering principle, narrative domain, and logistical constraint in *Alphabetical Africa?* His innovative play with the fixed elements of the alphabet constitutes in large part the "meaning" of the text.

The second level of ICONIC SPACE pertains to what many would consider the basic unit of literary semiosis—the word. As several theoreticians of fiction have pointed out, a literary narrative is "made of words," and some fictionists are acutely aware of this fact. In order to communicate this awareness to the reader (for any number of reasons), the fictionist may resort to various techniques that foreground the "wordiness" of fiction. The writer may choose language that is so opaque or obscure that the reader finds it difficult if not impossible to make the quantum leap from the signifier to the signified; the reader is restricted to the words themselves, "reading without comprehension" (John Ashbery's phrase in *Three Poems*). Or the writer can resort to language that is overdetermined, to words whose several meanings all fit the narrative context and which therefore signify so many things as to be insignificant; a pun is an elementary example of an overdetermined semantic space. Or the writer might make use of the aural aspect of a verbal configuration in such a way as to undercut its basic semantic information. John Barth does this continually in the stories in *Lost in the Funhouse;* a classic example would be the opening lines to "Autobiography: A Self-Recorded Fiction," in which the speaker is a tape recorder:

"You who   listen   give me life .   in a manner of speaking."

In each of these several techniques, the fictionist undercuts the semantic dimension of his language and thus draws attention to the words themselves. The realm of the signified is sacrificed to the play of the signifiers.

Another component of ICONIC SPACE pertains to the empty field on which the language of fiction is inscribed—the page. Most conventional fiction adheres to a natural, grammatical syntax that prescribes that the narrative unfold in linear, sequential, left-to-right articulations. Certain innovative fictions attempt to take advantage of the space of the page on which they are inscribed; the letters and words of the fiction are scrambled in heterogeneous fashion across the page, fre-

quently creating a pictorial image that either enacts or parodies
the semantic import of the narrative articulation; concrete
poetry is the verse analogue of this device. One of the more
important explorers of PAGINAL SPACE, Raymond Federman, ex-
plains the practice as follows:

> The space of the page (and of course all the pages that make the
> book) can either restrain the fiction and force the language to un-
> fold into a predetermined conventional syntax, or else liberate the
> fiction so that it may invent, create on the spot its own syntax as it
> progresses. The distinction is between a grammatical syntax which
> is the result of habit and reflexes, or a paginal syntax which is the
> result of spontaneity and chance—and of course, when I say syntax
> I also mean narrative since narrative is created by a succession of
> syntactical articulations (or, in the case of modern fiction, by a suc-
> cession of syntactical disarticulations).[31]

The attempt to generate spontaneously a paginal syntax constitutes yet another way in which contemporary writers liberate
narrative energies.

Federman's comment about the several pages that make the
book indicates the aspect of textuality that determines the final
component of ICONIC SPACE, that which I have termed COMPOSI-
TIONAL SPACE, in that it calls into question the ways in which the
various pages, chapters, or sections of the narrative are composed (in the etymological sense of *put together*) within the text.
A text arrays its narrative units in some format; a conventional
text adopts a left-to-right, top-to-bottom syntactic articulation,
page-to-page continuity, and textual irreversibility. The reader,
a consumer of the text, accepts the text as *these* pages in *this*
order. A paratactic text, one whose narrative motifs are discrete
and autonomous, by disrupting textual continuity calls attention to the ways in which texts are put together and thus creates
a degree of COMPOSITIONAL SPACE (which it inevitably "shares"
with the reader). The text deconstructs conventional notions of
textuality and demands that the reader assume a more active
role in narrative management. The reader must create his or
her own reading order for the narrative (the novel-in-a-box) or
imaginatively construct (not re-construct) the segmented fragments of the text into a satisfactory whole. This second type of
text Edward Marcotte refers to as "intersticed prose," a species
of contemporary writing characterized, he argues, by a segmentation of the narrative text into discrete entities or frag-

ments. The fact of fragmentation is not meant to imply incompleteness; as Marcotte notes, "the *intentional* fragment . . . is meant to be taken as in its way complete."[32] This type of writing creates some idiosyncratic effects: it drastically modifies the reader's notion of what constitutes a narrative unit; the spacing between units suggests that each unit is to be considered separate but equal (there is no hierarchy based upon relative importance of each unit); the discontinuity of the text de-emphasizes linearity and causality and temporality, and correspondingly privileges simultaneity and spatiality; the silences in the text—the gaps between fragments—offer themselves as "holes" to be filled; readers are invited to step in, to fill the gap, to make the missing connection, and perhaps to make fools of themselves; the structure of the narrative makes room for the reader as part of its narrative ontology. Marcotte speaks of this form of writing as "an attempt to bring about a fundamental reorganization in prose, the charting of a new stop in narrational space."[33] Although several modernist authors (e.g., Virginia Woolf in *The Waves*) employ this mode of writing partially and sporadically, some contemporary fictionists have adopted it as *the* compositional principle, both for short fictions (Donald Barthelme's "Views of My Father Weeping") and for entire novels (Burroughs's *Naked Lunch* and Ronald Sukenick's *Out*). The increase in the number of writers employing parataxis as ordering principle and the fact that the principle is applied systematically mark a qualitative change in narrative sensibility, a change that manifests itself not only in "intersticed prose," but also in experimentation with the various other components of ICONIC and DISCURSIVE SPACE.

As the above discussion indicates, the narrational component of any fiction is potentially a very complex system of types of signification. Although the discussion suggests the complexity of the matter, it might unfortunately also suggest that a particular narrative element can readily be isolated and identified as belonging solely to the realm of narration, that elements of NARRATIONAL SPACE are separate and distinct from elements of NARRATIVAL SPACE. Such is not the case. Any narrative unit may perform several functions within a total fictional space. A narrative unit from fragmented or intersticed narrative, for example, may contain information that contributes to the development of the skeletal STORY, at the same time as it marks and characterizes the presence of the speaker through manipulation of DISCURSIVE SPACE, and as it, as *intentional* fragment, helps to bring into being a degree of COMPOSITIONAL SPACE; the unit makes several contributions at once. Since a unit cannot be classified and pigeonholed once and for all, what should be of interest for the student of narrative is not the inalienable identity of any particular unit, but rather the preponderance of one (or more) functions throughout the texture of the entire narrative; any particular narrative generates its own dominant, that component of a literary system which "rules, determines, and transforms the remaining components" of the system.[34] In terms of our own vocabulary, one component of fictional space by virtue of its systematic elaboration tends to dominate the other components of the space and thus to establish a typologic character for the text.

Although the system of NARRATIONAL SPACE that I have mapped is already dismayingly complex and involved, it may well be argued that it is not complex enough in that it omits an element of fiction of considerable importance: point of view. This exception to, or qualification of, my discussion of narration must be answered. What establishes for a text its narrational character is not that it unfolds from the point of view of first or third person, but that the text is marked by either the presence or the absence of a speaking subject. The entire question of point of view should be broached from this axiomatic postulate. As a matter of fact, Lubomir Dolezel has attempted to approach the problem from this standpoint and has derived a typology of the narrator from it.[35] Dolezel's structural analysis, beginning with the fundamental distinction between texts with and without speakers, generates three basic types of narration (auctorial first person, personal first person, and objective) that bear some resemblance to standard tripartite divisions of point of view; what distinguishes Dolezel's discussion of the subject is his initial postulate, the systematic nature of his methodology, and (a consequence of the first two attributes) a typology of narrators that includes narrational types that have never been realized in the history of fiction (this last characteristic illustrates the predictive power of some contemporary structural analysis). In terms of my schema of fictional space, any text with a speaker has available to it the areas and types of signification outlined in my discussion of DISCURSIVE SPACE; the text may choose to occupy and exploit any or all of these areas and may be described in terms of these areas. The location of the speaker may be described in terms of the relation (or distance) between the space of the discourse (S_D) and the space of the fictional world (S_W). A text that systematically eliminates references to the presence and situation of the speaker "evacuates" DISCURSIVE SPACE and may be described without reference to it; as we shall see, the narrative functions performed by the components of DISCURSIVE SPACE are transferred from the speaking subject to the receiving subject (i.e., the reader).

IV

If you now ask whether in this way one ever gets to a specifically scientific interpretation, this question clearly implies a concept of science drawn from the natural sciences, more precisely, from physics. This so-called nomological concept of science has, meanwhile, been countered . . . by a dialogical concept of science which only an ideologue could consider "less scientific." The dialogical concept of science does not exclude the standpoint and activity of the subject, but rather includes him as the condition of knowledge, and this concept is to that extent specific to all sciences which would understand meaning, which proceed from the assumption that meaning is a yielded truth—and not a given one.

        Hans Robert Jauss, in Rien T. Segers, "Interview with Hans Robert Jauss"

I have outlined thus far the two major areas of signification obtaining to the text *per se*—the textual space available to the fictionist for expenditure of, and experimentation with, narrative energies. The unfolding TEXT SPACE of a narrative exists in dynamic relation with its *reader,* a relation determined by both the nature of that space and the competence of the reader. Readers have certain expectations about the nature and function of narratives in general, they have a more specific horizon of expectations about narrative fiction in particular, and they perform certain operations upon fictional texts to insure the fulfillment of those expectations. Readers anticipate satisfactions and gratifications predicated upon plenitude and sufficiency within fictional space, and they will supply these qualities if the fiction itself lacks them. If a fiction evacuates a portion of its conventionalized space, the reader will attempt to fill the resulting vacuum.

It should be clear that the space "occupied" by the reader is not of the same nature as that pertaining to the fiction; it has not the textual "presence" that characterizes the other two subspaces. The space of the reader may be described as PARASPACE in that it exists, as it were, in a separate dimension parallel to, or alongside of, the more tangible dimensions of TEXT SPACE. PARASPACE consists not so much in areas of signification as in processes or activities that the text elicits from the reader. Jonathan Culler, in his discussions of the reader's role in narrative, deliberately avoids the term *meaning,* which connotes a certain "thereness" within the text; he adopts the phrase *making sense,* which connects the notion of meaning with an active, creative process.[36] We shall see that making sense is merely one of several possible operations that a reader performs on the text (and one that is not solely the reader's responsibility), but Culler's point that meaning is less a property than the product of a process is a good one. In describing the reader's contribution to the space of the fiction, I shall be enumerating a series of activities that are generated by a horizon of expectations.

Every narrative addresses itself to a hypothetical audience; a story is narrated by someone for someone. The audience of which I speak is not the auditors who sometimes appear in narratives employing a tale-within-a-tale (the actions and characteristics of which sometimes parody the actual reading audience), nor is it the flesh-and-blood reader who sits in the easy chair with the text before him or her. The reader I refer to is a "metonymic characterization of the text,"[37] consisting of a set of textually conditioned and culturally sanctioned mental operations that are performed upon the text. These operations are predicated upon the reader's prior exposure to and familiarity with a narrative tradition, upon previous literary experiences that determine the competence of the "native reader."

The most elementary operation that the reader performs, and one that all narrative elicits, can be referred to as *actualization.* Before "doing" anything with the fictional space that they encounter, readers must endow the fictional configurations with a degree of imaginal substance. Like Hawthorne in his den, readers must *real-*ize a "tribe of unrealities" by investing fictional phantasms with dimensionality or "presence," thus giving them an imaginal actuality. Reading a Faulkner novel, a reader must bring Yoknapatawpha County into "existence"; beginning an Austen novel, a reader must gradually create from imaginative resources the image of a spoiled, immature, and willful Emma Woodhouse; poring over a Hemingway text, a reader reconstructs, *ex nihilo,* the image of an old man, a turbu-

lent sea, and a monster fish. In the actualization process, the
reader verifies the motifs that have been decoded by comparing
them with a pre-acquired encyclopedia of knowledge encom-
passing the models and laws of physical phenomena, the norms
of verisimilar behavior, and a compendium of "real world" information brought to the text. All narrative provokes this primary act of actualization; much narrative attempts to facilitate
it by supplying abundant concrete detail, smooth transitions,
and narrative continuity, all of which contribute to the ready
"naturalization" of the text by the reader. Some contemporary
fiction, on the other hand, assaults the very notion of fictional
worlds by continuously disrupting or complicating this elementary process of actualization.

Once a particular text has been actualized, it remains to be
understood; the reader must discover its "meaning." As was
noted above, fiction creates worlds that are *other* than the "real
world." There need be no correspondence between the topoi,
actants, and events of a fiction and those of empirical reality,
although there may be a relationship of similarity
(verisimilitude). The discovery of meaning consists of a process
of naturalization that is based upon what Culler refers to as
vraisemblance: the reader organizes the reading experience by
relating the otherness of the fictional text to "natural" models
of experience, models that the culture makes familiar and
certifies. The reader "recuperates" the text and puts it to use by
discovering the ways in which it conforms to *a priori* models of
"reality" and not to its own internal workings. And the "reality"
that the work is seen to correspond with should not be taken
monolithically as empirical reality. As Culler has shown in his
enumeration of models of *vraisemblance,* the reader naturalizes
a text by establishing its relation with "realities" that can be
empirical, cultural, and/or literary; the reader domesticates the
text by working out its connections with various models that are
known beforehand and culturally sanctioned.[38]

The activity of discovering meaning takes place on various
levels within the text, both microtextual and macrotextual.
Each narrative kernel is successively brought into relation with
appropriate cultural models, and eventually the entire narrative sequence is named. For example, the reader recognizes
Tom Jones's encounter with Lady Bellaston as an example of
"naive young man being led astray by older woman of the
world"; after recuperating this and the many other sequences

that constitute the novel *Tom Jones*, the reader may make sense
of the total experience by remarking its correspondence with a
cultural model that specifies that "benevolence must be tem-
pered by prudence in the character of the good man." Clearly
these two levels of meaning are interrelated; the reader works
back and forth between the micro- and macrotextual levels,
progressively organizing his or her experience of the text.[39]

The above example may suggest that the meaning discovered
by the process of *vraisemblablisation* will necessarily be singular,
but such is not the case. A text may, at the micro- or macrotextual level, generate separate but equal forms of meaning, based
upon different cultural models. Greimas terms these separate
forms of coherent meaning the text's "isotopies."[40] For example, Franz Kafka's *The Castle* has been severally interpreted as
depicting the quest of a soul for grace, the struggle of modern
man with the fact of Nothingness, the search of the son for the
absent mother, and the encounter between individual and bureaucracy.[41] Each of these readings can be supported by extensive evidence from the text; they are parallel interpretations of
a deliberately obscure situation. The fact of multiple readings,
of polysemy, is not in itself a cause for consternation for
readers; in many cases the play of meaning adds to the reader's
appreciation of the text in that it adds to the text's resonance
and challenges the reader to group the several meanings by
moving to a higher level of generality where a "total" meaning
is available.

I speak here of the meaning *of the text,* of the text's isotopies,
of its polysemy. All of these locutions underscore the fact that
meaning is to some extent an attribute of the text and thus not
solely the product of a reader's activity. Every narrative channels its readers into certain avenues of meaning, according to
the incidents it portrays and the rhetoric it employs. The DIS-
CURSIVE SPACE of a fiction, particularly in authorial narration, is
frequently used to focus or channel the interpretive energies of
the reader. A fictionist can, for that matter, choose to state
explicitly what it is that his narrative "means." Aesop's fables
(and fables in general) are imaginary narratives whose meaning, whose relation to the "real world," is specified by means of
an explicit moral. The speakers within Hawthorne's fictional
spaces often resort to explicit statements of meaning at the end
of their tales, particularly when the tale seems to have tenuous
or fragile connection with everyday experience.[42] One should

contrast the fable, which tends to "occupy" the space of meaning, with those mini-narratives that appear in the Gospels—the parables. A parable may be defined as a short fictitious narrative that is obviously pregnant with meaning, but whose creator (cf. Jesus, who is beleaguered by his disciples for the "true" meanings of his parables) refuses to reveal just what that meaning is. It should be noted that one of the generic characteristics of the mainstream of Western narrative in the modern world (the Novel since its inception in the eighteenth century) is its parabolic nature; the novel has generally refused to state explicitly just what its final meaning is. As Wolfgang Iser has argued in his text on the reader's role, "the meaning of the novel only materializes in the reader's reactions, since it does not exist per se."[43] The novel as a genre seeks to generate a total meaning; it even tends to circumscribe the semantic boundaries of that meaning; nevertheless it obstinately refuses to name that meaning. A reader comes to a novel with the understanding that there exists *some* relation between its fictional world (the components of NARRATIVAL SPACE) and experiential reality and that it will be his or her responsibility to discover the nature of that relation. The novel necessarily presents a world that is strange or other, but "the process of reading naturalizes and reduces that strangeness by recognizing and naming."[44] The fact of otherness creates a space of interpretation; the reader obligingly occupies that space.

The discovery of meaning is usually the most important of the reader's responsibilities in relation to the text, but it is certainly not the final one. An operation that is generally subsequent to the process of naturalization and attendant upon it involves evaluating the actants and events of the fictional world. Once a fiction is brought into relation with the "real world," once its meaning has been discovered, there is established in the reader's imagination a set of norms (derived from the real world and modified by the textual experience) that enables the reader to make evaluative statements about narrative realities. Characters may be labeled as good or evil or a mixture thereof, decisions seen as foolish or wise, accomplishments as glorious or trivial, events as catastrophic or fortunate. And at the macrotextual level, the reader may feel qualified to pass judgment on an entire fictional world. The act of interpreting the fictional experience establishes a normative framework with which that experience may be judged (and with which the reader might reevaluate extratextual existence). It a great many, but not all, reading experiences the processes of interpretation and evaluation occur simultaneously. One noteworthy exception is the fairy tale, which prescribes for the reader the proper normative responses to its actants and events ("once upon a time there was a *good* little boy who was forced by the death of his *gentle* parents to stay with *evil* stepparents who . . .") and at the same time fails to establish a circumscribed interpretive framework (the reader is hard pressed to discover models of *vraisemblance* for fairy tales); a fairy tale occupies its normative space and yet evacuates its interpretive space.

As I have noted above, the activity of interpretation frequently involves establishment of relationships between fictional and "real" worlds; the reader attempts to naturalize or recuperate elements of NARRATIVAL SPACE. The activity of evaluation, on the other hand, is more intimately connected with components of NARRATIONAL SPACE; the reader takes his clues about normative judgments concerning actants and events from discursive elements that situate the speaker in relation to the fictional world. In other words, aspects of DISCURSIVE SPACE shape the reader's normative response and thereby circumscribe the "normative space" of the fiction (creating a "rhetoric" of fiction), just as aspects of the fictional world circumscribe its "interpretive space."

There are yet two other operations that readers "naturally" perform upon texts to obtain the cognitive and sublimative satisfactions they seek from fiction. Readers expect not only that a fictional text will be significant, that it will have "meaning"; they also expect (and the fact of meaning is in part predicated upon satisfaction of this expectation) that the text will cohere, that they will be able to make transitions from motif to motif, from kernel to kernel, from sequence to sequence. In most cases the armature of plot (what we have termed the STORY of the fiction) provides the thread of continuity that insures narrative coherence. The final expectation of the reader's horizon of expectations consists in a desire for completeness, for the satisfaction that comes from the "sense of an ending." The desire for coherence seeks out (or if necessary invents) the text's unity, a unity generally provided by the continuity of its parts; the reader feels a "need to make everything in a . . . novel or poem part of an organic whole." The desire for completeness, on the other hand, seeks to endow the text with a teleology born of an ineluctable narrative movement from stable point *A* through unstable point *B* to the terminal stability of point *C;* in regard to completeness, a reader is "haunted by the need to produce or invent an absent telos."[45] The expectation of both coherence and completeness derives from the reader's pre-understanding that the fictional experience (unlike his or her existential experience) should be characterized by certain qualities, namely, fullness, termination, teleology, form.

It happens, as Culler notes in "Making Sense," that certain narratives do not satisfy the reader's expectations of coherence and completeness, that the reader's attempt to establish connections and to discover irreversibility is deliberately obscured and frustrated by the text's incompleteness and fragmentation. More traditional fictions of course inevitably leave gaps in their narratives; not every movement or every thought of every actant can be related (witness the problems that Tristram Shandy encounters when he attempts to do this); a speaker must leave something out. But traditional narratives make sure that the gaps, the inevitable spaces between events and movements, are readily recuperable. The amount of labor that the reader performs in making the transition from scene to scene is minimal because the path is clearly demarcated. In more contemporary texts, the connections between scenes or episodes are not nearly so evident or common-sensical, if they exist at all. In paratactic fictions, where autonomous narrative units are simply juxtaposed, the narrative itself is radically discontinuous and the connections between motifs are problematic. If the narrative is to cohere, the reader must supply the links. In similar fashion a contemporary narrative may choose not to come to a final resting point, to a moment of stasis. In this case the reader must provide the absent *telos,* which invests the narrative with directionality and irreversibility. The reader gives to the text the ending it never knew.

It should be clear from the foregoing that, although most texts submit to and satisfy a reader's expectations of completeness and coherence, these are qualities that are not necessarily properties of the fictional text; and that these qualities, should they be absent or problematic, are almost automatically supplied by obliging readers. Fictionists who wish to promote these activities on the part of the reader frequently resort, as we shall see, to experimentation with both STORY and COMPOSI-

TIONAL SPACE because they know that these interrelated components supply the presentational glue that holds the parts together. And radical disruption of STORY or COMPOSITIONAL SPACE necessarily implicates the reader in narrative management; it creates a "writerly" text whose reader becomes an active producer, not a passive consumer, of both meaning and structure.[46]

This survey of PARASPACE reveals that readers participate to some extent in the production of all narrative texts; in more radically experimental texts, the degree and nature of that participation changes considerably. And readers perform this labor—the mining for meaning, the judicial passage of sentence, the tedious restitching of a raveled plot—willingly, sometimes uninvitedly, because they wish to make of their reading experience an organic totality. The fiction comes to life in their minds in proportion to the degree that it becomes "total" in their imaginations. By total we mean that the action *represented* to the reader should be single (unified), complete (teleological), and significant (meaningful). To the extent that the fiction lacks these qualities, to the extent that it resists totalization,[47] to that extent will readers be dissatisfied. In most instances readers attempt to supply what the fiction has left out; they partially totalize even the most nontotalizing narrative. For it is hard to live with, much less justify, a species of fiction that seems totally unconnected with the way we live now. That kind of narrative will have to wait for a radical alteration in the readers' horizon of expectations.

Having completed this examination of the spaces of fiction, I should perhaps provide a "map" of the field in its entirety so as to review the ground covered and to establish a perspective (see p. 60). It should be noted that this diagram presents a static (and "spatialized") model of what I have insisted all along is a dynamic *process*. A fictional space consists of an unfolding field of complex interactions in which transformations in one part of the system (e.g., retreat of "authorial" persona, change in speaker, fragmentation of STORY) result in corresponding adjustments by the reader. But because a map necessarily renders in *space* (synchronically) the phenomena it is meant to *represent*, the diagram does not do justice to the diachronic aspect of the experience of narrative, in particular the element of STORY. As a matter of fact, the entire discussion of the space of the fictional world simply identifies this most important area of signification and leaves its articulation to the future. There remain to be written a grammar of stories, a typology of actants, and a typology of topographical spaces. The same reservation, of course, applies to the other components of fictional space.

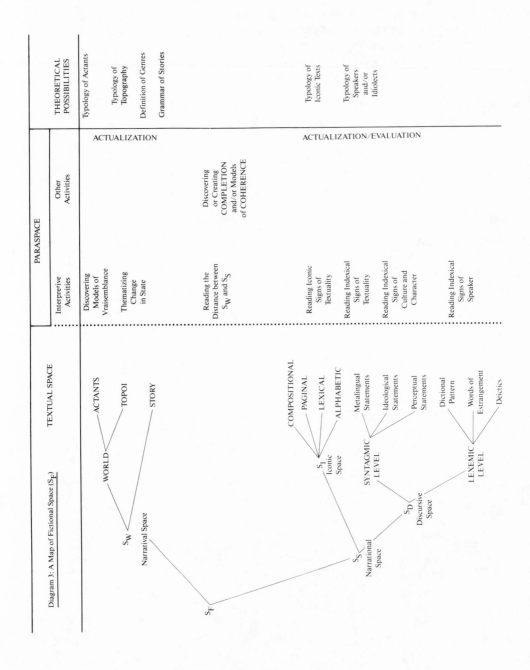

Diagram 3: A Map of Fictional Space (S_F)

	TEXTUAL SPACE	PARASPACE		THEORETICAL POSSIBILITIES
		Interpretive Activities	Other Activities	

ACTUALIZATION

ACTUALIZATION/EVALUATION

Textual Space:

- S_F
  - Narratival Space — S_W
    - WORLD
      - ACTANTS
      - TOPOI
    - STORY
  - S_S Narrational Space
    - S_D Discursive Space
      - S_I Iconic Space
        - COMPOSITIONAL
        - PAGINAL
        - LEXICAL
        - ALPHABETIC
      - SYNTAGMIC LEVEL
        - Metalingual Statements
        - Ideological Statements
        - Perceptual Statements
      - LEXEMIC LEVEL
        - Dictional Pattern
        - Words of Estrangement
        - Deictics

Interpretive Activities:

- Discovering Models of Vraisemblance
- Thematizing Change in State
- Reading the Distance between S_W and S_S
- Reading Iconic Signs of Textuality
- Reading Indexical Signs of Textuality
- Reading Indexical Signs of Culture and Character
- Reading Indexical Signs of Speaker

Other Activities:

- Discovering or Creating COMPLETION and/or Models of COHERENCE

Theoretical Possibilities:

- Typology of Actants
- Typology of Topography
- Definition of Genres
- Grammar of Stories
- Typology of Iconic Texts
- Typology of Speakers and/or Idiolects

Part II

Our task, on the other hand, is the description of that hollow structure impregnated by the interpretations of critics and readers. We shall remain as far from the interpretation of individual works as we were in dealing with the verbal or syntactic aspect. As before, we are concerned here as well to describe a configuration rather than to name a meaning.

Tzvetan Todorov, The Fantastic

Let me tell you something I once asked Einstein. I was questioning his effort to bring the laws that govern atomic particles into line with a general theory of relativity. What good does all this theory do I finally asked him unless we find a way of incorporating it into our own experience. . . . My dear skeptic, you are perfectly right. Only experience can restore that lost synthesis which analysis has forced us to shatter. Experience alone can decide on truth.

Ronald Sukenick, 98.6

Fictional Space and the Twentieth-Century American Novel

From a pragmatic standpoint, the real value of a theory rests in its capacity to describe and account for the empirical phenomena that generated it. A theory, in addition, should be able "to provide new organizing perspectives for a field of study."[1] In Part I of this text several theoretical advantages were attributed to the concept *fictional space*. For one thing the concept attempts to embrace the various centers of the literary experience—author, text, and reader. For another, the concept can be readily modified so as to encompass narrative discourse in general and thus to clarify the generic distinctiveness of forms of prose narrative. Finally, the concept should be able to account for the fact and shape of literary change; it should be readily adaptable to the needs of literary historiography. In the chapters that follow, the theory of fictional space will be used to generate "new organizing perspectives" for the phenomena that brought it into existence—the myriad forms of American fiction in the twentieth century.

American fiction has undergone incredible changes in this century. There is a marked difference between the convoluted but essentially "readerly" fictions of Henry James's major phase and the kaleidoscopic montage of Dos Passos's *U.S.A.* And there is an even more pronounced difference between the Dos Passos text and Raymond Federman's "spatial displacement of words" in *Take It or Leave It*. These radical differences in fictional forms derive from certain relatively simple transformations performed upon the subspaces of the texts, transformations that result in the evolution of new narrative "dominants," alter the narrative ontology, and create new responsibilities for the reader. Three major movements in the process of transformation may be distinguished—*modernist, paramodernist,* and *postmodernist,* terms referring more to types of sensibility than to matters of chronology. These movements can best be described through contrast with premodernist practice.

One of the most significant "interspaces" of a fiction consists in the potential distance between NARRATIVAL space and NARRATIONAL space, a distance that can be measured in terms of space (position of "authorial" privilege) and in terms of time (use of the epic preterit). Victorian authors tend to take the existence of this distance for granted; acting upon widespread cultural assumptions, they feel that they can contain or circumscribe a fictional space, can preside over it, *author*-ize it, a belief reflected in the narrative's coherence and intelligibility as well as in the speaker's magisterial position. The fictional speaker assumes a relation toward the fictional world that might be termed *determined*. Modernist authors, lacking the epistemological assurance of the Victorians, tend to relinquish traditional interpretive responsibilities. They do this by "flattening" the fictional space, that is, by reducing or eliminating the consoling distance between S_W and S_S. The resultant space appears to the reader as *underdetermined* because of the elimination of a "degree of interpretation." Paramodernist authors continue the transformation of fictional space in more radical terms, systematically leaving deliberate and visible gaps in their fictions, thus compelling the reader to take a different role in narrative management; their fictional spaces might be referred to as *undetermined*. Finally, postmodernist fictionists reoccupy previously evacuated or "exploded" subspaces of the fiction, but in an *overdetermined* fashion. By cheerfully and ironically donning the *author*-ial mask and acknowledging the "battle" for fictional space with the reader, they turn fiction against itself and explore the nature of fictionality.

2

The Evacuation of Fictional Space
The Retreat of the Post-Victorians

I

In 1900, Nietzsche died; Freud published The Interpretation of Dreams; *1900 was the date of Husserl's* Logic *and of Russell's* Critical Exposition of the Philosophy of Leibniz. *With an exquisite sense of timing Planck published his quantum hypothesis in the very last days of the century, December 1900. Thus, within a few months, were published works which transformed or transvalued spirituality, the relation of language to knowing, and the very locus of human uncertainty, henceforth to be thought of not as an imperfection of the human apparatus but part of the nature of things.*

Frank Kermode, The Sense of an Ending

The object of the novelist is to keep the reader entirely oblivious of the fact that the author exists—even of the fact that he is reading a novel.
Ford Madox Ford, in Ferguson, "The Face in the Mirror: Authorial Presence in the
Multiple Vision of the Third-Person Impressionist Narrative"

It is a generally accredited critical notion that there is something distinctive about the modern novel, that the modern novel is somehow "different" from its Victorian predecessor. What critics tend to debate, at length and without resolution (and this relates to modernism in general), is the nature of that difference.[2] Critics may argue as to the radicality of the transformation that fiction undergoes, but there is general agreement that there is "something happening" in the realm of narrative fiction. One critic singles out an increasing awareness on the part of novelists of the subjective nature of experience; another emphasizes the desire to present the fictional world dramatically, without the illusion-destroying interpolations of the intrusive narrator; yet another argues that the modern novel is characterized by a degree of "ethical openness" that precludes closure or finality in matters of ethical import; there are those who maintain that the distinctiveness of the modern novel rests on a loss of faith in a "stable and hierarchic society" where exterior signs and events can reveal interior realities; some generalize the notion of loss of faith and cite nihilism as the central preoccupation of all modern literature; and finally there are those who single out a general dissatisfaction with the novelistic "great tradition" of the Victorian age, a dissatisfaction that leads to an emphasis upon the autonomy of art and a fascination with the formal qualities of the novel.[3] Clearly these arguments (in which there is some confusion of causes and effects) are not mutually exclusive; each accounts partially or locally for literary upheaval and experimentation. Consider, for example, the line of reasoning that stresses the intraliterary origins of modernism and the modern novel, the prevalence of a feeling that traditional literary forms are outmoded or used up (a point of view championed by Ezra Pound in his proclamation to young poets to "Make It New"). This particular argument has been clearly shown to be partial by Russian Formalists like Boris Engelhardt and Jurij Tynjanov, who note that this theory can account only for the necessity for literary evolution and not for the direction that evolution will take.[4] Any argument that insists that the fundamental influence upon a literary movement is the literary tradition itself is subject to this sort of objection. Any comprehensive attempt to delineate the causes and manifestations of modernism needs must take into consideration the historical, economic, political, ideational, and cultural contexts in which the modernist sensibility is "cooked." What is needed to describe and explain modernism is a comprehensive culturology.[5]

It is beyond the scope of this work to analyze the complex cultural forces that generate the modernist sensibility. Any such study would have to examine in detail the ideational background of the time, the climate of thought that challenges and eventually topples the prevalent epistemological paradigm. The study would have to explore the serial and causal connections between all of the following ideational landmarks: the work of Nietzsche, Frazier, and Freud and its impact upon faith in the primacy of reason as well as its insight into the power and universality of the irrational; the philosophical disquisitions of Russell, Moore, and William James, which cast doubt upon notions of moral absolutism (a skepticism nurtured as well by the accumulating global field work done by anthropologists, sociologists, and ethnologists); the discovery of radical contingency in "Nature's plan" by Darwin and the geneticists who followed him; the introduction of notions of discontinuity and paradox into the physical world by Planck's quantum theory; and, of course, Einstein's reimagining of time and space as fundamentally interrelated and his concomitant recognition of the central role of the observer in the physical sciences. After this survey, the study would need to investigate contemporaneous historical, political, economic, and sociocultural developments. It is of no small interest to representational art, for example, that by this time photography had established itself as a legitimate art form and that the cinema revealed that "reality" may be broken down into a series of separate, discontinuous images. Developments in education, technology, and the media should similarly be taken into account.

At the onset of the twentieth century, evidence of change, rapid and radical change, was everywhere, and it was inevitable that the fact of change should register upon the literary sensibility. Virginia Woolf's idiosyncratic formulation epitomizes the awakening to new realities: "And I will now hazard a second assertion, which is more disputable perhaps, to the effect that on or about December 1910 human character changed."[6]

In another essay Woolf articulates an elementary aspect of that change. Speaking of the privileges of Jane Austen, she says: "To believe that your impressions hold good for others is to be released from the cramp and confinement of personality."[7] This particular belief is not available to modernist writers. This loss of belief is not limited to matters of personal "impressions"; a sense of uncertainty, born of increased awareness of relativism and subjectivity, pervades the world of objective fact, the communal faith in "eternal verities," and, significantly, the general understanding of the ways in which things are known—there is an epistemological crisis. The problematics of knowing and the possibility of knowledge become a very central concern for many authors. In this particular, modernist authors may be distinguished from their Victorian predecessors. Critics have for a long time remarked on the intrusive quality of the majority of Victorian narrators, and some have correctly sur-

mised that that intrusiveness at least partially rests in the episteme of the culture:

> In the heyday of the "liberal" novel (the 19th century) author-
> narrator-entrepreneurs ruled their fictional worlds as despotically
> as the laissez-faire capitalists ruled their factories. And beyond this,
> the benevolently despotic narrator was invariably committed to the
> most sweeping generalizations about human nature. He was always
> looking for the laws of behavior that governed the action of his
> puppets. The realism of the 19th century was characterized by the
> belief that the nature of reality is determinate and discoverable but
> has not been discovered until now.[8]

This certitude about the "know-ability" of knowledge, which
manifests itself in part in the form of magisterial intrusions,
covers at least two areas of cognition: (1) the author knows
things both about the fictional world and his characters, and
about the Real World, Culture, and Human Nature; and (2) the
author "knows" that the fictional world is designed so as to be
coterminous with the empirical world. Not only can the author
speak confidently about his or her creatures, but also he or she
can move readily from the "real world" to the fictional because
there are no sharp boundaries between. This faith in the contiguity of fictional and real worlds manifests itself in part in the
form of "ideological discursive statements," where the authorial
persona speaks from a position of privilege from and for the
culture depicted. Roger Fowler has said of these statements:

> A certain relevant culture is created (romantic, artistic, fashionable,
> privileged, socializing) to be shared by the narrator and his appro-
> priate reader—a reader for whom these citations have a coherent
> significance. They are literally citations—footnote references to a
> selected world outside the fiction. The narrative stance created by
> the invocation of these cultural codes joins narrator and reader in a
> compact of knowing superiority.[9]

Clearly, to eliminate such statements is to change the relation
between narrator and reader.

    This sense of community and the attendant assurance and
confidence modernist authors lack, and they tend to evacuate
that portion of fictional space generated by that confidence. It
is clear that this evacuation owes much to the practice of
Flaubert, who as early as 1857 argues for the "invisibility" of the

author, saying things like, "I don't even think that the novelist should express his own opinion of the things of this world. He may communicate it, but I don't want him to state it."[10] But what for Flaubert is one plank of an aesthetic program, and to some degree a matter of choice, becomes for modernist authors an ineluctable burden of sorts. As Daiches argues,

> In the modern novel . . . the novelist may have no assurance that it is the outward action which reveals the significant fact about his characters, nor is he even convinced that the public gestures provided by society—even by language, the most basic of all social instruments—can ever achieve real communication between individuals.[11]

Thus it is that a significant number of modernist novels become epistemological forays, explorations into the genesis of "significant facts," and examinations of the various tools of knowledge, in particular language. The leader of this new movement in fiction is Henry James.

II

It is not my fault if I am so put together as often to find more life in situations obscure and subject to interpretation than in the gross rattle of the foreground.
Henry James, in Todorov, "The Secret of Narrative"

I wish at first to put before you a general proposition; that a work of art is very seldom limited to one exclusive meaning and not necessarily tending to a definite conclusion.
Joseph Conrad, Life and Letters

Hemingway was evolving "a new theory that you could omit anything if you knew what you omitted, and the omitted part would strengthen the story and make people feel something more than they understood."
David Lodge, "Analysis and Interpretation of the Realist Text: A Pluralist Approach to Hemingway's 'Cat in the Rain'"

The obliquity of James's "major phase" is not the product of a willful and perverse desire to obscure or obfuscate, but rather is based upon a clearly defined and articulated theory of the strongest "subject" for fiction. Again and again in the prefaces written for the 1909 New York Edition of his works James speaks to this problem, and almost as frequently he falls back upon the notion of "bewilderment" as the necessary element in the generation of compelling narrative; one or more of the "subjects" of the piece must experience a degree of uncertainty if the fiction is to convey the impression of "felt life." The implications that this belief has for James's fictional techniques are admirably summarized by Wayne Booth: "There can be no intensity of illusion if the author is present, constantly reminding us of his unnatural wisdom. Indeed, there can be no illusion of life where there is no bewilderment, and the omniscient narrator is obviously not bewildered."[12] For James bewilderment is an essential aspect of experience at the end of the nineteenth century; the balance of experience rests not in the brute facts of experiential reality but in the way in which the perceiving consciousness construes (and misconstrues) those facts. This credo is reflected at the general level by James's almost programmatic use of a "central intelligence" as the dramatic focus for his later fictions and at the local level by his renewed interest in the ghost story, an interest quickened by a realization that one best renders ghosts not by scrupulously recording the particulars of their deviltry but by reproducing the effect they create upon their victims.[13]

As Booth's comment suggests, James's concerns at this point in his career necessarily entail certain consequences in narrative technique, particularly in the matter of the type of narrative situation. Omniscient narration almost by definition precludes the "enactment" ("showing" as opposed to "telling") of states of bewilderment. James is thus forced by his own preoccupations and beliefs to experiment deliberately with different narrative situations, an enterprise that after the fact can be seen to take two forms. At one extreme, James relies on forms of first-person narration and later perfects what one theorist has called the "figural" novel in order to approximate the pure dramatization of a human consciousness as it deals with the various "facts" of experience. At the other extreme James attempts total effacement of evidence of the author through "pure" scenic presentation. The former practice, exemplified in *The Turn of the Screw* (first person) and *The Ambassadors* (figural), has been institutionalized by critics like Lubbock[14] as James's major contribution to narrative technique and prefigures to some extent the stream-of-consciousness work of the great modernists. The latter practice, embodied in lesser-known works like *The*

Awkward Age (which consists in large part of conversation), pre-
sages the "pure objectivity" of later writers like Hemingway and
Anderson. These two experiments result in narratives of very
different texture, with very different aesthetic effects, but they
share an authorial intention to eliminate the author as a source
of truth and certitude within the fiction and thus to encode in
the text an inherent degree of bewilderment. In other words,
these *fin-de-siècle* works by James at one and the same time
mark, and precipitate on a more systematic basis, the author's
retreat (qua Author) from a portion of fictional space.

The nature and consequence of that retreat is embodied
most dramatically in that most controversial of all stories, *The
Turn of the Screw.* This *"amusette* to catch those not easily caught"
has quite literally done that from the moment of its publication
in 1898—critics have dangled helplessly on the tenterhooks of
its systematic ambiguity. The publication in 1976 and 1977 of
Christine Brooke-Rose's brilliant series of essays on the text[15]
should serve as a landmark of demystification in a mystified
critical atmosphere. Not only does Brooke-Rose accept and
demonstrate as explicitly encoded in the text the two major
readings (the ghosts are real/the ghosts are products of the
governess's imagination); she also convincingly argues that it is
"a text structured . . . on the same principle that neurosis is
structured" in that "the structure of a neurosis involves the
attempt (often irresistible) to drag the 'other' down into itself,
into the neurosis, the other being here the reader."[16] That is,
the text induces in its readers the very same tendencies that
inform its structure: "The critics reproduce the very tendencies
they so often note in the governess: omission; assertion; elaboration; lying even (or, for the critics, let us call it error)."[17] For
example, just like the governess, critics have a marked tendency
to slide from supposition to assertion, to assert as fact what they
have previously (and without adequate textual evidence) as-
sumed to be true. Part of the strength of Brooke-Rose's first
essay lies in the methodological rigor and systematic documen-
tation that she brings to her analysis of critical (mal)practice to
date.

What is of particular significance for this essay is the evidence
adduced by Brooke-Rose to demonstrate the text's duplicity—a
duplicity that has of late been more and more accepted.[18] The
text admits of at least two sets of interpretations, which at one
level are mutually exclusive. This duplicity, encoded in every

narrative unit of the text, is made possible by an inherent characteristic of first-person narration, a characteristic that may best be described by reference to NARRATIVAL and NARRATIONAL SPACE. In "authorial" narration, where the enunciation can be attributed to a speaker who enjoys the station, wisdom, and privilege of a fictional deity, NARRATIONAL SPACE may be said to exist in a plane different from the plane of NARRATIVAL SPACE. The former exists somewhere "above" the latter, at a spatial and temporal remove. From this position of privilege, the speaker has the *author*-ity to preside over the space of the fictional world; he or she is privileged to know characters' thoughts and motives, to move at will through topographical space, to articulate a controlling ideology, to manipulate the presentation of events, and in general to speak to the fictiveness of the inscribed world.[19] The presence of the authorial speaker particularly manifests itself in the form of perceptual, ideological, and metalingual statements of DISCURSIVE SPACE. That is, the Author pronounces sentences upon characters, upon the controlling beliefs, habits, or episteme of the fictional world, or upon the nature of narrative and its codes. The Author makes these comments in the form of discrete statements that can only be attributable to Him. DISCURSIVE SPACE acts as a sort of filter for the actants and events of the world, to no small degree channeling and directing the reader's response to that world. In first-person narration the ontology of NARRATIONAL SPACE changes drastically. In figurative terms, NARRATIONAL SPACE is "lowered" into the space of the world and shares the fictiveness of that world. All DISCURSIVE statements in the enunciation are "motivated"; they belong not to a privileged and disinterested speaker but to an interested character. A "first-person" speaker, whether simple spectator to, or spirited actor in, the narrative's unfolding events, is necessarily "engaged" in those events, and generally in a double sense: the speaker is affected by the story (otherwise there would be no reason to tell it); at the same time he or she mediates the story—the story is filtered through his or her consciousness or sensibility. The type of mediation might vary; usually the narrator speaks after the fact and, given the advantage of distance and perspective, supplies at least one degree of interpretation (such is the case with the governess in James's tale). But even if the mediation is of the form of "unmediated" perception (as in stream-of-consciousness), the story passes through a "human" and therefore potentially altering sensibility, one that possesses no special privilege in relation to the rest of the fictional world because it exists in the same narrative plane. This fact of purely "fictional" mediation is one of the great attractions of first-person narration: as Richard Gullon puts it, "One of the functions of the narrative 'I' is to produce this verbal space, to give a context for the motion which constitutes the novel; a space that is not a reflection of anything but, rather, an invention of the invention which is the narrator, whose perceptions (transferred to images) engender it."[20] As has been argued previously, the adoption by an author of a first-person narrator establishes *ex nihilo* a substantial NAR-RATIONAL SPACE, the space pertaining to the existence of a speaker within the fiction. Within any first-person narrative there are two equally pronounced systems of signification, the one pertaining to the actants and events of the fictional WORLD, the other to the enunciation itself. In most first-person narrative the latter dimension has been utilized primarily to make contributions to what Barthes calls the "semic" code. That is, the space of the enunciation contributes to the characterization of the speaker, who is, after all, a principal actant in the narrative. The enunciation is used to reveal the character's idiosyncrasies, idiolect, psychology, or other personal traits. James, however, is one of the first to comprehend all the implications of first-person narration; in particular, that NARRATIONAL SPACE is the property of a fictional entity (the "invention of the invention") and therefore at least twice removed from the "real world." The content of the enunciation need not coincide with the "content" of the fictional world.

A detailed examination of the governess's "occupation" of NARRATIONAL SPACE might help to clarify this point. Any first-person narrator (defined as a speaker who is also an actant within the fictional world) has the entire spectrum of NARRA-TIONAL SPACE at his or her disposal. In traditional first-person narration, the speaker normally relies heavily upon DISCURSIVE SPACE in order to locate and circumscribe the unfolding fictional world. The governess is no exception. The first two words of her enunciation, "I remember . . . ," serve as deictics, identifying a first-person discourse and locating the narrative action somewhere in the circumscribed past.[21] Throughout her enunciation the governess employs adverbs of time like *today* or *now* to emphasize that she is looking back at prior events. Deictics can even take the form of interpolated clauses: "I have not seen Bly since the day I left it" (p. 9); "It was an immense help to me—I confess I rather applaud myself as I look back" (p. 28); "It was not, I am as sure today as I was sure then, my mere infernal imagination" (p. 50). Such clauses locate the scene of writing at a distant temporal remove from the time of the narrative events and testify to the governess's confidence and reliability at the moment of the enunciation.

An important aspect of DISCURSIVE SPACE involves narrational commentary, statements made by the speaker about the characters, the society in which they move, or the very act of composing a narrative (respectively termed "perceptual," "ideological," or "metalingual" statements). The governess's use of this aspect of DISCURSIVE SPACE is distinctive. In the first place, although her enunciation is littered with references to other novels, romances, "story-books and fairy-tales" (p. 10), "grey prose," (p. 19), and the like, it contains only one explicit metalingual statement: "So I saw [Quint] as I see the letters I form on this page" (p. 17). This is not surprising, because metalingual statements, which address the codes and conventions of the narrative act, serve to remind the reader of the artificiality of the narrative in process. Ironically, the governess uses this one metacommentary to substantiate one of her previous "visions." What is perhaps more surprising is the fact that nowhere does the governess resort to ideological statements (e.g., by comparing Miles to a societal type or by propounding a general truth). As has been argued, ideological statements are based upon contiguity and congruence between real and fictional worlds; a speaker typically makes a general statement about society and proceeds to apply that statement to the fictional world. The total absence of such commentary in the governess's enunciation serves to sever Bly, its inhabitants, and its events from the outside world. Bly is, quite literally, like nothing else.

If the governess's enunciation lacks ideological and metalingual commentary, it almost makes up for the lack in perceptual commentary. Her perceptual commentary takes two forms: observations, consisting of general statements about the characters (including the governess), and interpretations, consisting of attempts to decipher what these characters' actions signify. Both types of commentary are often introduced by words of estrangement like "it seemed" or "I felt" and occur very frequently in the text.

Soon after recounting her arrival at Bly, the governess introduces Flora in the following way:

> The little girl who accompanied Mrs. Grose affected me on the spot as a creature too charming not to make it a great fortune to have to do with her. She was the most beautiful child I had ever seen and I afterwards wondered why my employer hadn't made more of a point to me of this. (p. 7)

The governess here begins with a general observation about Flora's beauty, but she continues with a question as to why it had gone unremarked by the master. She moves, in other words, from perception toward interpretation (of, in this case, a related phenomenon). In the same paragraph of the text, she notes that Mrs. Grose had been glad to see her, but had been "on her guard against showing it too much" (p. 7), and the governess wonders why.

The governess's typical pattern, then, is to go from perception to speculation and ultimately to interpretation. In the second sighting of Quint, for example, she "sees" Quint at the window, sees that he sees her, sees that he looks elsewhere in the room, realizes that he's looking for someone else, and jumps to the conclusion that he's looking for Miles. Later, she takes the final step in this process and asserts as fact that which had previously been only interpretation—Quint is after Miles; Flora "saw"; the children are "talking horrors." As a result of this process, the governess's entire commentary is made problematic. The reader cannot be sure if any given perception, interpretation, supposition, or "fact" corresponds to a given "reality" within the fictional world.

In a case where the first-person enunciation has been made problematic, how does the reader know if the speaker is reliable? Usually the appropriate response to any particular first-person enunciation is channeled through metatextual signals drawn from shared cultural codes. For example, the reader knows, by relying on certain ethical codes, not to agree with Huckleberry Finn that he's "going to hell" when he decides not to turn Jim in. Signals like these, however, are often open to multiple interpretation, based on the code selected.[22] A more reliable way to signal the veracity and fidelity of the first-person speaker is to provide some sort of extratextual endorsement or testimonial. This witness to the speaker's character usually takes the form of a framing device. A narrative frame does just that: at one and the same time it limits the scope of the object to be viewed, creates a spatial enclosure or envelope, establishes the angle of vision, and testifies as to the "character" of the narrator. James seems to have been aware of the multiple functions of frames; in any case, he provides *The Turn of the Screw* with an elaborate frame, one that deserves another turn of the screw of analysis.

Critics have frequently noted the elaborate frame for the story; there are no less than four storytellers in the novel— Griffin, the nameless narrator ("I" is his only designation in the text), Douglas, and the unnamed governess. Griffin does not actually speak in the text; he has just finished his story ("The story had held us . . ."), and his function is to introduce the genre of the story to follow (one dealing with some kind of "gruesome visitation"). The first official speaker, who remains mostly uncharacterized, both introduces readers to the third speaker, Douglas, and gives him a "character reference." That is, through his sympathetic attention to and interest in Douglas's words, the "I" lends credence to the story Douglas has to tell. The original nameless narrator refers to Douglas as "our friend," and seems to read his mind from time to time ("I see. She was in love." "You *are* acute. Yes, she was in love"), and generally indicates that there is a communion between the two: "It was to me in particular that he appeared in propound this— appeared almost to appeal for aid not to hesitate" (p. 2). This introduction induces the reader to adopt a similar sympathetic attitude toward Douglas.

Douglas, like the narrator who precedes him, serves a double function: he introduces the following (and final) speaker and vouches for her character. At first reading the words he speaks in her behalf are completely unambiguous. He states flatly that she was "the most agreeable woman I've ever known in her position; she'd have been worthy of any whatever" (p. 2). He mentions that he found her "awfully clever and nice" and admits candidly that "I liked her extremely and am glad to this day to think that she liked me too" (p. 2). Douglas speaks so enthusiastically of her person that his auditors infer with some reason that he was in love with her (p. 3). The reader is prepared to lend a very sympathetic ear to the governess's story after his report.

His testimony is so unequivocal that the reader is led to overlook certain problematic or questionable aspects of his presentation. These aspects surface only at a second, closer scrutiny, one perhaps precipitated by the ambiguity of the governess's version. The points in question are mere touches as it were, but they tend to accumulate. In speaking of the previous story, Douglas tosses off, "Griffin's ghost, or whatever it was" (p. 1). There is the peculiar matter of the time element, the fact of a double reticence. Douglas has waited forty years to tell this story (p. 3), and Douglas asserts that the episode itself happened "long before," and that the governess herself had kept silent during the intervening years. One wonders about the motivation for these periods of silence. And if Douglas gives the governess an exceptional reference, he gives her predecessor an almost equally good character, stating that the master of the children had found only "the best people" to attend them and referring to Miss Jessel specifically as a "most respectable person" (p. 5). When one of his auditors then asks a sarcastic question about the predecessor's character, Douglas seem to tell a lie. He says that the cause of her death will come out, a piece of information that the narrative does not supply. In a similar vein, when asked by Mrs. Griffin whom the governess was in love with, Douglas responds, "The story *won't* tell . . . not in any literal vulgar way" (p. 3) (a statement that has metatextual resonance as a summary of the story as a whole). But the governess freely admits that she was carried away in London and several times confesses she hoped to win the master's favorable regard. And in giving the governess's history, Douglas supplies details that undercut the reader's estimation of her qualifications: she was a "fluttered anxious girl out of a Hampshire vicarage" (p. 4)—"young, untried, nervous" (p. 6). In her own narrative the governess admits that her life to that point had been "small" and "smothered." She adds that it was the first time "that I had known space and air and freedom, all the music of summer and all the mystery of nature" and that these circumstances were particularly beguiling for her imagination (p. 14). The remoteness of Bly and the governess's absolute dominion there imply a sort of "neutral territory" where the boundaries between fact and fiction may be confused, where the governess's fancy (a favorite word of hers) may be set free.[23] The fact that the original events are far away in both space and time adds to the reader's sense that all he or she gets is a version, far removed from its origin, obscured by the intervening space and time. This sense of distance is much compounded by the fact that the story passes through not one but three sets of human hands. The opening frame, although tending to corroborate the veracity of the narrative to follow, contains a number of equivocations and ambiguities and does not conclusively endorse the governess's "reading" of the events she reports.

Since, as has been shown by Brooke-Rose and others, the story itself does not tell, each of its narrative articulations being susceptible of at least two readings, what recourse has the reader who desires to verify or disconfirm the truth of the "matter"? In normal circumstances the reader can rely for information not only on the opening of the frame but also upon its closing, once the central narrative has run its course. The closing of the frame offers the reader an opportunity to see what impact the embedded story has had upon its auditors.[24] At the same time the auditors' response to a certain extent speaks for the credibility of the central narrator. The closing of the frame thus functions to bring the narrative to a satisfactory rest, to close off its semantic possibilities, and to indicate the appropriate response. A narrative with a full frame might well be diagrammed as follows:

$$
\begin{array}{ccc}
& \text{enunciation of} & S_s \\
\lbrack \text{--} \rbrack \\
& \text{fictional world} & S_w
\end{array}
$$

where brackets represent the functions served by the all-important frame. In a fully-bracketed fictional space, the closing of the frame serves to guarantee a degree of convergence or congruence between the commentary of the speaker and the events of the fictional world. If one accepts the above representation, then the equivalent diagram for *The Turn of the Screw* would be:

$$
\begin{array}{llll}
\lbrack N^1 & & & R_x \\
\quad \lbrack N^2 & & & \\
& \lbrack \text{------} & \text{governess's enunciation} \quad S_s \\
& & \text{of fictional world of Bly} \quad S_w \\
& & & R_y
\end{array}
$$

where N^1 and N^2 represent the original narrator and Douglas who serve both to "authorize" the tale to come and to separate it substantially from the "real world"; and where R_X and R_Y represent the two major sets of readings generated by two characteristics of the narrative: (1) the collapse of the space of the speaker (S_S) into the space of the fictional world (S_W), and the resultant possibility that the two systems might be congruent or incongruent, since the nature of a fictional "fact" becomes entirely problematic; and (2) the absence of some sort of closing of the frame that could provide both aesthetic and semantic closure. The result is a thoroughly ambiguous text. James's failure (or refusal) to provide the second set of brackets can be seen as a symbolic gesture marking and heralding the opening of a portion of fictional space, the portion circumscribed by the traditional singularity of meaning. Readers are placed in a position very similar to that of the governess. Like her, they are left without recourse to a master of any kind. Like her, they are dropped into a somewhat "unnatural" situation with instructions to "take the whole thing over and let [the master] alone" (p. 6). And like her, readers take the "facts" presented and read into them or behind them the meaning that particularly suits their subjectivity. As one critic puts it, "The reader's involvement in the work is its meaning."[25] Readers occupy the space of meaning that the duplicitous text fails to clarify, and the manner of their occupation may well be a matter for his (the master's) amusement.

If one way to eliminate an authorial speaker with his privileged position and his magisterial prerogatives is to replace his enunciation with that of one of the actants, thus collapsing S_S into S_W, another way consists in simply removing the more conspicuous evidence of his presence, thus creating a narrative that aspires to the condition of drama (all "show" and no "tell"). This project James undertakes in *The Awkward Age*. In his preface to the text, James himself suggests that "the beauty of the conception" rests in the approximation of the form "to the successive acts of a Play." James goes on to explain:

> The divine distinction of the act of a play—and a greater than any other it easily succeeds in arriving at—was, I reasoned, in its special, its guarded objectivity. This objectivity, in turn, when achieving its ideal, came from the imposed absence of that "going behind," to compass explanations and amplifications, to drag out odds and

ends from the "mere" storyteller's great property-shop of aids to illusion.[26]

The speaker of *The Awkward Age* does not have the privilege of "going behind," of revealing characters' thoughts and motivations or being privy to their secret desires. James thus specifically notes that his speaker will not have access to what has been termed the "perceptual" component of DISCURSIVE SPACE. As a matter of fact, the speaker of this novel retreats completely from the statement level of DISCURSIVE SPACE; this speaker is unable (or unwilling) to pronounce upon matters characterological, ideological, or metatextual. Nowhere does the speaker reveal himself at the level of the sentence; everywhere the speaker maintains a "guarded objectivity."

James is too much a "scientist" of consciousness to refrain entirely from forays into the minds of his characters. The problem for him in *The Awkward Age* consists in allowing his speaker to suggest what lies "behind" without in any way conferring *author*-ity upon that speaker. James accomplishes this somewhat tricky end by the systematic deployment of "words of estrangement" (at the lexemic level of DISCURSIVE SPACE). That is, the speaker prefaces all incursions beneath the surface with lexical markers that obviate any authority or privilege the statements might confer upon the speaker. The text is heavily marked by verbs of speculation like *it seemed* or *it appeared* or *there might have been*, and by words of speculation like *apparently, perhaps,* and (the speaker's especial favorite) *as if.* Taken in combination, these words create what Uspensky has termed a synchronic narrative situation. The speaker presents himself as merely an observer present on the scene, one whose scope of knowledge is as limited as that of any "normal" observer. That this is the effect James intends is clear from a remark such as, "Mrs. Brook, for some minutes, had played no audible part, but the acute observer we are constantly taking for granted would perhaps have detected in her, as one of the effects of the special complexion, today, of Vanderbank's presence, a certain smothered irritation" (p. 228).

Remarks like this indicate the special problem James confronted in *The Awkward Age.* He very much wished to have the text approximate the condition of drama, but he did not wish to relinquish entirely the complexities and nuances that the addition of a mediating consciousness makes possible. James was able to accomplish this complex effect by evacuating the statement level of DISCURSIVE SPACE while at the same time leaning heavily on words of estrangement. In two ways *The Awkward Age* can be seen as a pivotal text. First, it serves as a prototype for fictions in which the method of "scenic presentation" is carried even farther by the more systematic evacuation of DISCURSIVE SPACE—the "impersonal" fictions of Hemingway and the like. Second, the text prepares James for a more important type of drama—the dramatization of consciousness in *The Ambassadors.*

Writing to Hugh Walpole in 1912 about his turn-of-the-century work *The Ambassadors,* James castigates his friend for a failure of reading: "how can you say I do anything so foul and abject as to 'state'? You deserve that I should condemn you to read the book over once again!" It seems then that James's avowed purpose is to "state" nothing, to achieve the "stuff of drama."[27] One way to approximate the conditions of drama would have been to present the entire action scenically, in the sense of one dramatic scene after another, as had been done in *The Awkward Age.* But James confesses in another place a "preference for dealing with my subject matter, for 'seeing my story,' through the opportunity and the sensibility of some more or less detached, some not strictly involved, though thoroughly interested and intelligent witness or reporter, some person who contributes to the case mainly a certain amount of criticism and interpretation of it."[28] The addition of this one degree of interpretation contributes substantially to the "intensification of interest." One way to accomplish this dramatization of consciousness is to adopt a first-person narrator, but James specifies in his preface that that narrative situation did not serve his purposes for this text. He notes that first-person narration is "foredoomed to looseness" in a long piece (p. 10) and that the "terrible *fluidity* of self-revelation" does not suit his "exhibitional conditions" (p. 11). Although James's wording is characteristically abstract and indirect, he seems to have two objections to first person in this instance: it inherently admits the inclusion of extraneous material because the narrator necessarily wishes to incorporate all the relevant information (in a long piece a complete autobiography, presumably); and, consequently, the focus of the drama becomes a total personality rather than the impression created by a circumscribed chain of events. The author, in effect, sacrifices a measure of aesthetic

control in first-person narrative. James speaks of the necessity
to "encage" Strether so as to prevent him from becoming both
subject and object of the narrative. What is to be exhibited is
not an entire personality, but a "process of vision" (p. 2)
wherein a discriminating intelligence is confronted with an ambiguous situation; it is to be a "drama of discrimination" (p. 7).[29]

In order best to make the narrative approximate the condition of drama, James clearly had to eliminate as much as possible the intrusions of the mediating speaker. As was the case in
The Awkward Age, the speaker had to efface himself. Although
there has been critical disagreement[30] as to the extent of authorial intrusion in the text, from the vantage point of the overall
texture the speaker is conspicuous mainly by (his) absence. A
quick perusal of any page reveals the evident care that James
took to locate the action in his mediating consciousness:

> he felt even as he spoke . . .
> he had made up his mind . . .
> he had a fear . . .
> this confirmed precisely an interpretation of her manner . . .
> her voice seemed to make her words . . .
> he had made up his mind . . .
> his pleasure was deep now on learning . . .
> as his finding himself thus able . . .
> He supposed himself to have supposed. . . .

These locutions can be found in the space of two paragraphs in
the text (pp. 174–75), and the same two paragraphs contain no
explicit reference to the speaker and only one phrase that indirectly announces his presence ("The end of it was that half an
hour later . . ."). Conspicuously absent from the text are those
discursive statements (perceptual, ideological, or metalingual)
which signal the speaker's proprietorship over elements of the
fictional world. That James from time to time deliberately reveals a speaker's presence is undeniable; the mere existence of
the reiterated phrase *our friend* (Tilford counts 65 appearances)
signals the speaker's presence at the lexemic level of discourse
and to some degree channels the reader's sympathy. But it is to
James's aesthetic purpose to reveal the speaker's guiding hand.
The speaker wishes to announce his presence so as to increase
the distance between the reader and Strether's consciousness,
to make the latter the "subject" of the story—that is, the object
of the reader's scrutiny (compare this relationship with the

identification frequently fostered by first-person narrative). In this way consciousness itself is to be dramatized. And "dramatized" is the right word because in no explicit way does James's speaker comment on or critique the workings of that consciousness; he encourages the reader to attend to it ("our friend"), but he keeps it at arm's length. At one point in the text the speaker refers to himself as "chronicler" (p. 43); that word aptly summarizes his relationship with the fictional world—he is a recorder of (mental) events whose greatest problem seems to be in *transcribing* those events in their rapidity and complexity (e.g., pp. 43, 91). By putting a consciousness onstage, retaining vestiges of authorship for purposes of aesthetic distance and yet eliminating the descriptive and normative aspects of authorial intrusion, James creates what Stanzel calls a "figural" novel in almost pure form.[31] Given the predominance of this form in the first half of this century, it is an important landmark in modern fiction.

Part of the greatness of *The Ambassadors* rests in the fact that the thematic content generated by the STORY of the novel enacts (and therefore reinforces and clarifies) the very concerns embodied in the carefully wrought narrative situation. In terms of content, several critics have noticed that James's later fictions often deal with situations that duplicate fairy-tale formulae. Christof Wegelin has said of *The Ambassadors:* "The task for which Strether has been sent to Paris resembles the traditional test which the fairy prince has to pass before he wins the hand of the princess."[32] Most interpretations of the text begin with this formula and apply it directly to Strether's experience, concluding variously that he passes or fails the test.[33] Critics tend to overlook the important signals given in the "Preface," the "Project for Novel," and the text itself, which specify that Strether as *discriminating consciousness* and not Strether as man is the hero of the novel. Strether, the "man of imagination," is quite literally Imagination personified within the context of the novel.[34] The entire apparatus of the plot can be translated into this more allegorical (and, to some extent, reductive) reading: The Imagination is bidden by some force in position of power (Dispatcher) to go from Here (the kingdom of the Familiar) to There (kingdom of the Strange, the Other) to bring back the Desired Object (in this case, the correct Reading of the situation presented by the Other). The reader is presented with a "drama of discrimination" in which the Imagination/hero encounters a succession of obstacles in the form of problematic events that it is his task to comprehend. The novel duplicates or reenacts the process of Reading itself and thus foregrounds James's awareness of the importance of Reading (reading with Imagination and Discrimination) in an age of uncertainty and bewilderment.

This more generalized reading is supported by the way in which James depicts Paris in the novel. Paris is not so much a place as an experience, one involving exposure to Difference.[35] The city is described as a gleaming jewel (p. 64) that continually acts as a spur to the imagination (p. 69). It is an experience the sense of which is "quite disconnected from the sense of [Strether's] past" (p. 20), an experience to which he must give himself up (p. 27). Once he has done this, he experiences an "extraordinary sense of escape" (p. 59), and soon comes to feel that "all the windows of his mind" are opened (p. 120). As James notes in his "Preface," Paris and its denizens constitute "a mere symbol for more things than had been dreamt about in the philosophy of Woollett" (p. 8).

As is suggested in this last phrase, Woollett is to be contrasted with Paris. If Paris represents the Other, the Unknown, the Unfamiliar, then Woollett represents that which is *a priori* known, that which is accepted without reflection. Woollett is very much the place of conventionalized "philosophy," whose ambassadors invariably "come out" loaded (in both senses of that word) "with a moral scheme of the most approved pattern" (p. 7). If Paris can be seen as a text embodying Otherness, then Woollett comes to stand for that which one inevitably brings to such a text, a "reality principle" that seeks to manage or domesticate that Otherness by submitting it to rigid codes, categories, formulae, or schemes. When the second wave of ambassadors comes out in the second half of the book in the form of Sarah Pocock and her retinue, Strether fears their arrival (p. 201), fears that She ("larger than life") will chastise him for his indiscretions and liberties. He knows that she has come to make "the contribution of the real" (p. 212). Sarah Pocock is truly her mother's ambassador, for the shadowy Mrs. Newsome, that "whole moral or intellectual being, or block" (p. 298), *is* the principle of reality, maintaining a strong presence in the text, but only as "affirmed influence, only in her deputed, represented form, . . . always absent, yet always felt" ("Project," p. 379).[36]

Seen in these terms, the novel becomes a record of the process in which the reading imagination, both detached and engaged, continually finds itself in the presence of "new facts" (p. 193) and gropes its way to a series of provisionally satisfactory interpretations.[37] The first six books, in particular, present the reader with a number of readings that Strether (often with the help of Maria) comes up with in an effort to name and thus to domesticate his Paris experience.[38] Strether comes out armed with the notion that Chad needs protection from life (p. 54), but his exposure to little Bilham and Miss Barrace eats away at his certitude; he begins to feel that he "knows nothing" for sure (pp. 72–73), that he is, in fact, "at sea" (p. 78). He speculates that Bilham has been planted there by Chad as some sort of trap (p. 76), and that he is the victim of some sort of conspiracy (pp. 87–88), which is of course a correct reading. His initial meeting with Chad only increases his bewilderment and sets off a chain of provisional explanations. Convinced that the Chad he meets is not the Chad he knew or expected (p. 90), that Chad has been "made over" into an "absolutely new quantity" (pp. 95–96), Strether falls back on a number of stereotypical categories: Chad is successively a "man of the world" (p. 97), an "irreducible young Pagan," and, most wonderful of all, a "gentleman" (p. 102). In his efforts to digest this strange phenomenon, Strether finally concedes that he lacks the requisite clues and needs to remodel his plan (pp. 102–4). His conversation with Maria Gostrey at this point does convince him that there is more to it than meets the eye, that some "uncanny" force lies behind the transformation. The two of them come to the conclusion that Chad is not free (p. 106) and that it is Chad's female attachment who is responsible for his remarkable improvement. This set of interpretations is closely followed by the announcement that Strether is to meet two females to whom Chad is much indebted, an announcement that precipitates a whole host of possible interpretations on the part of the two confidants (pp. 114–17). Of course, the interpretations are wide of the mark, based as they are upon very limited data. This news, however, results in the shift of Strether's interpretive energies from Chad himself to his relation with the women who had remade him. The remainder of the first half of the novel charts his struggle with the problems of this relationship.[39]

The first six books, as a matter of fact, adhere very well to the formulae prescribed by the fairy-tale plot. The hero is sent by a dispatcher to perform a task (which, by the way, the dispatcher may misconstrue, as is the case here), in this modern instance the achievement of a "total" reading. At the very beginning of his journey, he acquires the assistance of two Helpers, in the form of two different "readers" of Europe—Waymarsh and Maria Gostrey. Waymarsh is patently a rather poor reader, blind to the beauties and nuances of his experience. The first six books detail the gradual shift in allegiance by Strether from the poor reader (at the beginning of Book Three Strether still identifies his point of view with that of Waymarsh) to the good reader (after his period of tutelage, Maria abruptly leaves him, for reasons of her own, insisting that he can now manage on his own). The first half of the book is particularly marked by uncertainties, gropings, and wrong guesses on Strether's part, but at the midway point he has achieved a satisfactory account of the state of affairs: he senses, first, that Madame de Vionnet "has saved" Chad (p. 167), and, second, that theirs is "a friendship, of a beautiful sort" (p. 168). Of course, his reading is partly right and partly wrong.

At this point in the text, Strether's role in the course of events changes. Having arrived at a tentatively acceptable reading, he switches from passive interpreter to active "manager" of events. In an attempt to "save" Mme. de Vionnet, he persuades Chad *not* to return to Woollett and thus precipitates the "coming out" of the next set of ambassadors, the Pococks. The shift in Strether's relation to the world of Europe, it might be argued, symbolically represents James's awareness that the act of reading, which begins in passive observation, necessarily moves toward active involvement—the reader becomes the producer of texts. The change also signals an increase in aesthetic distance between the reader and Strether. In the first half of the text Strether stands outside of the unfolding events, at a vantage point very similar to that of the reader. As the text unfolds, he gradually moves inside the text, as it were. He becomes the reader's "ambassador" within the text. This movement is reflected in the recurrence of a set of images related to the theater. At the outset of the novel, Strether feels himself surrounded by players (p. 43), just like a spectator at the theater. Throughout the second half of the narrative he wonders about his own odd "part" in the performance of "Europe" (p. 226). By the tenth book he is identified as the "hero of the drama" by Miss Barrace—and so he is. The Reader has become Actor, because his drama is to be one of reading, and the extratextual reader must adopt the same relation toward Strether's drama as "our friend" adopted toward the drama of "Europe" in the first part of the book—interested and yet detached. In climactic Book Eleven, Strether quite literally steps into a work of art, as James goes to some pains to remind the reader (pp. 301, 305, 308), and experiences his final peripeteia. He learns that he has been guilty of a "too interpretative innocence" (p. 315), that what he has witnessed does in fact conform in some respects with the "typical tale of Paris" (p. 315). And yet Strether does not repudiate his new allegiances; he has, in effect, been changed by his "reading experience."[40] He comes back, as he must, empty-handed, with no tangible reward, but in terms of increase of consciousness he is a conquering hero. Readers of *The Ambassadors* are meant to undergo a similar sea-change. Like Strether, they return from their experience empty-handed. Like Strether, they are in some sense "losers," for they "come out" where they inevitably *are* (cf. the last words of the novel), at a place that lacks the security and comfort of "ideas" (in the sense of preconceived notions of any kind).

One of Strether's last comments in Maria Gostrey is, "I *have* no ideas. I'm afraid of them" (p. 344). The phrase echoes closely T. S. Eliot's insight into the nature of James's own genius: "James's critical genius comes out most tellingly in his mastery over, his baffling escape from, Ideas; a mastery and an escape which are perhaps the last test of a superior intelligence. He had a mind so fine that no idea could violate it."[41] Both the form and the content of *The Ambassadors* contribute to the creation of this state of being for the reader. The carefully contrived narrative situation presents, without editorial interpolation or guidance, a human consciousness as at once central character and locus of action. The story itself—it might be referred to as a *Leserroman* or as the "Portrait of the Reader as an Elderly Gentleman of Imagination"—recapitulates the process of reading and thus speaks to the terms in which the novel is to be read and to the role that "reading" plays in an age in which things fall apart and the center will not hold. The reader, like Strether and James, is to be dispossessed of his Ideas, is to accept the story in his imagination on its own terms, "all tragically, all comically." This process of dispossession bequeaths to the reader all the exhilaration and insecurity of freedom.

It may be argued, by way of conclusion, that the fictions of James's major phase mark the inception of the "modernist" novel, insofar as they transform the traditional notion of the Author as a source of ideas and arbiter of value. In these fictions, the Author has been effaced, by the abdication of Authorial prerogatives or responsibilites, or replaced, by the voice or consciousness of one of the actants. In either case the fictional space has been "flattened," because NARRATIONAL SPACE has been evacuated or deprived of its position of privilege. The reader confronts more *im*-mediately the fictional experience, having in effect been abandoned by the Author. At the same time the interpretation of NARRATIVAL SPACE (the space of the fictional world) is bequeathed to the reader, whose interpretive responsibilities in the text serve as a model for necessary extratextual activities in a world in which all the "eternal verities" have been undermined. Readers are invited to step in, to make up their own minds, to take chances, perhaps even to make fools of themselves.

III

I do not consider that any creative artist is anything but contemporary. Only he is sensitive to what is contemporary long before the average human being is.
                            Gertrude Stein, *"Transatlantic Interview"*

It is obviously best if you can contrive to be without any views at all; your business with the world is rendering, not alteration.
                            Ford Madox Ford, Joseph Conrad, A Personal Remembrance

You have got to accept a complete difference. It is hard to accept that, it is much easier to have one hand in the past. That is why James Joyce was accepted and I was not. He leaned toward the past, in my work the newness and difference is fundamental.
                            Gertrude Stein, *in Copeland,* Language and Time and Gertrude Stein

[Picasso] understood that a thing without progress is more splendid than a thing which progresses.
                            Gertrude Stein, *in Fitz, "Gertrude Stein and Picasso: The Language of Surfaces"*

Cézanne conceived the idea that in composition one thing was as important as another thing. Each part is as important as the whole, and that impressed me enormously, and it impressed me so much that I began to write Three Lives.
                            Gertrude Stein, *"Transatlantic Interview"*

William Gass has written very tellingly of the problems presented modern criticism (particularly New Criticism) by the example of Gertrude Stein.[42] Stein is generally acknowledged to be a major figure in the modernist movement, as evidenced by the express indebtedness to her on the part of writers like Hemingway and Sherwood Anderson, and great attention is paid to the events of her life, her role in the circle of Paris expatriates, some of her poetic aphorisms, the question of her influence, and her unusual lectures and essays. But very little is said about her literary works themselves, and much of that is self-evident, repetitive, or simply wrong. Gass perceptively puts his finger on the source of this "failure"; Stein's works, he notes, systematically frustrate the critic "bent on explication." They intransigently resist any and all attempts to discover or reveal "hidden" meanings—her writings insist that they simply be experienced. Gass summarizes the critic's predicament as follows: "Modern criticism has lived like a shrew upon paraphrase and explanation. Literature, it holds, is made of signs and the significance of literature, especially prose, lies in the meaning of these signs. The whole tendency of Gertrude Stein's work is to deny this. She was right to do so. Art is not a form of simple communication."[43] The obvious lesson for critics who heed Gass is that Stein's work requires a new critical methodology, one not based upon the signified, one free of excessive emphasis upon meaning. What is needed to deal with the entire Stein corpus is a reimagining of a neglected genre, a new poetics of the prose poem. The theory of fictional space, in that it is a discourse-oriented theory (i.e., takes as its object of study an extended narrative discourse), can illuminate Stein's procedures in her earlier narratives. It is less helpful in relation to the experiments of Stein's "middle phase," in which the object of "presentational immediacy" becomes the word.

As Stein suggests again and again in interviews and essays like "Composition as Explanation," the collection of three stories published as *Three Lives* marks the beginning of a new phase in her writing (and perhaps in narrative in general), and the centerpiece story, "Melanctha," represents the culmination of this stage of experiment. As a formal experiment in technique, the story merits attention.

As argued above, Henry James created new narrative dominants and new readerly activities by experimenting with the relations between NARRATIVAL and NARRATIONAL SPACE. He managed to deprive NARRATIONAL SPACE of its position of privilege either by relying on first-person speakers or by eliminating the Author as presiding deity over the fictional world. The result is narratives that aspire to the condition of drama (all "show" and no "tell"). Stein's experiments in *Three Lives* take another form (although they produce similar effects). Her innovations, for one thing, do not involve the evacuation of DISCURSIVE SPACE.[44] The narrator of "Melanctha" feels qualified to make both general statements about Negro culture and personality and normative statements about her characters. What is in question here is not the presence of a speaker's voice, but rather the character and nature of that voice.

As outlined in the first chapter, speakers reveal themselves at the statement level of DISCURSIVE SPACE in three possible forms: perceptual statements, ideological statements, and metalingual statements. There are no metalingual statements in *Three Lives.* Of the other two types of "intrusions," the latter type consists of abstract predications of "global" force, statements of "truth" about the culture or society in which the fictional world is inscribed. The former consists in "local" evaluations of specific motifs within the fictional world. The narrator of "Melanctha" occupies both of these regions of DISCURSIVE SPACE. At the ideological level she feels free to speak of the "wide, abandoned laughter that makes the warm broad glow of negro sunshine" (pp. 86, 92, 111, passim) and of "the simple, promiscuous unmorality of the black people" (p. 86).[45] Two things should be noted about Stein's use of ideological statements in "Melanctha." First, the number of such statements, particularly when compared with the number in the framing stories, "The Good Anna" and "The Gentle Lena," is very small.[46] Furthermore, the statements themselves tend to lose their ideological force when they are repeated in the narrative; they become like the restful refrain at the end of a ballad; they become more an idiosyncratic aspect of the story's texture than global statements about human nature.

One cannot say about perceptual statements in "Melanctha" that they are few and far between; they constitute the bulk of the text, to the extent that the act of narration becomes the narrative dominant.[47] The story begins with the description of the relationship between Melanctha Herbert and Rose Johnson, a description loaded with normative commentary (particularly strings of adjectives) characterizing the two women and qualifying their relationship. Melanctha "tended Rose, and she was patient, submissive, soothing, and untiring, while the sullen, childish cowardly, black Rosie grumbled and fussed and howled and made herself to be an abomination and like a simple beast" (p. 85). A peculiar aspect of these statements lies in the fact that the reasons for these traits are never explored. The novella is made up almost entirely of predicative statements like these, but basic questions—like the reason for the attraction between Rose and Melanctha—are left unanswered. As a result, the reader never comes to "know" the characters.[48] Their qualities are simply given, in a way that compels the reader to accept them as self-evident and thus to remain on the surface.

Yet another peculiar aspect of the discourse might be referred to as the "dissolve" of voice. The reader listens to the description of the characters and immediately posits a controlling narrative voice. A page later that voice repeats with some modification her summary of the situation ("Why did the subtle, intelligent, attractive, half white girl Melanctha Herbert love and do for and demean herself in service of this coarse, decent, sullen, ordinary black childish Rose . . . ?" p. 86), but the paragraph that follows seems to locate this summary in the mind of Melanctha Herbert: "Sometimes the thought of how all her world was made filled the complex, desiring Melanctha with despair" (p. 87). This process of "dissolve" happens continually in the story. The reader is presented with a perceptual statement about character that he ascribes to the central speaker. Moments later this speaker dissolves, and reveals the presence of a mediating character. Over the course of the narration the effect of these "dissolves" is the effacement of central speaker through fusion with characters and reader. As one critic aptly puts it, "It is as though Stein wanted to fuse character, experience, and author into oneness."[49] The reader's answer to the Barthesian question of "who is speaking?" can only be "*we* are." The end result of this achieved intersubjectivity is a sense of "presentational immediacy," the hypostasis of the reading experience itself.

Another oft-noted characteristic of Stein's narrative technique in "Melanctha" is the use of certain repeated refrains to identify and qualify characters, a practice that critics have rightly attributed to Stein's belief in the stability of character. Donald Sutherland summarizes this argument succinctly:

> If character does not change, if its interior and exterior history has no important influence upon it, and if it is the definition and description of types of character that interest the writer, the problem is one of projecting character in time without a sequence of events. . . . This leads naturally to repetition, the constantly new assertion and realization of the same simple thing, an existence with its typical qualities, not an event.[50]

At the same time that Stein repeats a motif, she often modulates it slightly to give the narrative a (small) degree of movement. A good example of this process can be seen in development of the relation between Jefferson Campbell and Melanctha Herbert:

> He felt no desire to know more about this girl (p. 113).

> He never found that he thought much about Melanctha. He never found that he believed much in her having a good mind, like Jane Harden (p. 113).

> He had no feeling, much, about her. He did not find that he took any interest in her (p. 114).

> Dr. Campbell began to feel a little, about how she responded to him. Dr. Campbell began to see a little that perhaps Melanctha had a good mind (p. 116).

> Jefferson was beginning to know that Melanctha certainly had a good mind and he was beginning to feel her sweetness (p. 126).

> Jefferson knew now very well that she had a good mind (p. 131).

Numerous other instances could be cited. The aesthetic reasons for and effects of this technique of repetition with incremental variation are perhaps of more significance than their basis in a theory or character. That is, these reiterated motifs impart a feeling not only of recurrence but also of stasis to the narrative. The narrative does not seem to be "getting anywhere"; it seems to be starting all over again and again. Events happen, but they don't "add up." This is particularly underscored by the repetition of this description of Melanctha: "Melanctha Herbert was always seeking rest and quiet, and always she could only find new ways to be in trouble." The phrase first appears in the initial description of Melanctha (p. 89), is repeated throughout the summary of her adolescence (pp. 92, 93, 99), disappears during her extended relation with Jeff Campbell, but then disconcertingly reappears at the end of that relation (pp. 207, 228). The reader responds somewhat uncomfortably with the feeling that nothing has happened. This recurrence and the effect it creates are, of course, entirely to Stein's purposes. In a series of lectures in America, Stein characterized her work as "an effort to escape from this thing to escape from inevitably feeling that anything that everything had meaning as beginning and middle and ending."[51] She praises American writing because, she says, it "has been an escaping not an escaping but an existing without the necessary feeling of one thing succeeding another thing."[52] The story "Melanctha" marks her first concerted attempt to create a kind of writing that is merely "existing." This sense of existing, the here-and-now-ness of the narrative, is produced, above all, by deliberate frustration of beginnings and endings, by elimination of causes and effects. The result is a totally new type of narrative: "When one used to think of narrative one meant a telling of what is happening in successive moments of its happening. . . . But now we have changed all that we really have. We really now do not really know that anything is progressively happening."[53] And repetition is the cornerstone in "Melanctha" for this new mode of narrative. The recurrence of familiar refrains suggests that the text is continually rebeginning, that the reader is to experience not a progress but a process. As Stein suggests in "Composition as Explanation,"[54] all the action takes place within a "continuous present," a present that is always beginning and always in the middle of happening, a condition Stein particularly tries to create by resorting continually to the present participle of verbs. The narrative world unfolds, moment to moment, before the reader's eyes; there is no momentum or teleology. The STORY's movement is frustrated, its plot dismantled. The end result is a narrative that resists interpretation based upon the armature of STORY, a narrative in which all information must be weighed equally.

This sense that each and every narrative moment is separate but equal is reinforced by the simple syntax of the discourse. Many of the sentences are simple sentences, and those that diverge are generally compound. The order of the sentence is invariably the standard Subject/Verb/Predicate, the length of the sentences coming from interpolated adverbs, strings of adjectives, or compounded subjects or predicates. The primary unit of this narrative is obviously the simple sentence, perhaps because "a sentence has not really any beginning or middle or ending because each part is its part as its part."[55] The moment the writer moves beyond the sentence, she shifts the focus from the sentence/object itself and sequences of thought begin—there is movement, direction, teleology. And that is just what Stein wishes to prevent. "One and one and one and one and one. That is the natural way to go on counting."[56] For Stein there should be no movement away from the thing that is "existing," and especially no "thinking" (this is Jefferson Campbell's problem) about the experience. The products of thinking—assembling, totaling, comparing, remembering, interpreting—take the reader away from the experience itself and thus impoverish its plentitude. Stein's syntax, language, and style continually bring the reader back again and again and again and again to the immediate and apparently unmediated narrative moment, the "continuous present."

It is this emphasis upon the "continuous present" that is the source of critical frustration with Stein's narrative method. "Melanctha" employs all the elements of traditional narrative: authorial speaker, a story, characters, a fictional world. But these elements are so impoverished or transformed as to resist the application of critical methods predicated upon conventional notions of their nature and function. There is a conventional plot to "Melanctha"—it is, after all, a love story—but the technique of recurrence and continual beginning again so debilitates the plot that the reader feels that nothing of any moment has happened. Story implies a movement from point *A* to point *B*, a change in state that of itself is thematically significant. There is no such movement in "Melanctha." The space of the speaker seems to belong to some omniscient, sympathetic deity, but that deity seems to know only what the actants say and do and are, not what the speeches, actions, or qualities betoken, leaving the reader with narration without depth (all "tell" and no "show"). The fictional world, contaminated by the contagious but unlocatable narrative voice, becomes not a circumscribed There, but an undifferentiated Here. The reader is left only with a notion of character; it is no accident that critics invariably speak of Stein's ability to capture and render character.

In the previous section it was argued that by manipulating the distance between the space of the speaker and that of the fictional world James is able to undermine the speaker as a source of authority and ideas within the fiction. The fictional experience is given over to the reader to "read" and interpret. Using other methods, Stein achieves similar effects—she changes the shape of her fictional space. The elimination of momentum and teleology within the STORY, the conflation of speaker's and characters' voices into an undifferentiated presence, and the recurrence of descriptive semes all combine to create a fictional space that, not unlike James's, has been "leveled" or "flattened," in a way that recapitulates the flatness of experience. Gass has described Stein's way of looking at the world as follows:

> The earth might be round but experience, in effect, was flat. Life might be long but living was as brief as each breath in breathing. Without a past, in the prolonged narrowness of any "now," wasn't everything in a constant condition of commencement? Then, too, breathing is repeating—it is beginning and rebeginning, over and over, again and again and again.[57]

Confronted by a fiction that is beginning and rebeginning, over and over, the reader, like Melanctha, must simply "give herself to this experience" (p. 109) in all its presentational immediacy. Stein attempts in "Melanctha" a narrative that overthrows most of the reader's expectations as to the constituents of narrative; her sentences try to "force themselves upon you, make yourself know yourself knowing them."[58]

In James's later novels, transformations in the ontology of NARRATIONAL SPACE transfer to the reader greater interpretive responsibilities. In Stein's "Melanctha," aspects of NARRATIONAL SPACE subvert interpretation, "for her verbal configurations are set up precisely to manifest the arbitrariness of discourse, the impossibility of arriving at 'the meaning' even as countless possible meanings present themselves to our attention." In Stein signifiers are detached from their conventional signifieds as "speaking loses its relational force."[59] If James's later novels herald the advent of modernist fiction, then Stein's *Three Lives* anticipates those forms of postmodernist literature which strive for a systematic exemption of significant depth, which sacrifice the signified for the play of the signifier.

IV

So far we have established that Space as an explicit component enters perceptual experience only in the particular cases in which relations between independent spatial systems are considered. These relations require an independent system of their own, not identifiable with any object.
                                    Rudolph Arnheim, "A Stricture on Space and Time"

The scientific and practical development of the technique of perspective bears witness to the gradual awareness of an interpretive subjectivity pitted against the work of art. Yet it was equally certain that this awareness had led to a tendency to operate against the "openness" of the work, to favour its "closing out." The various devices of perspective were just so many different concessions to the actual location of the observer in order to ensure that he looked at the figure in the only possible right way.
                                    Umberto Eco, "The Poetics of the Open Work"

It was, as you say, thirteen ways of looking at a blackbird. But the truth, I would like to think, comes out, that when the reader has read all these thirteen different ways of looking at the blackbird, the reader has his own fourteenth image of the blackbird which I would like to think is the truth.
                                    William Faulkner, Faulkner in the University

In his later years, at the university or in interviews, William Faulkner frequently refers to *The Sound and the Fury* as his "most splendid failure," a somewhat incongruous epithet for what many consider his one unqualified success.[60] Faulkner insists that, unlike *As I Lay Dying,* this work should not be seen as a mere technical *tour de force,* that he was simply trying to tell one story that moved him very much, and that the very fact that he failed four times is the source of the tenderness he feels for the novel.[61] If Faulkner sees the work as a failure, it must be that it fails in terms of his original intention. His comments about that intention are in this respect very interesting. Having figuratively shut the door between himself and the publishers, Faulkner states that he felt a new freedom within which to write: "So I, who had never had a sister and was fated to lose my daughter in infancy, set out to make myself a beautiful and tragic little girl."[62] The book then represents a vain attempt to create *ex nihilo* that which Faulkner was denied in life; it is an assault upon the impossible, an effort to fill a gap in his life, to capture through art that which nature has denied. Like *Moby Dick,* the novel attempts to capture in the nets of language an archetypal emblem of Significance—in this case a girl/woman named Caddy. It is a mark of his modernism that Faulkner can only imagine this repository of *omni*-significance as absent, missing, gone. As André Bleikasten notes of the general Faulknerian corpus, it is made up of "novels *about* lack and loss, in which desire is always intimately bound up with death. And it is clear too that they have sprung *out* of a deep sense of lack and loss—texts spun around a primal gap."[63]

When asked by a student why there was no section devoted to Caddy's point of view, Faulkner responded somewhat cryptically, "That's a good question. That—the explanation of the whole book is in that."[64] Caddy is at once more and less than a character in the novel; she (and her child) are from one standpoint the "subject" in that she inspires and fills the dreams of the others, but at the same time she remains a shadow without substance. She is never described, but remains a "word" that is filled by the significations of those who dream her privately and solitarily. She is that unnamable Other into which various selves project their self-images, fears, and frustrated desires. The novel consists in a discontinuous series of asymptotic approaches toward that Other, which remains its shadowy and unrealized center.

The Other can be actualized only in the minds of those who intend to conceive Otherness, and this fact dictates certain aspects of Faulkner's narrative method. The novel gives the reader a series of essentially static and separate consciousnesses that alternately illuminate and are illuminated by the "primal gap" of the narrative, the irremediable absence of Caddy. Each of the four sections presents different modes of apprehending and dealing with this central lack. That these modes are essentially separate and distinct is emphasized by the radical discontinuity of the text, both between sections (between pp. 92 and 93 the reader is abruptly transported from one highly idiosyncratic consciousness to another and from 1928 to 1910) and within sections (particularly in the disjointed monologues of Benjy and Quentin).[65] The sections are meant to be experienced as separate, unmediated glimpses into functioning minds, all presented as driven by a regressive desire to "possess," to hold onto that which is ephemeral because subject to the laws of change. Between the sections there exists what one critic calls a "no-man's land of unformulated connections,"[66] which despite having only an intratextual existence seems thick, dense, pregnant with significance. The density of the narrative derives from the imaginative (and occasionally imaginary) connections that the reader necessarily interpolates in the "space" between the sections so as to make of them a continuous and coherent whole. The narrative "fractures" its fictional space in such a way as to enact the motif of Absence and to implicate significantly the reader in matters of narrative management and meaning.

In terms of fictional space, *The Sound and the Fury* may be described in the following manner. By adopting what has been generally termed the stream-of-consciousness method of presentation (for three-fourths of the narrative), Faulkner gives to his NARRATIONAL SPACE two essential features. First, as in other "first-person" forms, the enunciation of the speaker is "dropped" into the space of the fictional world that it "shares" with the actants, topoi, and events of the fiction (whether those events be empirical or mental). This transformation of S_S may be described as follows: S_S (authorial) $\rightarrow S_S$ (actantial). Second, in contrast to traditional "first person," where the speaker is aware of the fact that he is narrating *to someone* (who may even exist within the fictional space), the enunciation here, consisting of an "unedited" and *im*-mediate flow of consciousness, can be said to have the predicates [+ MENTAL] and [+ SIMULTANEOUS].[67] The speaker "speaks" without his knowledge and to no one in particular, and the speech act seems to coincide temporally with the moment of the narrative (even if that act dwells on events that have happened in the narrative past). The epic preterit employed here in the stream-of-consciousness sections does not signify "pastness" in the same way that it does in conventional first person. There it betokens perspective, control, and a degree of understanding. Here there are no such implications; the preterit indicates only that the mental event happened some time in the past. These features of NARRATIONAL SPACE themselves transform the reader's relation to the narrative. As is the case in "Melanctha" (despite the extreme difference in narrative texture), the reader is dropped into an as it were unmediated and undifferentiated flux, without the consolations of an authorial personal or the control implicit in the conventional epic preterit. This unmanaged space of consciousness guarantees no logical or smooth links between sentences, ideas, or narremes; narrative units are juxtaposed and often linked only by association. The consciousnesses of Benjy, Quentin, and Jason register, more or less passively, the "raw materials" of the fictional reality; the degree of interpretation is minimal (except perhaps in the Jason section).[68] The technique of juxtaposition and the absence of aesthetic distance compel the reader to devise his or her own interpretive strategies, to "name" each sequence and discover its significance.

It should be noted that the final section, though not the unmediated perceptions of any one of the characters, achieves an effect similar to the previous sections through a technique similar to James's in *The Awkward Age*. The speaker exists somewhere apart from the characters, but shares several qualities with them, like limited knowledge, no foreknowledge or control of events, and reliance upon speculation (a trait signaled by the speaker's use of words of estrangement like *as if* and *seemed*). The result is what Uspensky terms a "synchronic" narrative situation,[69] one in which the speaker stands in the arena of action but alongside or apart from the actants involved. From this position he must speculate as to the motivations, behavior, and feelings of the actants involved. In general, the speaker, like the reader, is restricted to a role of detached, if intelligent and sympathetic, observer.[70]

The changes in NARRATIONAL SPACE are overshadowed by even more profound changes in NARRATIVAL SPACE, the combination thereof creating a uniquely shaped modernist text. *The Sound and the Fury* retains the conventional elements of a fictional world, like actants, topoi, and story, but inserts them into a new kind of structure. The structure of the text, for example, drastically deforms the *fabula* (the events of the narrative in the order they occur—the skeleton of STORY) into the presentational order of the *sujet*. The deformation is signaled by the section titles: "April Seventh 1928," "June Second 1910," "April Sixth 1928," and "April Eighth." These titles warn readers that they are to be displaced abruptly, if only in time. The reordering of STORY (both between sections and within sections, according to the movement of consciousness) challenges readers first to identify the events that occupy these idiosyncratic consciousnesses and second to establish their place in an extratextual chronology, a task that Faulkner makes difficult but not impossible.[71] Once readers identify Caddy as the absent center of the narrative, they begin to discern a narrative skeleton built on significant events in her life. These events and their repercussions provide the glue that connects the otherwise free-floating and self-sufficient sections. As one critic has pointed out, the narrative assumes a significant degree of continuity once one identifies Caddy as its heroine.[72]

The *fabula* of the story necessarily asks to be remade, to be reconstructed out of its shattered parts by the reader. The narrative is incoherent unless the reader recognizes for example that $Quentin_1$ is not the same as $Quentin_2$, that $Quentin_2$ is female and the illegitimate child of Caddy, that Mr. Compson and Jason share the same first name and so on. The clues, both linguistic and narrative, for the reconstruction are there. For example, Faulkner carefully provides the names of Benjy's different Negro attendants in many of the disparate Benjy "narremes" so as to enable the reader to locate the event with greater accuracy. In other words, the *fabula* is encoded within the text of the novel. One who looks for a "story" there will find it.

But the novel, just because of its arrangement in four disparate, achronological sections, offers itself as an object for study from another vantage point. It presents itself as a synchronic structure of four components in motion around an empty center as well as a diachronic tale of a family in decay.[73] By virtue of their (absent) common center, the separate sections are thrown into relation of juxtaposition, and the reader is encouraged to establish thematic, structural, and other correspondences between them. The density of the novel shifts from within the sections (limited and partial) to the space of signification between sections (an intratextual plenitude almost as fertile as the reader's imagination). In this way the principle of order and significance shifts from the text to the intratext and consequently to the reader. A local and empirical way to establish connections rests in identifying congruences, resemblances between separate scenes, such as Quentin's and Jason's similar response to female relatives in comparable states of undress. By mapping and ordering these congruences, the reader establishes the boundaries of the novel's subsystem of themes; that is, the brothers' respective responses reveal an attitude toward women that is simultaneously prudish and prurient. This theme may then ultimately be related to a tendency on the brothers' part to regard the Other as object to be possessed rather than autonomous self. In this way the reader moves from local congruence to global interpretation. Or the reader might begin with an extraliterary schema and demonstrate how that schema brings the sections into significant relation; Carvel Collins produces two different sets of coherence for the novel in this way, first by borrowing a Christian paradigm and later resorting to a Freudian paradigm.[74] Or the sections themselves can be inductively generalized into a self-regulating whole; witness Wolfgang Iser's discussion of the novel as a series of phenomenological reductions of the interplay between self and world.[75] In any case, what becomes the critic's primary concern is the space between the sections, the hermeneutic "play" (in the sense of "give") of the novel.

Arnheim has said of fragmented narrative in general:

> The shattering of the narrative sequence challenges the reader or viewer to reconstruct the objective order of events. In trying to do so, he tends to assign the scattered pieces to their place in a structurally separate system. However, if the reader or viewer would limit his effort to this reconstruction of objective reality, he would miss the entire other half of the work's structure. Although discontinuous and therefore disorderly with regard to objective reality, the presentation must also be understood as a valid sequence of its own, a flow of disparate fragments, complexly and absurdly related to one another.[76]

In *The Sound and the Fury,* the multiplication of discursive modes, the consequent deformation of *fabula* into *sujet,* and the relationship of juxtaposition (as opposed to chronology) between narrative segments results in a narrative structure that elicits simultaneously two different readerly activities: the reconstructions of the "natural" narrative according to its "objective reality," and the formulation of systems of coherence accounting for "these sections in this order." The gaps between the sections assert themselves as significant and dramatic parts of the narrative ontology. The space of the WORLD begins visibly to dilate, as if to make room for readers who can connect the parts, fill up the wholes, give to the fiction the center it structurally seems to lack, creating the little girl that is not there.

The Sound and the Fury and *As I Lay Dying* have frequently been treated by critics as a kind of matched set, probably because of both the proximity in date of composition and the similarities in narrative strategies. Structurally the two novels resemble one another somewhat, the latter appearing to take the fragmentation of the former one step farther, so that the reader is confronted with fifty-nine ways of looking at a blackbird rather than a mere four. But the titles of the individual sections signal an important difference: where the former novel assigns dates to the various sections, the latter assigns the name of the individual spectator or actor. It is as though the former wishes to announce that time is the basic index of its dislocations whereas the latter takes space (in the form of the space between characters' perspectives) as the fundamental discontinuity; where the most significant dislocations in *The Sound and the Fury* involve the space of the WORLD, those in *As I Lay Dying* involve the number of speakers and the "distance" between them. This difference is reflected in their respective treatment of STORY. In the latter novel the reader is not confronted by a *fabula* that has been radically deformed in the *sujet;* with the exception of a couple of troublesome prolepses (flashforwards) and an occasional filling-in of the past (Darl on the history of Jewel and the horse; Addie on her relation to Anse), the "story" is presented in chronological order. The reader has no problem deciphering or recuperating the events and actants that make up the STORY of the novel. It might be argued, for that matter, that the relative coherence of the narrative line encourages readers to view the novel in traditional ways—that is, as a traditional "journey" narrative, one to be evaluated in terms of success or failure of the journey's object. In this light the journey is at once the principle of coherence and the source of meaning in the novel.

The notion that space and not time is the *ne plus ultra* of the narrative is reflected not only in its treatment of STORY, but also in the temporal perspective adopted within many of the sections (the time of the discourse). The traditional distance between the narrated story (NARRATIVAL SPACE) and the act of narration (NARRATIONAL SPACE)—a distance generally predicated upon an implicit amount of time and signaled by the epic preterit—is collapsed here; the enunciation is contemporaneous with the fictional "reality." As one critic puts it, "the reader sees the functioning mind, but it is not exhibiting experience *for* the reader; it is simply experiencing."[77] The disappearance of the epic preterit betokens a world in process, and therefore a world unmanaged. The insecurity that the reader feels because of this is encouraged by the rapidity of the shifts in perspective. The reader is not immersed in any one character's consciousness long enough to identify with the narrator. By means of the abrupt shifts, the reader is kept in the position of a spectator, viewing the unfolding of a "rapid montage of contrasting snap-shots."[78] The use of the present tense for the enunciation and the technique of rapid montage combine to militate against the expected three-dimensionality of the fictional world, substitut-ing for volume and continuity the less "readable" or predictable facts of surface and simultaneity.[79]

What, in effect, occurs is an evaporation of "significant depth" in the novel. One critic summarizes the situation as follows: "*As I Lay Dying* is to be 'seen,' not understood; experi-enced, not translated; felt, not analysed. . . . There is thus in the novel a fundamental silence that is truly terrible. For what is more mysterious, finally, than immediacy? Explanations tranquilize wonder, and *As I Lay Dying* contains no explana-tions."[80]

In "Melanctha," Stein creates a "flattened" fictional space by continually beginning and beginning again, by refusing to "add" up the various units of her story, by repeating motifs with incremental variation, by ignoring the motivations (the psycho-logical "depth") of her characters; hers is a flatness produced stylistically within DISCURSIVE SPACE. Faulkner, on the other hand, achieves ultimately a similar effect within his DISCURSIVE SPACE in a manner that may be described as "structural." First he segments a fairly continuous narrative into a rather large number of self-sufficient segments, the distance between the segments predicated upon the abrupt shift to a different and idiosyncratic speaker—the reader must negotiate a gap in time, in space, in perspective, and in idiolect. The individual enunci-ations themselves, unfolding as they do in basically present tense (thus DISCOURSE is contemporaneous with STORY) and rendering for the most part an uninterpreted experience, as-sert themselves as isolated moments of "uncooked" experience, each moment of equal weight in the narrative. The overall effect such a structure has on the reader is not dissimilar to that of a photo album. The text is experienced both statically, as isolated but vivid pictures of significant narrative moments, and serially, as a series of such photos informed by various princi-ples of continuity. DISCURSIVE SPACE tends to stand still, while STORY forges on.[81] The text presents a fictional reality that is at once simultaneous and sequential, and the reader feels the ten-sion between the two perspectives.

The overriding impression that the text makes derives from this segmentation into shifting and overlapping frames, a fragmentation unlike that in *The Sound and the Fury* because it involves elements of DISCOURSE rather than of STORY and thus creates a different effect. In *The Sound and the Fury* segmentation creates intratextual gaps that seem pregnant with significance; the reader searches for congruence between the disparate sections. In *As I Lay Dying* connections between segments are implicitly encoded; the STORY provides the narrative glue. But the type and amount of segmentation and the *immediacy* of presentational format produce a leveling effect among narrative segments. Confronted by fifty-nine separate but equal intensely visual images of a fictional reality, the reader's first impulse is to negotiate the space between speakers, to establish hierarchies of speakers—Addie, Darl, Cash as privileged spokespersons—in order to create systems of meaning, or a "totalized" reading. Regardless of what that total reading might be, the reader of *As I Lay Dying* experiences a radically different discursive structure, one that forces upon him or her new types of interpretive activities, activities that anticipate the challenges presented to the reader by a second form of narrative tranformation—the experiment with PARASPACE.

V

Although the fictions of James, Stein, and Faulkner are structurally, stylistically, and thematically very disparate, they can be linked in terms of their respective elimination of "authorial" speaker as source of wisdom and arbiter of value within a fictional space. James accomplishes the "retreat" of the author basically through his management of the interspace between S_S and S_W. In James's later fictions DISCURSIVE SPACE is either subordinated to or subsumed within the space of the WORLD. In "Melanctha" Stein creates a narrative whose DISCOURSE dominates its WORLD. The enunciation of "Melanctha," by repeating recurrent motifs and continually beginning again, subverts the STORY; the reader is left with predication without explanation. Faulkner, in *The Sound and the Fury* and *As I Lay Dying*, attempts a systematic assault upon, respectively, the temporality of STORY and the unimodality of DISCURSIVE SPACE. In both fictions the fact of segmentation and the reliance upon actantial enunciations result in narrative structures in which meaning "shifts" from text to the intratextual gaps. Each of these narratives, by leveling or flattening one or another of its fictional subspaces and thus creating a narrative without volume, transfers to the reader interpretive responsibilities that authorial fictions tend to assume themselves. In the modernist texts of these and other writers, the fictional space is underdetermined; the reader must determine the semantic dimensions of these texts by "reading out" or "naming" the space of meaning that the authorial speaker has evacuated or emptied out.

Prologue to Chapter 3

My attitude to subjects and expressions, the angles of my vision, my methods of composition will, within limits, be always changing—not because I am unstable or unprincipled but because I am free. Or perhaps it may be more exact to say, because I am always trying for freedom—within my limits.

Joseph Conrad, Life and Letters

To read well, that is, to read true books in a true spirit, is a noble exercise and one that will task the reader more than any exercise which the customs of the day esteem. It requires a training such as the athletes underwent, the steady intention almost of a whole life to this object.

Henry David Thoreau, "Reading"

Formal invention in the novel, far from being opposed to realism as short-sighted critics often assume, is the sine qua non *of a greater realism.*

Michel Butor, "The Novel as Research"

For, far from neglecting him, the author of today proclaims his absolute need of the reader's cooperation, an active, conscious, creative assistance. What he asks of him is no longer to receive ready-made a world completed, full, closed upon itself, but on the contrary to participate in a creation, to invent in his turn the work—and the world— and thus to learn to invent his own life.

Alain Robbe-Grillet, For a New Novel

The criterion of truth resides in the enhancement of the feeling of power.
Friedrich Nietzsche, in Holland, "Human Identity"

3

Making Room for the Reader
The Experiment with Paraspace

The painting is finished when the idea has disappeared.
        Georges Braque, in Josipovici, The World and the Book

Blank space, the pure and simple juxtaposition of two paragraphs describing two events far apart in time, thus appears as the fastest possible form of narrative, a speed which effaces everything. Within this "blank," the author may introduce a notation which will force the reader to spend a certain time in proceeding from one paragraph to the next, and especially to establish a certain scale between this reading and the time of the adventure itself.
        Michel Butor, "Research on the Technique of the Novel"

Pousser has offered a tentative definition of his musical work which involves the term "field of possibilities." In fact this shows that he is prepared to borrow two extremely revealing technical terms from contemporary culture. The notion of "field" is provided by physics, and implies a revised vision of the classic relationship posited between cause and effect as a rigid, one-directional system: now a complex inter-play of motive forces is envisaged, a configuration of possible events, a complete dynamism of structure. The notion of "possibility" is a philosophical canon which reflects a wide-spread tendency in contemporary science: the discarding of a static, syllogistic view of order, a corresponding devolution of intellectual authority to personal decision, choice and social context.
        Umberto Eco, "The Poetics of the Open Work"

Modernist authors, partly because of epistemological insecurity, partly because of their distrust of abstractions of any sort, and partly because of a reawakening to the pleasures inherent in the surfaces of things—in experience unmediated by intellection or reflection—progressively relegate Ideas and Idealism to an inferior status within their narrative spaces.[1] In some radical

109

instances, authors attempt to banish Ideas entirely from their fictional space, suspecting that Ideas, because of their nature as mental constructs, automatically reduce, dissipate, or destroy the palpability of the fictional experience. Their goal is to make the reader forget that he or she is in fact reading a fiction, to make the reader's immersion in the "destructive element" nearly as total as possible. One way to accomplish this end is to abolish signs or evidence of the Author as a mediating presence, and pursuit of this end results in fictions characterized by the "disappearance" of the author and by scenic presentation. Other authors, accepting the inevitable role that ideas play in the life of the mind, try to preempt the *author*-ity of those ideas by ascribing them to actants within the field of the fiction. Thus modernist fictionists frequently adopt first-person narration or stream-of-consciousness or what Stanzel refers to as the "figural" narrative situation; after the fact, critics speak of such narrative subgenres as the "modern psychological novel" or the "stream-of-consciousness novel."

The elimination of the author as both source of moral wisdom and as interpolating and interpreting consciousness can be accomplished through a number of transformations of fictional space. In "authorial" narration, narration not directly attributable to an actant within the fiction, the speaker can achieve relative effacement by an evacuation of the NARRATIONAL SPACE of the fiction, especially the DISCURSIVE component of NARRATIONAL SPACE, since in conventional narrative the ICONIC component is generally overlooked. First and foremost, the speaker abandons the syntagmatic level of DISCURSIVE SPACE, which is generated by statements of a perceptual, ideological, or metalingual nature (see chapter 1). These descriptive and normative statements of person, society, and textuality announce the speaker's presence and reveal his or her epistemological assurance; in some modernist fiction these statements are entirely eliminated from the narrative. In similar fashion the author removes any deictics (words referring to the enunciation); the moment of enunciation is to give way to the moment of the narrative. This is not to say that the narrative is not mediated, that it achieves the immediacy of drama. The retention of the epic preterit as the primary verb tense signals that the experience recounted in the text has been digested and circumscribed. And these narratives are often diacritically marked by frequent resort to various words of estrangement. An example is Faulkner's narrative stance in the fourth section of *The Sound and the Fury:* "Ben ceased whimpering. He watched the spoon as it rose to his mouth. It was *as if* even eagerness were muscle-bound in him too, and hunger itself inarticulate, not knowing it is hunger" (emphasis added). These phrases at one and the same time announce indirectly a speaker's (observer's) presence, indicate his epistemological uncertainty, and allow him to offer suggestions that "pure" impersonal narration would not admit. Finally, as the example of Faulkner clearly shows, the speaker in an impersonal narration is revealed by the idiosyncratic locutions he adopts, the syntax he uses, the vocabulary he employs (even though the distinctiveness of these dictional and linguistic patterns can be minimized, as in some of Hemingway's short stories). These qualities create the tone of the fiction and ultimately indicate the "personality" of the speaker.

Impersonal narration, by nature a form of narrative in which the speaker is dehumanized and deintellectualized, obviously does not appeal to authors who desire to retain introspection and sympathy within the narrative fabric as more than just subjects of conversation. To retain a "personalized" narrative these authors may resort to either a first-person or figural narrative situation, in which, as if by prestidigitation, the very nature of DISCURSIVE SPACE is transformed. In "authorial" narration the speaker mediates between the fictional world and the world of the reader; the space of DISCOURSE is not located on the same plane as the space of the fictional world, the NAR-RATIVAL SPACE. DISCOURSE is located at a different, *privileged* plane. The reader instinctively relies on the vantage point provided by the plane of DISCOURSE to gain perspective on the fictional world. In first-person and figural narrations, the space of DISCOURSE is relocated at an unprivileged position *within* the fictional world itself; speech acts about the fictional world assume the same degree of fictionality (in the sense of "made-up-ness") as the elements and constituents of that world. DISCURSIVE SPACE is appropriated by the "character" who is speaking or by the consciousness that is being dramatized. In terms of fictive ontology, the difference between *histoire* and *discours* is abolished, the space between NARRATIVE and NARRA-TION collapsed. These two spaces are separate and distinguishable, but they exist on the same ontological plane (it is this fact that James makes such great use of in *The Turn of the Screw*).

In this case the "actantial" speaker (or the mediating consciousness) may resort to the spectrum of DISCURSIVE statements to articulate his views of the fictional world; the reader must, however, keep in mind that those views are "motivated" and therefore not privileged. Or the author may choose to present narrative events (elements of NARRATIVAL SPACE) as they impinge upon the mediating consciousness and thus to minimize the DISCURSIVE component of the fiction. The narrative presents the reader with a world that is unmediated and undigested—an immediate present.

In the modernist novel, then, the traditional notion of the Author as a source of Ideas and a repositor of Value has been transformed: the Author has either been eliminated, through abdication of authorial responsibilities, or replaced, by the voice or consciousness of one of the characters. The result is a narrative with a "zero degree" of *author*-ized interpretation. The novel consequently becomes more an *experience* and less an exposition; there is a corresponding emphasis upon the surfaces of events, things, and experience, and a concomitant de-emphasis of depth, essence, meaning. This is not to say that narrative units no longer *signify,* but that their significations remain almost completely unarticulated. One critic, borrowing his words from Plato, puts it as follows: "written speech is bound to speak and signify, in the absence of his father, and without his father's assistance."[2] The abdication of authorial interpretive responsibilities does not signal the end of interpretation; those responsibilities are merely transferred to the reader. In the modernist novel, the fictional experience is still meaningful; the author is, however, unwilling or unable to specify just what that meaning might be. Thus there is generated within the modernist text a significant and substantial interpretive space whose management and description falls to the reader. The fiction no longer specifies its relation to "reality"; that relation must be *discovered* by the reader, who is given no guarantee that the relation is either simple or singular. But because readers come to the novel with expectations of significance (expectations that the author shares and approves of), they willingly or compulsively occupy that interpretive space, making the connections and forging the "reading" that the author was unable to do.

The circumstance for the author who "comes after" the modernist author is significantly different. The epigones of mod-

ernism share the modernist sensibility—in particular the
epistemological insecurity and the counterbalancing faith in the
redemptive power of Art—and learn from the modernist literary experience. Where modernist writers were, in a manner of
speaking, *forced* to evacuate a portion of their fictional space,
paramodernist writers[3] willingly disrupt their fictional space,
acting upon two basic assumptions: that the progressive "dila-
tion" of the space of the fiction automatically activates the
reader's imagination as a coproducer of the aesthetic experience; and that this activation constitutes the *raison d'être* of the
work of art. Umberto Eco, speaking of the poetics of the "open
work," has said of the contemporary artist that "rather than
submit to the 'openness' as an inescapable element of artistic
interpretation, he subsumes it into a positive aspect of his production, recasting the work so as to expose it to the maximum
possible 'opening.' "[4] Given the fact that he or she can no longer
contain or circumscribe fictional space, and aware of the virtues
of openness, the paramodernist author creates a more radically
"open" text, whose function it is to enlarge the reader's powers
of imagination and/or to mirror more closely the discontinuous
"feel" of contemporary experience. No longer limited to hermeneutic activities, the reader becomes part of the formal furniture of the house of fiction.

In order to make the fiction a more open system, the
paramodernist author relies on a number of strategies. The
greatest single obstacle to "open" narrative is continuity and the
kind of movement that continuity presupposes—the gradual,
predictable, and irreversible progress from point *A* to point *B*.
The vehicle for this movement in the traditional novel is STORY.
As argued above (see chapter 1), STORY functions as the glue
that endows fictional space with coherence, continuity, and teleology, and that guarantees the text's readability. Most modernist fiction retains some sort of minimal plot (be it the events of
an ordinary day in June 1904, a postponed trip to a lighthouse,
or the burial of a dead relative), though it tends to experiment
drastically with the form of its presentation. Paramodernist
fiction, on the other hand, occasionally dispenses entirely with
conventional STORY, presenting the reader instead with a series
of independent units recounting apparently unrelated events
or scenes. Jurij Lotman, speaking of the mechanism of plot in
traditional fiction, has described its nature as follows. The space
of a fictional world consists of mutually nonintersecting topoi,

between any two of which there exists a "boundary"—"the most important topological feature of space." In traditional narrative, plot is based upon transgression of these boundaries by one of the characters; for example, Sister Carrie goes to Chicago, Joseph Andrew goes to the country, Red Riding Hood goes into the forest. Lotman goes on to say that a text may be characterized by the ways in which boundaries divide it into topological subspaces.[5] What happens, however, when a STORY consists of discrete and independent narrative segments, when the "boundary" between topoi takes the shape of a *blank* page? The only one who can "transgress" this type of boundary is the reader.

And such is the case in some paramodernist fiction. The space of the fictional world is "pulverized" almost beyond recognition; into the systems of actants, topoi, and STORY, into the very fabric of the text, there are introduced factors of discontinuity, often in the form of empty space. It is as if these writers were attempting to adhere to Gide's plan for *The Counterfeiters:* "Never take advantage of the impetus that has been acquired. This is the rule of my game."[6] STORY, itself the skeleton of NARRATIVAL SPACE, is transformed from a unidirectional, irreversible "flow" to a field of relationships between independent narrative segments. The number and kind of these relationships are to a large extent dependent upon the reader's imagination. In this sort of fiction, there is no development, only distribution, and notions of hierarchy and progression are undercut—each narrative segment assumes equal weight and importance.

Continuity in fiction is implicit not only in the notion of story but also in the shape of the discourse. The linearity of prose— its successivity and regularity and predictability—inevitably suggests a condition of seamlessness; in Roland Barthes's phrase, "everything holds together." The insertion of blank spaces in the text, even in the form of chapter endings, necessarily creates a gap across which the reader's imagination must leap. If that gap serves as a transition between different times in the narrative, different speakers in the narrative, or different kinds or modes of narrative, the reader's imagination is "thrown" into that breach to fill it with appropriate connections. In paramodernist fictions these gaps are often so multiplied as to give the narrative a distinctive, "discontinuous" look. More important, however, the types of connections that are available in modernist fictions (thirteen ways of looking *at a blackbird,* fifteen ways of viewing *a corpse*) are not authorized by paramodernist narrative segmentation. Sections are so disparate in form and content that the gap-filling that the reader does becomes problematic if not fraudulent.

Yet another way to "dilate" the space of a fiction is to open the boundaries of the fictional world to alien entities of various kinds. The world may, for example, be extended to include other forms of literary art, such as the poem, diary, or essay; or it may incorporate elements and techniques drawn from other media, like graphic art, cinema, or newspaper. Nathanael West has said, for example, of *Miss Lonelyhearts* that it was an attempt to approximate the form of the comic strip.[7] In this way the repertoire of fiction is enlarged, and the possibility of intratextual relationships is increased. Paramodernist authors also attempt to expand the field of fiction by abolishing the separateness of fiction and reality. As Gertrude Stein has noted, in the twentieth century "the way of living had extended and each thing was as important as any other thing."[8] In order to encompass this "surplus" of reality, paramodernist authors feel constrained to incorporate it, virtually undisguised and untransformed, in their fictional space. These fictions may be characterized as "bi-referential," in that they contain a double field of reference, "the internal unified field of fiction mapped out within the book" (Internal Fields of Reference) and the "external configuration of facts verifiable outside the book" (External Fields of Reference).[9] Paramodernist use of empirical fact or reality should not be confused with that of realistic fiction. In the latter, the introduction of verisimilar, verifiable, or recognizable fact serves to confirm the mimetic contract, to give what Barthes calls "the effect of the real." In the former, facts and "real-life" personages are incorporated (but not necessarily assimilated) to expand the fictional world, to destroy the boundaries between the fictive and the real, to convert the fiction into an "open dynamic system in active tension with the experiential world outside the book."[10] The fiction mixes, without fusing, realities belonging to different orders—formal and material realities—much as the techniques of collage in painting brings together visual elements drawn from different levels of experience.

The notion of collage, in fact, is instrumental in an understanding of the technique and objectives of paramodernist fiction. Harold Rosenberg has said of collage that it is both a child of technology and a form born of reservations in our time about the ART/LIFE dichotomy, that a work of collage "appropriates the external world," and that the object in collage is suspended, as it were, between its extratextual reality and its formal location within an artistic whole.[11] His description of artistic collage is highly applicable to the ways in which paramodernist authors use fact in narrative. The empirically verifiable "piece" of fact (the newspaper headline or story, the literary fragment, the "real-life" character) is inserted into the fictional space, and at one and the same time fractures the space, thereby generating areas of intratextuality, and transforms the shape and substance of the fictional world. The boundary between fictional world and real world is obscured (but not obliterated as in the nonfiction novel), the two fields overlapping and generating semantic possibilities. The space of the fictional world becomes polymorphous (like the new technological reality it seeks to evoke), an amalgamation of "pieces" drawn from different realities, different levels of consciousness, different types of discourse.

By admitting into the space of the fictional world materials drawn from different orders of experience, by juxtaposing elements of fact and fiction in the same fictional plane, and by introducing discontinuity into the conventional components of fiction (plot, character, setting), paramodernists create "narratives" consisting in large part of discrete and independent units. The texture of these texts forces upon the reader new activities. As Lotman says, "Juxtaposed units that are incompatible in one system force the reader to construct an additional structure in which the incompatibility is eliminated."[12] Fictional space approaches the condition of a field of possibilities, a field for which the reader must create harmony and order.

William Gaddis's *JR:* The Novel of Babel

Above all, the unreadable book will humiliate, confound, and rout the reader. This is the essential aim of "final unreadability" (l'illisibilité finale).
                                        George Steiner, "Books: Crossed Lines"

But few Americans will be able or willing to read JR.
        J. D. O'Hara, "Boardwalk and Park Place vs. Chance and Peace of Mind"

But it is 726 pages, and the codes are oblique; I may, or may not, have missed something.

Malcolm Bradbury, "Hello, Dollar"

At the very end of the nineteenth century Henry James wrote a novel called *The Awkward Age*, a curious novel in which conversations are at once the form and the content, as Todorov has convincingly shown.[13] About thirty years later Ernest Hemingway wrote a number of stories such as "Hills Like White Elephants," "The Killers," and "A Clean, Well-Lighted Place," in which conversations compose the bulk of the narrative events. In these works and in others like them, the method of scenic presentation is refined to a high degree. The texts consist of a series of disembodied voices, who speak apparently without authorial guidance or assistance and usually without authorial comment, and the reader is constrained to "flesh out" the characters and the situations from the (frequently laconic) conversations themselves. Stories like these aspire to and approach the condition of drama, in that they so dispense with the DIS-CURSIVE SPACE of the fiction that the narrative action is presented almost unmediated. And unlike the theatergoer, readers do not have the character before them to help them "read between the lines." These fictions *do*, however, give the reader considerable help in reconstructing the narrative action and the fictional world, in the following ways:

(1) by specifying the narrative locale (which can be metatextually symbolic): "The hills across the valley of the Ebro were long and white. On this side there was no shade and no trees and the station was between two rails in the sun. . . . The American and the girl with him sat at a table in the shade, outside the building."[14]

(2) by specifying the nature or kind of involvement or participation by the characters (and thus indirectly contributing to their characterization): "His interruption was clearly too vague to be sincere, and it was as such that, going straight on, she treated it."[15]

(3) by clearly identifying the speakers (and thus keeping the lines of communication clear): "'They look like white elephants,' she said. 'I've never seen one,' the man drank his beer."[16]

(4) by providing discursive authorial transitions between narrative episodes (and thus glueing the narrative together): "When, after dinner, the company was restored to the upper rooms, the Duchess was on her feet as soon as the door opened for the entrance of the gentlemen."[17] These techniques endow the fictional space with density and continuity, bringing the fictional world into correspondence with the empirical world.

In 1975 William Gaddis published his long-awaited second novel, *JR*, a voluminous text that perhaps extends the principle of scenic presentation through elimination of authorial intrusion to its ultimate configuration. The 726-page text is almost exclusively made up of talking, of the speeches, mutterings, dialogues, conversations, interruptions, and harangues of a panoply of characters. Because those speeches are strung together almost entirely without "authorized" interpolation, the text contains a "zero degree" of S_S, the space of the speaker. William Gass, in a short note about the novels of 1976, has said of *JR* that it is "perhaps the supreme masterpiece of acoustical collage."[18] Gass's description is particularly apropos in that it singles out perhaps the distinctive quality of the text—its "shape." The various "speeches" (the word is appropriate since no one seems to be listening to what anyone else is saying) of the text are presented in simple sequential juxtaposition (just as the pieces in collage are juxtaposed in space), without the benefit of authorial interpolation at all. The result is an undifferentiated, undiscriminated "acoustical" fictional space, and what one critic has referred to as a "difficult narrative surface."[19] It is as if the narrative method consisted in the verbatim transcription of tapes taken from a stationary tape recorder, which has been equipped with a microphone of limited range sensitive only to human voices.

The resulting "seamless web" of narrative voices causes a series of problems for readers looking for coherence and a narrative line, and their attempts to solve these problems implicate them strongly in narrative management. In the first place the reader must "learn" to identify just *who* is speaking. In rare instances the speaker is specified, by means of impersonal, "telegraphic" dialogue tags: "—PRwise it can't hurt us educationwise, Miss Flesch got in through bread."[20] Such interpolations assist the reader in identifying other speakers in the conversation, if only by process of elimination. In most cases the reader is provided no direct signals, and can sort out individual strands in the stream of voices only by mastering various idiolectal codes; each speaker may be identified by linguistic idiosyncrasies or by personal hobbyhorses. For example, some of the more cacophonic conversations transpire in the principal's office at the school JR attends, where there may be gathered at any one time a wide assortment of characters—teachers, school board members, Congressmen, salespersons, Foundation representatives, the principal himself. The reader learns who is present from perfunctory introductions and greetings, but he or she must assign speeches to individual speakers by recognizing their distinctive idiolect. Mr. Whiteback, the principal of the school and president of the local bank, may be identified by the hesitations that punctuate his speech and by his tendency to fall back on modern educational jargon: "—But you both ahm, Mister Gall yes you might want to see this next lesson in terms of a good deal less ahm, less unplanlessness than the one we've just . . ." (p. 44).[21] In similar fashion Major Hyde, the mercenary school board member, may be identified by his brusque, colloqial idiom ("—I don't think Vern's head's screwed on Whiteback . . ." p. 23; "The foundation is committed up to its, it's deeply committed," p. 26); and Davidoff, the pushy PR man, by his reliance upon clichés, especially the expression "putting out brush fires." But more than on linguistic signals, the reader relies on personal hobbyhorses that inevitably worm their way into the characters' speech acts. One recognizes Hyde by his concern to get the school to pay for his elaborate and expensive air-raid shelter, Mrs. deCaphalis by her promiscuity and her selfish concern with her various "art" projects, slatternly Rhoda by her obsession with her body, Mr. Crawley by his wild dream to stock American national parks with African game, and so on. Of the cacophony of voices the reader makes a managed and manageable fugue.

The reader's activity in the text is not limited to the identification and elaboration of voices; he or she must likewise locate and imaginatively reconstruct the fictional milieu. In this regard the method of transition between narrative locales bears further investigation. The first scene-shift in the novel takes the reader from the living-room of the Bast sisters' house in the fringes of a Long Island suburb to a bank and then a school more centrally located in the community. The "narrator" does not allow himself the freedom to effect this spatial transition without "motivation"; rather, he must rely on some sort of neutral vehicle to "carry" the recording transcriber from one spot to the other. The transition itself, the actual act of movement, is then selectively but neutrally described, the mediating technological instrument being a camera lens fitted with a kind of impressionistic lens. In this particular instance the vehicle upon which the camera is mounted happens to be the car of the attorney Mr. Coen:

> was gone in a swerving miss for the pepperidge tree towering ahead, past shadeless windows in a naked farmhouse sprawl at the corner where the road trimmed neatly into the suburban labyrinth and things came scaled down to a wieldy size, dogwood, then barberry, becomingly streaked blood-red for fall.
>
> Past the firehouse, where once black crepe had been laboriously strung in such commemoration as that advertised today on the sign Our Dear Departed Member easy to hang and store as a soft drink poster, past the crumbling eyesore dedicated within recent memory as the Marine Memorial, past the. . . . (Pp. 17–18)

The camera rolls on recording sight after sight until it, as if by accident, notices and zooms in on a man in pastel (Whiteback), standing in front of the bank (the reader later learns that he is both principal *and* bank president) and "crowding the high-bosomed brunette at the curb" (Amy Joubert). Abruptly the recorder is turned on again and the space reverts from visual to acoustic. This method is employed throughout the text as the vehicle for spatial movement, the resulting text becoming a textural hybrid of lengthy passages of acoustic transcription punctuated infrequently by visual registration of scenic transition. Once the scene has been shifted, the reader frequently has only the vaguest idea what the new setting might be and often no notion at all how many or who are its participants.

Passage of time in the text likewise occurs in a subtle, understated fashion. Here is the first passage in the text in which the passage of time is noted:

> and they entered the car out of sight behind its filthy windows as its lights too receded and became mere punctuations in this aimless spread of evening past the firehouse and the crumbling marine memorial, the blooded barberry and the woodbine's silent siege and the desirable property For Sale, up weeded ruts and Queen Anne's laces to finally mount the sky itself where another blue day brought even more the shock of fall in its brilliance, spread loss like shipwreck on high winds tossing these oaks back. (Pp. 74–75)

The reader who is not alert may well miss the fact that an evening has passed and that the conversation soon to follow transpires on the following day. In effect, the camera has panned away from the train station through the suburb to the sky, where the reader watches the color change from darkness to blue, and then the camera recapitulates its journey back to the train station, where the reader encounters Mrs. Joubert trying to herd her charges onto the train for their field trip to Manhattan. The reader must infer the unstated passage of time if the narrative is to make sense.[22]

There is another way in which the reader is implicated in narrative management, the matter of general context(s) for the speech acts.[23] In any narrative consisting primarily of unencumbered dialogue, the reader must necessarily construct the context for the speech acts; for example, in "Hills Like White Elephants," the reader must deduce that the two characters are speaking about pregnancy and the feasibility of abortion. Now in any instance where the context is singular, where the speakers share a common context, a degree of communication takes place—information or opinion is exchanged. In *JR* the contexts for a series of consecutive speech acts are so multiplied that communication is minimized; locked in his or her own context, no one hears what the other person is saying. The resulting "conversation," from the vantage point of the reader, is pure noise, and if the reader wishes to make sense of any of it, he or she must reconstruct the divergent contexts. In this way the reader acts against the entropy of the text, tying together speech acts that, in terms of their direction and manner of presentation, tend to disperse, wander, dissipate, dwindle, disappear.

The activities outlined above all take place at the microtextual level. The reader must expend energy merely to figure out who is saying what to whom and where and why, while what is taking place. This type of "readerly" activity is not generally required by other narrative texts. The speaker of a traditional text generally tends to locate and specify the actants and topoi of the fictional world; the speaker attempts to facilitate the reading process. The "dehumanized" speaker (really a complicated recording mechanism) of *JR* makes the "actualization" of this fictional world as much the reader's responsibility as possible. Within the text, the world consists only in a "thin" acoustic surface, without materiality, dimension, or substance.

The reader must quite literally give flesh to a disembodied narrative surface, at both the microtextual and the macrotextual level. From hints given in the foregrounded acoustic surface of the text, the reader must infer the total narrative background, the substance of the fictional world, the configurations of NARRATIVAL SPACE. From the bits and pieces of fragmented and oblique conversations, the reader charts a WORLD and a STORY, basically the tale of a series of failures (in the form of suicides, separations, divorces, accidents, random fornication, and so on) counterpointed by the phenomenal success of the JR Family of Companies.[24] The reader's success in "filling in" the narrative background is obstructed by the basic narrative technique: the recorder and microphone can be in only one place at one time, and therefore the events and conversations occurring at other places go unrecorded. These unrecorded events must be (re)constructed by the reader; there is no all-knowing author to provide brief and succinct summaries of the unrecounted episodes. The reader, through diligence and care alone, "actualizes" or "concretizes" the fiction by occupying NARRATIVAL gaps and by reading through the blizzard of noise to the fictional reality that generates the noise.

In this respect the telephone conversation becomes an important metaphor *in* and *for* the novel. At numerous places in the novel the reader (not to mention the characters) is put in the position where he or she must listen to one character carrying on a phone conversation. For example, JR conducts most of his business with Edward Bast over the phone. Here is a portion of one of his conversations:

> I mean the more you spend the more you get, see? I mean that's the whole . . . no well sure but . . . no I know I was always yelling about low-cost operations see but . . . no but listen a second hey I mean how do you think the telephone company works where they're always yelling how they have to spend all this here money so they need to raise the rates I mean the more money they can think of how to spend it someplace they get to take this here percent where they keep raising the rates till they're like almost bigger than the gover . . . no but wait, see the . . . No I know you don't mean I mean I'm just coming to that hey . . . no well I just mean we like we the company, like not really anybody see so . . . No but see that's the whole thing Bast see it's not money anyway it's just exchanging this here stock. (P. 465)

And so on. Readers have trouble enough working their way through JR's colloquial and redundant idiom to the substance of his speech, but their task is severely complicated by the fact that they must "supply" the other half of the dialogue. This particular situation may be generalized to describe readers' relation to the entire text (and perhaps, from Gaddis's standpoint, their necessary relation to works of Art); the text of *JR* presents readers with one half of a phone conversation; they must supply the other half if their experience is to have meaning or coherence. Gaddis's point, of course, is that meaning and coherence are less properties of a text than they are products of activities performed upon it. *JR* takes a form that necessarily demands and fosters these activities.

The need for these activities extends beyond the realm of textuality. At one point Jack Gibbs reads the following passage from his work-in-progress: "A remarkable characteristic of the Americans is the manner in which they have applied science to modern life Wilde marveled on struck by the noisiest country that ever existed" (p. 289). Like the reader of *JR*, the average person is continually bombarded and assaulted by walls of noise (in both the literal and information sense)—electronic, technological, and human. This deafening bombardment "softens" the receiver, in the long run transforming him or her into a passive recorder of sensations, a human machine.[25] Responding to Bast's complaint that his magnum opus is too hard to read, Gibbs delivers the following harangue: ". . . problem most God Damned readers rather be at the movies. Pay attention here bring something to it take something away problem most God damned writing's written for readers perfectly happy who they are rather be at the movies come in empty-handed go out the same God damned way" (pp. 289–90). Reading *JR* is not like going to the movies, and Gaddis seems to think that it can be a more meaningful and humanizing experience. To master the text, the reader is at every moment compelled to penetrate its seamless wall of language, to transform its noise into information, to resist its entropy, to construct from the words as "reality" that is sensible, in the many senses of that word. And it is just this imaginal activity that Gaddis wishes to promote because "nothing's worth doing till you've done it and then it was worth doing even if it wasn't because that's all you" (p. 715).

Anaïs Nin's *Collages:* The Paratactic Novel

The function of those micro-units is . . . to emphatically underline the intransitiveness of this type of fiction, to deny it any continuum, to do away with the two fundamental imperatives of traditional fiction, the double necessity . . . of having a beginning and an end.

   André Le Vot, "Disjunctive and Conjunctive Modes in Contemporary American Fiction"

It is a curious anomaly that we listen to jazz, we look at modern paintings, we live in modern houses of modern design, we travel in jet planes, yet we continue to read novels written in a tempo and a style which is not of our time and not related to any of these influences. The new swift novel could match our modern life in speed, rhythms, condensation, abstraction, miniaturization, X rays of our secrets, a subjective gauge of external events. It could be born of Freud, Einstein, jazz, and science.

   Anaïs Nin, The Novel of the Future

Collages was inspired by seeing Varda work with his little bits of material. I began to think about the people that I knew in Los Angeles and they suddenly formed a pattern of dreamers. They were all absolutely possessed by some myth or some dream. . . . I put them all together and that formed a collage of dreamers who couldn't possibly talk to each other because each one was pursuing his own fantasy. So they were like little pieces in a collage. They never absolutely could meet each other, but each one was completely possessed by a different kind of fantasy. I had the Japanese woman, and Varda also was one of the characters, creating his own world. When I started I couldn't see any design or pattern or anything, but then I suddenly realized that the pattern and theme was a collage.

   Anaïs Nin, A Woman Speaks: The Lectures, Seminars, and Interviews of Anaïs Nin

  The title page of *Collages* identifies the text as "a novel" by Anaïs Nin. One critic, however, less than enchanted with the entire piece, complains about that nomenclature and suggests that the text "might be more properly described as a collection of short stories with a single common character, a woman painter named Renate."[26] Clearly the text does not satisfy his expectations as to what a novel should be, at least partly because of its "shape." The text is divided into nineteen discrete units, each of which tells an abbreviated but yet complete "story" about Renate or one of the "characters" that she meets. This degree of fragmentation in the novel does continually frustrate the reader's expectations of continuity and momentum and completion. And the process of fragmentation is not limited to the separate "chapters"; it infiltrates the stories themselves. In the first chapter, for example, the reader is rather abruptly dropped into Vienna, the city of statues, and introduced to the child Renate, who is "convinced that people did not die, they became statues."[27] The text moves without warning from a description of the young girl to her father and continues in the following manner:

> Renate's father built telescopes and microscopes, so that for a long time Renate did not know the exact size of anything. She had only seen them diminutive or magnified.
>
> Renate's father treated her like a confidante, a friend. He took her with him on trips, to the inauguration of telescopes, or to ski. He discussed her mother with her as if Renate were a woman, and explained that it was her mother's constant depression which drove him away from home.
>
> He relished Renate's laughter, and there were times when Renate wondered whether she was not laughing for two people, laughing for herself, but also for her mother who never laughed. She laughed even when she felt like weeping.
>
> When she was sixteen she decided that she wanted to become an actress. (p. 8)

And so on. The chapter goes on to describe an argument became Renate and her father about her career and then suddenly shifts focus to her tutor/uncle who insists that he has no marrow in his bones. The narrative thus consists of minimally connected and relatively autotelic "narremes," whose interrelationships the reader is at liberty to speculate about. For example, the reader may surmise that Renate's mother is constantly depressed because her husband is a philanderer (her father is fond of actesses), and that her father and uncle carry on a somewhat unhealthy sibling rivalry, but such readings are not in any way authorized by the text. Furthermore, the effects that these familial realities might have had upon the adolescent daughter are completely passed over. Once the "stories" of the father and the uncle are told, these characters disappear from the text, never to appear again, even by way of influence. In fact, the entire text of *Collages* dispenses in large part with cause-and-effect relationships; sequences are simply juxtaposed, and causal relations must be inferred, perhaps unjustifiably.

Traditional narrative arranges its sequences hypotactically,

with successive narremes linked implicitly or explicitly (connectives provided) according to relations of chronology, dependency, or subordination. The primary principle of
arrangement, of course, is chronology, a principle that is
codified in narrative fiction as plot. In traditional narrative, plot
consists in a series of consecutive and irreversible events charting a movement from state A to state B, this movement in itself
carrying thematic weight.[28] In a text like *Collages,* however, and
in many paraspatial fictions, the principle of arrangement is not
hypotaxis but parataxis.[29] That is, discrete narrative units are
placed side by side, without the benefit (and perhaps possibility)
of connectives. The narrative is distributed rather than developed. A text like *As I Lay Dying* fractures its STORY without
transforming its nature—the principle of arrangement is still
chronology, and the plot can be "read" thematically. And even
"novels" in the form of collected short stories, like Anderson's
Winesburg, Ohio or Hemingway's Nick Adams stories, are *informed* by a "deep structure" based on some kind of irreversible movement or "transgression of boundaries" (such as
initiation or maturation). A text like *Collages,* on the other hand,
totally reconceives its STORY, eliminating elements of chronology and causality and shaping principle, and presenting its narrative units as separate, discrete, equal. The shape of *Collages,*
in this respect, anticipates the fragmented postmodern narratives of authors like Barthelme and Sukenick (the main difference being that in these later works the principle of collage is
treated ironically).

Because of its paratactic principle of arrangement, the un-
numbered sections that "compose" *Collages* may be read in any
order, especially once one has read the first section dealing with
Renate's adolescence. The first four sections, although they all
focus on Renate, seem to be arranged less according to chronology than geography. They in effect give the reader snapshots of
Renate's on-again/off-again relationship with Bruce from
Vienna, Mexico, Holland, and California. Once Renate "set-
tles" in California, the narrative shifts focus from her to the
collection of dreamers—Count Laundromat, the Seal-Man,
Henri, Varda, Nina, Nobuko, and so on—that she seems to
attract. The "stories" of these dreamers, each one occupying
mainly one narrative section, might be read in any order; in at
least one of the sections Renate is not even mentioned (the first
Varda section, pp. 59–61), and in many others she makes only a

perfunctory appearance so as to "naturalize" the story to follow (e.g., she picks up the Seal-Man hitch-hiking on Pacific Palisades).

This transformation of STORY demands from the reader rather different activities from those demanded by more traditional fiction. Having traveled from point *A* to point *B* of the conventional plot, the reader necessarily establishes those two points as states of rest and automatically compares them to determine movement that can then be read metatextually as meaning. Traditional plot thus becomes one armature for the reader's interpretive activities, one that is not available in a text like *Collages*. Since the text does not depict a movement from *A* to *B*, since it frustrates the reader's expectation of an ultimate *telos*, since it frequently reminds the reader both that "an interruption [might be] more eloquent than a complete paragraph" (p. 11) and that "nothing is ever finished" (pp. 91, 92, 97), the reader necessarily seeks out principles of unity other than continuity and teleology. In particular, the reader attempts to establish the text's COHERENCE by discovering what the disparate micro- and macrosequences have in common. This search for coherence is not necessarily a task that is more difficult than recuperating a plot, but it is a *different* activity, and one particularly well suited to the discontinuous "feel" of contemporary experience.

With respect to *Collages*, the principle of coherence that presents itself immediately to the reader is the artist Renate, who acts like a magnet for the other characters, drawing them to her and then eliciting their stories. But the emphasis in the text is on the stories themselves, and not on Renate's response to them. As mentioned above, the stories stand alone, separate from her response to them (a response that often goes unremarked). Renate is merely a vehicle to introduce the strange assortment of dreamers. The reader must consider Renate a *terminus a quo*, not a *terminus ad quem*. But Renate is central in that her own story establishes a pattern for the stories of the others. The first page of the text introduces Renate as the character who brings statues to life, one who transforms that which is cold, motionless, and lifeless into living, breathing creatures with histories.[30] This power of transformation becomes the central motif of the novel, the quality that links the otherwise heterogeneous cast of characters. All the various dreamers are able, by means of diverse talents or unusual qualities, to make of their everyday and mundane reality something special or wonderful, to live out their fantasies, "to make their dreams concrete."³¹ This power becomes the unifying thread of the novel.

Nin's almost self-evident point is that this power to bring dead statues to life, to dream and realize one's dreams, is a valuable one, one that her readers ought to cultivate. More important, however, is the fact that her prose and narrative method themselves foster this quality. There is, for example, an identifiable speaker in *Collages,* one who reveals herself not only through her distinctive idiolect ("[Varda] often spoke of paradise. Paradise was a distillation of women panoplied with ephemeral qualities. His collages taught how to remain in a state of grace of love, extract only elixirs, transmute all life into lunisolar fiestas, and all women, by a process of cut-outs, to aphrodisiacs. He was the alchemist searching only for what he could transmute into gold," p. 60), but also through her discursive commentary. Like modernist authors in general, she refrains from using ideological discursive statements, those which are based upon cultural and epistemological security. But Nin very frequently falls back on perceptual discursive statements, of an idiosyncratic nature, especially to reveal the inner tropisms of her characters. Here are a number of these statements from the first section:

—She laughed even when she felt like weeping (p. 8).
—Renate spoke vehemently, and as she spoke her sense of injustice grew magnified. It took the form of a long accusation (p. 8).
—She did not talk like a child angry that her father did not believe in her talent, but like a betrayed wife or mistress (p. 8).
—But Renate had spoken unconsciously a brief for an unloved wife (p. 9).

What is distinctive about these discursive statements is that they prompt many more questions than they begin to answer. The reader is told that Renate laughs even when she feels like weeping, but not what this fact signifies; that she upbraids her father accusatorily like a rejected lover, but not why she would behave like this; that Renate's mother was "unloved," but not why this should be. In general, the reader is presented with a psychological *fact*, deprived of both context and motivation. Given only the *what* of the psyche, the reader is encouraged to discover or "fill in" the *why*, reading between the lines first for motivation and then for significance. The statements and events that compose the fiction come to seem like the tip of an iceberg, with its real weight and moment beneath the surface. The fictional world in general is endowed with a noumenal quality; its truth, like the truth of the statues that whisper to Renate, lies behind, beneath, or beyond its surfaces.

The noumenalistic feel of Nin's narrative does not of itself make it distinctive; after all, the Novel itself has traditionally been a parabolic form, pregnant with a significance that remains unarticulated and therefore to be discovered. Nin, like various modernist authors before her, merely extends the inarticulateness of fiction to a logical extreme. The feeling of incompleteness "contaminates" not only the microtextual sequences but also the very structure of the novel. The nineteen unmotivated and unconnected sections of the text become as a constellation of nineteen stars, whose configuration and "history" the reader is free to design. The truncated microtextual sequences contribute to the *mood* of the narrative, a mood that fosters in the reader both freedom and creativity. Nin's own remarks about the genesis of the fiction are significant in this regard: "I allowed myself to live out a mood and see what it would construct. Once the mood is accepted, the mood makes the selection, the mood will give fragments a unity, the mood will be a catalyser. And so, this book, which should have been a novel or another book of short stories, became something else, a collage."[32]

As the title indicates, the notion of collage is central to Nin's purposes. Collage, as an artistic technique, is particularly interesting in terms of the relation it establishes between the artwork and "reality." A collage apprehends heterogeneous bits and pieces of extratextual reality and relocates them within a textual framework where they retain their concrete particularity *and* contribute to the aesthetic totality. The resultant artwork possesses two special qualities: first, it does not adhere to mimetic or illusionist aesthetics, insisting rather that art is "added" to the world, since there is no equivalent for the collage in nature; second, it presents itself as a more "open" system, one whose boundaries are arbitrary and crumbling, since other bits of "reality" could be substituted or added on. Nin's verbal collage shares these qualities. In *Collages*, Nin appropriates *real* people, like Renate the painter and Varda the collagist and Tinguely the sculptor, *real* conversations, like Varda's advice to his daughter or Judith Sand's words to Dr. Mann, and *real* experiences, like Renate's relation to statues or her own (Nin's) LSD trip; she takes this material and transcribes it, with little or no modification, within a fictional framework, the various *real* fragments loosely knit together and juxtaposed. The reader is invited to extract from the "pieces" of *Collages* (and the plural in the title is significant) a coherent vision of his or her own, to construct from the fragmented STORY a personal and "total" collage.

For Nin understands that collage is more a process than a product, a making and remaking. *Collages* is written to make its readers into artists like Varda: "For I myself, I need unformed women, unfinished, undesigned women I can mold to my own pattern. I'm an artist. I'm only looking for fragments, remnants which I can co-ordinate in a new way" (p. 71). *Collages* gives the reader a series of fragments without necessary design with the intention that he or she should remake them, supplying his or her own design, and remembering that the pleasure lies more in the act of collage than in the product of collage. This remaking of the text is implicit in the ending of the text when Judith Sands begins to read from her own manuscript. Her text recapitulates the first words of *Collages* and thus throws the reader back to the beginning. But Sand's text is not identical to "Nin's." One word is changed—"top" becomes "tip"—as if to underscore the fact that Sand's text will diverge from the original as she reimagines it. The reader's "version" should likewise diverge from the original. Lacking cultural or empirical models of *vraisemblance* with which to "naturalize" the text, the reader necessarily creates his or her own. And the process of discovery is more important than the message discovered. Nin has said that "we know now that we *are composites in reality,* collages of our fathers and mothers, of what we read, of television influences and films, of friends and associates. . . ."[33] From the standpoint of a slightly different aesthetic, the text of *Collages* can be said to be "mimetic" in that its texture reproduces the discontinuous "feel" of identity and experience in advanced technological society. The exercise that "athletic" readers get from assembling Nin's *Collages* helps them to make of their own experience a significant whole.

Dos Passos's *U.S.A.*:
The Polymorphous Novel

As for me I should not like to cut at all. Please understand; I should like to put everything into my novel.

André Gide, The Counterfeiters

When I started writing Manhattan Transfer *thirty or more years ago, my aim was to contrive a highly energized sort of novel. I wanted to find some way of making the narrative carry a very large load. Instead of far away and long ago, I wanted it to be here and now. . . . I felt that everything should go in—popular songs, political aspirations and prejudices, ideals, delusions, clippings out of old newspapers. . . . It was that sort of impulse that produced the three* U.S.A. *novels. Somewhere along the line I'd been impressed by Eisenstein's contrived documentaries, such as* Potemkin. *"Montage" was the word used in those days to describe the juxtaposition of contrasting scenes in motion pictures. I took to montage to try to make the narrative stand up off the page.*

John Dos Passos, in Chametzky, "Reflections on U.S.A. as a Novel"

What Dos Passos created with The 42nd Parallel *was in fact another American invention—an American thing peculiar to the opportunity and stress of American life, like the Wright Brothers' airplane, Edison's phonograph, Luther Burbank's hybrids, Thorsten Veblen's social analysis. Frank Lloyd Wright's first office buildings. . . . We soon recognize that Dos Passos' contraption, his new kind of novel . . . is in fact* the greatest character in the book itself.

Alfred Kazin, introduction to U.S.A.

The perplexity that modernist writers seem to suffer derives not only from the epistemological insecurity contingent upon an awareness of relativism and irrationality, but also from the changing fabric of reality itself. Confronted by the degree of technological breakthrough that marked the end of the nineteenth and the beginning of the twentieth century, by the mechanisms and conveniences the new technology produced, by the new media it spawned, by the changes it wrought in the social fabric, the modernist author—particularly the American modernist, for change here was quicker and more visible— must have felt a bit of apocalyptic excitement; the appearance of phenomena like the steam engine, the light bulb, the phonograph, the radio, the airplane, the automobile, the cinema, the American plan, interchangeable parts, and new urban centers threatened to change the very face of society, to replace the old world with a new one. As writers like Stein, Dos

Passos, and O'Hara have noted, the very *amount* of reality in the twentieth century seems to have increased, its various shapes and forms to have proliferated, its tempo to have accelerated, its rhythms to have quickened. Fictionists who feel that it is fiction's responsibility to record and comprehend these monumental changes are constrained to incorporate somehow this surplus of reality within their fictional space. The space of the fiction must be enlarged to accommodate multiplying heterogeneous elements and thus to reproduce the accelerated rhythms and alien "feel" of twentieth-century reality.

The most obvious way to "possess" and master reality is to appropriate it wholesale within the fictional space. The trilogy *U.S.A.* attempts just this. Dos Passos reimagines the limits and nature of the space of the fictional world (S_W), dissolving the conventionalized boundaries between the autonomous aesthetic artifact and contingent empirical reality. This merging (collapse, not fusion) of fictional and empirical realities is particularly evident in his use of particular and verifiable historical incident, or what is generally termed "fact" in narrative. Conventional fiction traditionally employs factual frames of reference that designate signifieds with verifiable extratextual existence (exfrs); these exfrs are sometimes arrayed into externally verifiable Fields of Reference (ExFRs) designating entire historical segments, such as the Napoleonic wars in *War and Peace.* In conventional fiction, all ExFRs are subordinated to or subsumed within the counterfactual Internal Fields of Reference (InFRs). The fictionist takes a verifiable historical fact or event and works a number of "magical" changes upon it. First, these facts are assimilated into the texture of the fictional world, the process of assimilation altering their ontic status. As Murray Krieger suggests, "Tolstoy's Kutusov—or, for that matter Shakespeare's Henry V—has a different 'material' status from that of history's Kutusov (or Henry)."[34] The "truth" of these characters, their "wholeness" and integrity, rests ultimately not in their empirically verifiable reality outside the text, but rather in their integration within and relation to a unified aesthetic structure. Their figuration accords with the configuration of the fiction. Because of this, facts in fiction have a subordinate status within the fictional world. The needs of the fiction (the InFRs) dictate the selection, location, and the "truth" of the fact. As has often been noted, empirical facts have frequently been slanted, twisted, or changed to serve the purposes of the fictionist. Finally, facts in traditional narrative serve a number of purposes: they confirm the mimetic contract by standing as points of contact between fictional and empirical worlds; they also endow the narrative with density and specificity by giving substance to an imaginary world. Dos Passos in *U.S.A.* adds several wrinkles to the nature and function of fact in narrative, alterations that "infect" the very character of the text but that manifest themselves particularly in the Biographies and Newsreel sections of the text. In fact, the Newsreel sections represent a kind of model for the use of fact in *U.S.A.* They present the reader with distinct series of facts, trivial and not so trivial, domestic, national, and international. But these facts exist alongside, not within, the internally coherent Fields of Reference of *U.S.A.;* that is, the fortunes and misfortunes of its invented cast of actants. These facts are neither assimilated nor subordinated; they occupy a separate but equal portion of fictional space. They assert themselves as significant entities, as *facts* themselves, not as "elements" in a unified, hierarchical, coherent field. Correspondingly, they function not only to contribute to the density of the text, but to increase its intratextuality by causing gaps in the narrative and, more important, to dilate the fictional space by making it both in- and out-referential and thus a multimodal system.[35]

The distinction between traditional fiction's and Dos Passos's use (as well as that of other paramodernists) of fact can be summarized as follows:

Fact in Narrative

	Traditional	*U.S.A.*
Nature	assimilated	unassimilated
Status	subordinated	separate and equal
Purpose	vraisemblance/ density	density/dilation of fictional space
Metaphysics	noumenalistic	noumenalistic

The final category, the metaphysics of the use of fact, is included to point out a very significant similarity between traditional and paramodernist fiction, the common assumption that behind the fact, *in*-forming the fact, lies a comprehensible pattern of some kind, an inner logic. In traditional fiction this pattern inheres in the fictional field itself—it is the shaping principle to which the facts are subordinated, for which they

take a back seat. But in Dos Passos's unassimilated, unsubor-
dinated, apparently uncontextualized facts, this inner logic is
not spelled out and so must be supplied by the enterprising
reader. Dos Passos gives the reader "the facts, and nothing but
the facts," and the reader must discover the absent *telos* inductively. Of course, in this undertaking the reader is aided considerably by the example of the Internal Fields of Reference
(the interlocking stories of its invented characters, which I shall
term the "fiction" of the text; see below), but this fact under-
scores the possibilities inherent in the text's intratextuality. As
one critic has noted, "One of the most brilliant things about Dos
Passos' trilogy is the way in which the fictional and historic
characters come together on the same plane."[36] Within the plan
and plane of *U.S.A.*, fiction and history meet as equals.

The extent of innovation in *U.S.A.* is not limited to experiments with fact in fiction; it infects the very shape of the narrative. Dos Passos intuits that literary discourse itself must be
reconceived in order to accommodate the multiplying shapes of
reality. A novelistic text may itself subsume a number of old or
new literary forms, the fictional world becoming polymorphous, like the empirical reality it seeks to replicate. Dos Passos's
trilogy is composed of four different kinds of writing, each of
which, as John Wrenn has observed,[37] roughly corresponds
with a form of literary discourse, namely, history, fiction, autobiography, and biography. Each of these forms exists on the
same plane within the text, each obeys its own inner laws of
coherence and continuity, each presents its own preoccupations
and perspectives. But the larger text of *U.S.A.*, the one that
embraces all these forms, consists less in what is in each of them
than in what lies betwen them, the space of intratextuality.[38] In
order to define more precisely the boundaries of that space, as
well as to analyze the distinctiveness of the forms, it is necessary
to look at each of them in turn.

The text of *U.S.A.* begins with a Newsreel, appropriately
enough, because the Newsreel sections present the reader with
the unprocessed, unassimilated facts of history, and history is
the stuff that *U.S.A.* is made on. More important, however, is
that the form and method of the Newsreel presage the form
and method of the larger text. Learning to read the Newsreel is
learning to read *U.S.A.*, and that lesson consists in mastering the
principle of montage (as Dos Passos's comments on the novel

suggest). Dos Passos admits that he borrowed the technique from Eisenstein, who describes it as follows:

> The point is that the copulation (perhaps we had better say, the combination) of two hieroglyphs of the simplest series is to be regarded not as their sum, but as their product, i.e., as a value of another dimension, another degree; each, separately, corresponds to an *object*, to a fact, but their combination corresponds to a *concept*. From separate hieroglyphs has been fused—the ideogram.[39]

What is of particular interest here for the technique of *U.S.A.* (and that of paraspatial fictions in general) is the notion that the juxtaposition of two concrete entities gives birth to (the word *copulation* is, I think, exactly right) a third entity of a *different* nature, a *mental* event. For this is the method of the Newsreels and, in fact, the method of the trilogy itself. In the Newsreels Dos Passos juxtaposes disparate and distinct concrete elements (events, songs, speeches, headlines, etc.) so as to give rise to an Idea, *in the reader's mind.* The beginning of the first Newsreel serves as a representative example:

> "It was that emancipated race
> That was chargin' up the hill
> Up to where them insurrectos
> Was afightin' fit to kill"

CAPITAL CITY'S CENTURY CLOSED

> General Miles with his gaudy uniform and spirited charger was the center for all eyes, especially as his steed was extremely restless. Just as the band passed the Commanding General, his horse stood upon his hind legs and was almost erect. General Miles instantly reined in the frightened animal and dug in his spurs in an endeavor to control the horse which, to the horror of the spectators, fell over backwards and landed squarely on the Commanding General. Much to the gratification of the people, General Miles was not injured, but considerable skin was scraped off the flank of his horse. (*The 42nd Parallel*, p. 27)

The simple juxtaposition of a song drawn from an imperialist venture, a headline announcing the beginning of the new century, and a news report about a parade produces a narrative texture that can be almost endlessly explicated. In general terms these opening segments bring to mind all the optimism and energy that usually mark the beginning of a new century and hopefully mark a new "era." There are suggestions here of new frontiers, and military glory, and the pomp and circumstance of parade. These intimations of optimism and unity are underscored later in the same Newsreel when bold headlines proclaim severally that noise, labor, and churches all greet the new century. This act of celebration is, however, counterpointed by the events of the parade, the heavily symbolic tumble that the general's horse takes. In effect, the meanings that this opening section generates prefigure the larger meaning of the text, at the same time as the method of the sequence establishes the reading procedure. Charles Marz argues that "the Newsreels are ultimately verbal objects—"world and word debris," "the residue of the natural world, divested of original functions and contexts, wrenched from public and private occasions."[40] It may well be that the Newsreels supply the "noise of history," but at the same time they invite the reader to turn that noise into information, to make sense of the impress of history. In the Newsreels, contrastive historical "facts" are juxtaposed in such a way that their significations are multiplied. And these significations are purely connotative and therefore must be supplied by the reader; the text is silent in this respect.

The Newsreels, since they present the historical matrix against which the other sections of the text are to be measured, perform another function. They establish not only the tempo of the text, but also the ambiance of the respective volumes of the text. Although the Newsreels do not undergo any appreciable change in shape or format, they noticeably change their accumulated "pressure," each set of Newsreels setting the tone or atmosphere for the individual volumes. The Newsreels in the first volume show great variety both in subject matter and in possible implications, reflecting the sense of hope, the restlessness, and the widening vistas that characterized the beginning of the new century. On occasion, bits of stories are run together; for example:

> lady angels are smashed   troops guard oil fields America tends to become empire like in the days of the Caesars   five-dollar poem gets rich husband   eat less says Edison   rich pokerplayer falls dead when he draws royal flush   charges graft in Cicero   (*The 42nd Parallel,* p. 76)

In this way the narrative conveys the feeling that so much of such a disparate nature is happening that the Newsreel is hard pressed to contain it, much less to order it. The Newsreels in *Nineteen Nineteen,* by way of contrast, concentrate on a reduced number of topics and generally present these instances in more discursive form. Again the opening section may serve as a model. It presents the reader with nine different "items." Of the nine, six relate material drawn from the war, two speak of the interests of Wall Street and capital, and one tells of a labor strike. These three will be the big themes of the volume, with the story of the war predominating, but eventually giving way to the interests of postwar business and finance. Labor is presented throughout the volume in a subordinate and adversary role. The final volume, *The Big Money,* not surprisingly stresses in its Newsreels the mad scramble for the big money, the wild world of Wall Street and the stock market, and the confused life styles that evolve in this world. The Newsreels frequently relate suicides, homicides, and other asocial forms of behavior, as if to emphasize the disintegrating social fabric; the historical backdrop becomes markedly hysterical. At the macrotextual level, then, the Newsreels chart a progressive channeling and diminution of energies, the closing-off of possibilities, the betrayal of the promise of the new century, and thus act as a paradigmatic model for the movement of *U.S.A.*

Literally embedded in this sweep of events are the lives of the fictional characters of *U.S.A.*—J. Ward Morehouse, Eleanor Stoddard, Joe Williams, Eveline Hutchins, Charley Anderson, and so on—who populate what I shall call the "fiction" of the text. This "fiction" has qualities that should be noted. First, it is narrative whose DISCURSIVE SPACE has to a large extent been abandoned by the author. As several critics have noted,[41] Dos Passos presents his fiction neorealistically, by viewing his subject from without, journalistically, without the intervention of sentiment or sympathy. The result is a bare, factual presentation of outward movements   and chronicled events. All narrative syntagms that are even vaguely discursive are stylistically marked as belonging not to the narrator but to the character involved, as in the following excerpt taken from a section dealing with coarse Joe Williams:

> The *darn kike sawbones* tried to *hold him up* for another twentyfive bucks to complete the cure, but Joe said to hell with it and shipped

as an A.B. . . . . He was *sick* of the cold and the sleet and the grimy
Brooklyn streets and the logarithm tables in the course on the table
he couldn't get through his head and Mrs Olsen's *bullying jolly*
voice; she was beginning to act *like she wanted to run his life for him.*
She was *a swell woman,* but it was about time he *got the hell out.*
(*Nineteen Nineteen,* p. 73; emphasis added)

This method of scenic presentation contributes to a more
peculiar quality of the "fiction" of *U.S.A.,* one that Sartre discovers while investigating the "queer and sinister" feel of the
text. As Sartre notes, in the trilogy *U.S.A.,* "everything is told as
if by someone who is remembering." Sartre goes on to point out
the peculiarities of this memory. It recalls its events as though
they were past, but never does it establish causality in that past.
"Each event is irreducible, a gleaming and solitary *thing* that
does not flow from anything else, but suddenly arises to join
other things. For Dos Passos, narrating means adding."[42] The
fiction itself seems to consist in a series of interrelated but unconnected events that *happen to* the actants. As Sartre notes, the
lives of the fictional characters are transformed into "destinies,"
with their individual fates imposed from without by unnamed
and unknown forces, or perhaps the inexorable movement of
history itself. Confronted by this kind of bare, deterministic
fiction, the reader switches his or her energies from the meaning of each individual life to the immanent pattern informing
the movement of history itself. Nowhere is that pattern, the
"sense" of history, authoritatively given; readers must discern it
themselves. The "fiction" approaches the condition of simple
historical chronicle, a form to which Dos Passos deliberately
aspired.[43] In this regard, the laws of the fiction (which are based
upon cultural conventions) give way to the "laws" of history. As
one critic notes, the disappearance of Fenian MacCreary from
the fiction midway through the first volume is dictated not by
the logic of the fiction (which logic it in fact contravenes—the
reader expects to find out what eventually happens to Mac), but
by the logic of history, which decrees that the Wobblies soon
disappear as a significant social force.[44] In similar fashion minor
characters like Ike Hall (Mac's road companion for a time)
disappear abruptly and absolutely—"That was the last he saw
of Ike Hall" (*The 42nd Parallel,* p. 97)—and major characters
like Joe Williams and Daughter die unexpected and senseless
deaths (compare the symbolic deaths of Charley Anderson and
Eveline Hutchins). In each instance, "fiction" bends to the cir-

cumstances of "history," and consequently the purpose of history is foregrounded.

Critics have sometimes complained that the "Camera Eye" sections are misnamed since what the reader encounters therein are not the purely "objective" registrations of visual realities but rather subjective renderings of sights and sounds and smells as they impinge upon the senses of a youth coming of age in America—the Camera Eye gives the reader a phenomenology of the process of growing up in the twentieth century. But the title is appropriate because it takes for granted the fact that no camera eye is neutral or objective (compare the "eyes" of Bergman and Fellini), and it implies that what will be given is simply the view of the "scene" from one limited perspective. This particular "camera eye" is, moreover, exceptional in that it grows and changes, like the world around him. The fact of growth is reflected in both the form and content of the sections.[45] The sections in the first volume chronicling the young boy's travels in Europe and his eventual settling on the Chesapeake Bay are taken up with the almost mechanical registration of sensory data:

> under the counter it's dark and the lady the nice Dutch lady who loves Americans and has relations in Trenton shows you postcards that shine in the dark pretty hotels and palaces O que c'est beau schon prittie prittie and the moonlight ripple ripple under a bridge and the little reverberes are alight in the dark under the counter and the little windows of hotels around the harbor O que c'est beau la lune. (*The 42nd Parallel,* p. 30)

Here the quality of the narration almost literally approximates the quality of a camera, an instrument that records the sights and sounds of the scene before it without comprehending their significance. The self that provides the perspective for these sections (from time to time "he" is referred to as Jack) gradually matures as they unfold. Soon this self is marked by consciousness and self-consciousness ("and I wonder what the old major thought about and what I thought about . . ."; *The 42nd Parallel,* p. 115), and eventually by an awareness of its own difference and apartness or alienation ("I wished I was home but I hadn't any home"; *The 42nd Parallel,* p. 240). This sense of estrangement remains with the youth throughout his maturation and especially qualifies him to become a "professional" observer of American society, a calling that is formalized in his choice of

career as artist/reporter. The ultimate fruit of prolonged observation is assessment or evaluation; perception gives way to
reflection, reflection to understanding, and understanding to
evaluation. And this ability to judge what is going on in
America in the twentieth century is, of course, what the Camera
Eye achieves.[46] In sections 49, 50, and 51—the last of these
sections in the text and the portion some critics have singled out
as the narrative climax—the Camera Eye sings out its indictment of what America has become: "America our nation has
been beaten by strangers who have turned our language inside
out who have taken the clean words our fathers spoke and
made them slimy and foul" (*The Big Money*, p. 468).

The reader is quite understandably tempted to endorse this
particular reading of the American story, partly perhaps because of its placement and its rhetorical flourish. The reader
should remember, however, that this normative pronouncement exists as an isolated element in the plane of the fictional
space and for that reason merits no special privilege. It is
merely one idiosyncratic, limited camera eye; since it does not
mediate between the reader and the fictional world (as elements of DISCURSIVE SPACE normally do) but rather constitutes a
distinct part of that fictional world (which is, as I have said,
polymorphous), it has a purely fictional ontology that undercuts its *author*-ity. What should be more interesting to the
reader than its validity as a judgment is its multiple relations to
the other forms of the fictional world. The Camera Eye depicts
a consciousness that grows from perception through reflection
to evaluation. This is a course that the reader is encouraged to
take.

What lies on the other side of evaluation? The answer to this,
I think, is at least partly given by the Biographies, which many
critics assess as the most brilliant writing in the trilogy.[47] On
either side of evaluation lies vision, which naturally finds expression in the prose poetry of the Biographies, writing that is
in every way *informed* by a vision of America and designed to
convey aesthetically and articulately that vision to the reading
audience. The ethical pattern that the reader quickly discerns
involves a frighteningly inverted or perverted reformulation of
the truism that "character is fate." Historical figures whom the
Biographies expose as venal, short-sighted, greedy, or obtuse—
the Wilsons, Morgans, Hearsts, Taylors, and Fords—almost invariably thrive and prosper in the land of opportunity; whereas

those figures noted for their generosity, compassion, idealism, sincerity—the Debses, Haywoods, Reeds, Hills, and Veblens—are eventually chewed up and plowed under by the system. The Biographies, in the oracular tones of the oral poet, render painfully clear the decline and defeat of America.

The reader of *U.S.A.* experiences a gamut of discursive "prose" forms—history, "fiction," autobiography, and biography—each discursive form distinct in modality, shape, and "feel." And, not surprisingly, each form demands of the reader a different kind of activity and/or response: the Newsreels need to be actualized and then ordered (who is doing what to whom and when); the "fiction" to be interpreted (what is happening to these actants and why); the Camera Eye to be experienced (what does it "feel" like); and the Biographies to be responded to (how does one judge this spectacle). Of course, this kind of analysis constitutes an oversimplification in that reader response is a very complex phenomenon, but it points out the fact that the proliferation of forms within a fictional space concertedly mobilizes a variety of readerly activities and thus exercises and conditions what Barthes terms the lexeographical muscles.

What these various modes clearly have in common throughout the three volumes is the quality of discontinuity. Not only are the forms multiplied, but they are fragmented, both internally and externally. The facts of the Newsreel are obviously discontinuous; the various stories of the "fiction" are broken up and juggled; the Biographies are autotelic entities whose very typeface reveals the principle of (poetic) discontinuity; the Camera Eyes consist in the stringing together of associated images or impressions. Fragmentation at the micro- and macrotextual levels is *the* dominant principle of the narrative. Dos Passos has said of the novelist that "no matter how much legwork you do, you can't see it all yourself. You're dealing with scraps and fragments. A lot of it has to be second-hand. The fictional imagination depends on being able to reconstruct the whole unseen animal from a tooth and a toenail and a splinter of skull."[48] The method of *U.S.A.* is intended specifically to foster the "fictional imagination" in its readers, to make them anthropologists of America. In order to resist a reality that dominates and dehumanizes its populace (Janey Williams is almost literally turned into a typewriter), the reader is encouraged to "master" reality by taking its bits and pieces, the things it turns up, and discovering the principle of coherence, the relations between its parts. This principle is not given; at the surface level everything develops and nothing relates. But the disparate sections tend to converge,[49] and the reader is invited by this sense of convergence to endow the inert, indeterminate *thereness* of the text with a logic, an inner necessity, and thus to convert Dos Passos's *chronicle* into a real history.[50]

Dos Passos makes two major changes in the space of his fictional world to give it its unique configuration. First he conflates a variety of fictional modes—history, fiction, autobiography, and biography—within his polymorphous S_W in order to "get everything in." At the same time, he "pulverizes" the discursive presentation of those modes in order to replicate the discontinuous feel of twentieth-century experience and to generate meaning through the random collision of voices. It is given to the reader, who stands both in and outside history and the text, to extract meaning and value from the experience of *U.S.A.* by decoding and transcending its chronicle of fragmentation, dehumanization, and determinism.[51]

John Hawkes's *Second Skin:* The Fictional World Erased

I began to write fiction on the assumption that the true enemies of the novel were plot, character, setting, and theme, and once having abandoned these familiar ways of thinking about fiction, totality of vision or structure was all that remained. And structure—verbal and psychological coherence—is still my largest concern as a writer.
                                                         John Hawkes, Enck interview

But obviously we tend to appreciate in European writers what we sometimes fail to recognize in our own writers—the absolute need to create from the imagination a totally new and necessary fictional landscape or visionary world.
                                                         John Hawkes, Enck interview

I don't know where fiction ordinarily directs itself, but I am quite deliberately addressing myself to the whole area of what we call dreams.
                                       William Burroughs, interview in Writers at Work

In the textual space of a fiction, there are two main systems of signification: the space of the fictional world, or NARRATIVAL SPACE; and the space occupied by the speaker, or NARRATIONAL SPACE. In what might be termed authorial fictions, NARRATIONAL SPACE exists on a different plane from NARRATIVAL SPACE, within

the narrative ontology. The space of the speaker exists somewhere "above" (cf. the tendency to use the phrase *aesthetic "distance"* for these fictions) the space of the fictional world,
containing or circumscribing it, managing it, presiding over it.
To occupy this space is, in effect, to assume *author*-ity over the
fictional world and to guarantee its relevance and significance.
Lacking faith in these qualities, the modernist author is forced
to abandon this system of signification or somehow to rob it of
its position of privilege. One way to accomplish the latter is
simply to "drop" NARRATIONAL SPACE into the space of the
fictional world, a stratagem effected merely by making the
speaker an actant in that world. This relocation of the speaker
immediately changes the status of the enunciation; elements of
DISCURSIVE SPACE belong not to a mediating authorial persona,
but to a purely "fictional" invention.

It should be noted that modernist authors were not the first
to rely on first-person narrative situations. The Novel in the
Western world, from Defoe's "discovered" narratives to
Richardson's epistolary novels, first surfaced as a first-person
form. The difference in modernist usage lies not in the form
but in its function. Defoe prefaces *Robinson Crusoe* with a "publisher's" guarantee that the manuscript that follows is a "just
history of fact," and the adoption of first person serves to validate that guarantee. Mark Twain relies on first person in *Huckleberry Finn* for purposes of verisimilitude, for idiomatic license,
and for the aesthetic and thematic possibilities inherent in this
particular narrator. In either case the first-person narrative
situation serves in some way to verify and authenticate the narrative contract. Modernist use of first person is motivated not
only by reasons of verisimilitude; modernist authors, led by the
example of James, are aware of certain possibilities inherent in
the unique status of such narrators. James, in *The Turn of the
Screw,* reveals the possibilities inherent in this narrative situation by encoding a possible duplicity in everything that the
governess says. In so doing he demonstrates how the essence of
the speech act changes in first person. Authorial narration may
be diagrammed as follows:

where S_R = space of the reader; S_S = space of the speaker; and S_W = space of the fictional world. The system S_S filters, clarifies, and manages the input from system S_W, and thus reduces the gaps to be filled, the space to be occupied, by the reader (S_R). In a first-person narrative situation, the relations between spaces are transformed.

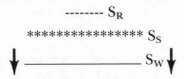

The space of the speaker "collapses" into the fictional world, and the reader is presented with the possibility of discrepancy between the narrator's report and the fictional "reality." The reader must measure the statements of the narrator against his or her own "reading" of fictional events, against the "context" of the fictional world.

One way, then, to rob S_S of its authority is to subsume it within the fictional world, and a number of modernist authors like Conrad, Ford, and Faulkner take advantage of this fact to encode a degree of textual uncertainty or ambiguity and thus to introduce interpretive "play" in the fiction.

It follows logically that the reverse procedure will work as well. That is, the fictional world may be subsumed within the space of the speaker, as follows:

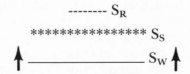

This is not quite the same thing as the former strategy, for the activity performed by the reader alters slightly. In the former the reader uses as his or her base the presumable "content" of the fictional world and evaluates the statements of the speaker against this base. A major question becomes the "reliability" of the speaker, such reliability to be determined by comparing the quality of the speech act against the quality of the fictional world. In the latter narrative situation, the fictional world (S_W) is subsumed within the space of the speaker (S_S), and the question of the "truth" of S_W becomes irrelevant and immaterial. The distinction between external and internal realities, between fictional event and enunciative rendering thereof, is blurred, and the reader "comprehends" the fiction by submitting to the mood created by the idiosyncratic and "romantic" enunciation. The dominant system is the space of the speaker, and the "subject" of the fiction is not so much the events of the fictional world (which naturally become purely problematic) as it is the fabulating imagination of the speaker. This latter type of fiction—which can be termed S_S-dominated first-person— generally causes real problems for critics who confuse it with an S_W-dominated first-person narrative.

A fine example of S_S-dominated fiction is John Hawkes's *Second Skin*.[52] The majority of critical readings of this text mistake it as an S_W-dominated text, and go back and forth arguing about the reliability or unreliability of Skipper, his heroism or cowardice, his success or failure, the veracity of the events he chronicles. Such readings ignore Hawkes's explicit extratextual remarks as well as encoded textual signals. Hawkes has said in an interview that his fiction is concerned "to lead [readers] into the realities of the imagination" and, more specifically, that "*Second Skin* is about the imagination. There is no doubt in *my* mind that Skipper's floating island is totally real. The landscape of the imagination is real in that fiction, whether it's projected as the idyllic, wandering tropical island or the rock-rooted, cold, barren New England island."[53] What is in question here is not the reality or unreality of the events Skipper reports,[54] but the quality or tonality of the imagination that reports (transcribes? transforms? invents?) those events.

Hawkes attempts to make his true subject clear within his text by foregrounding the system of the speaking subject. Skipper, the speaker of the text, frequently indulges in illusion-destroying metalingual commentary. Time and again Skipper reminds the reader that he or she is listening to only his version of the events: "here I mention my triumph, here reveal myself and choose to step from behind the scenes of my naked history" (p. 48); or "and so I have already stepped once more from behind the scenes of my naked history and having come this far I expect that I will never really be able to conceal myself completely in all those scenes which are even now on the tip of my tongue and crowding my eye" (p. 99). Time and again Skipper reminds the reader of his uncanny power to transform an ugly situation into some sort of aesthetic tableau. As Hawkes has said, Skipper "in all his weakness is supposed to embody the strength of knowing that there is nothing else in the world except what he creates and the figures he discovers in his creation."[55]

Because the dominant system in the fiction is that of the speaking subject rather than that of the fictional world, the reader must rely on different models of vraisemblance to retrieve the fiction. Culler has argued that the most available models of vraisemblance are those derived from "reality" itself, the "naturally" real.[56] In S_S-dominated texts such models are not useful since the "reality" of the actants and events of the fictional world is entirely problematic. The reader necessarily must find other models of vraisemblance, drawing them from other texts or perhaps inventing them himself. Of course, one can reduce the strangeness of the text by simply asserting that the text is "about" the imagination itself, and then develop this insight by trying to describe the particular quality of this imagination. Hawkes seems to suggest that such a procedure is appropriate when he says that Skipper is talking to keep himself alive, or that the last words of the fiction reproduce "the sound of a man articulating his own death."[57] This kind of reduction does enable the reader to extract "meaning" from the text, but it certainly sacrifices the force of the text's otherness. It is wiser perhaps to let go of notions like theme and meaning and to "read" the text in a novel way. Hawkes has said in an interview that "paradoxically, soon after I began to write, I knew that I wanted to keep the reader out of the fictional experience, wanted to resist the reader so that he would participate more fully."[58] Hawkes's peculiar narrative situation accomplishes just that contradictory goal. The narrative world, in that it consists in the fantastic concoctions of a strange imagination, is hermetically sealed from the intrusions of "reality" or the reader; it is totally Other. But at the same time as this otherness resists readerly recuperation, it tends to reproduce itself in the reader's imagination—the reader becomes the Other. The ultimate function of such fiction is not so much to impart a message as to create a mood. The fiction takes the reader from Here to There not so he or she may return to Here with a bit of wisdom gathered There, but that he or she may make Thereness a part of a way of life. Skipper's account demonstrates time and again how he uses language as a defense mechanism against the pain and fear in his life, how his imagination transforms the exigencies of a brutal reality into the idylls of an island paradise.

In chapter 1, for example, Skipper asserts that his mortician father "staged" his suicide for his (Skipper's) benefit—to begin Skipper's "knowledge of death as a lurid truth"—but that his mother arranged her departure so as to impart a vision—"the promise of mystery" (p. 8). Skipper goes on to describe in poetic prose his mother's serene and graceful exit in a "small open yellow machine with wooden wheels, white solid tires and brass headlamps," a description whose coda, significantly enough, is: "A waxen tableau, no doubt the product of a slight and romantic fancy. Yet I prefer this vision to my father's death" (p. 9). Skipper "deals" with the traumatic experience with Miranda on the frozen Northeastern island in a similar fashion:

> Because I know and have stated here, that behind every frozen episode of that other island—and I am convinced that in its way it too was enchanted, no matter the rocks and salt and fixed position in the cold black waters of the Atlantic—there lies the golden wheel of my hot sun; behind every black rock a tropical rose and behind every cruel wind-driven snowstorm a filmy sheet, a transparency, of golden fleas. No matter how stark the scene, no matter how black the gale or sinister the violence of Miranda, still the light of my triumph must shine through. (P. 48)

Skipper continually triumphs over the bleakness of "reality" by transforming it with language and imaginative vision. In Tony Tanner's words, Skipper converts "a nightmare of utter powerlessness" into a "dream of pure freedom."[59]

This power, to use language to *create* realty, to draw on the imagination as a source of healing, is the quality that Hawkes wishes to nurture in his readers. To accomplish this end, he "erases" his fictional world and submerges readers in the hermetic landscape of a poetic imagination. Hawkes understands the Romantic notion that a true poet makes poets of his readers, and he manages his fictional space in such a way as to create the conditions—in particular the alchemical mood—for that transformation.

William Burroughs: The Undetermined Text

When people speak of clarity in writing they generally mean plot, continuity, beginning middle and end, adherence to a "logical" sequence. But things don't happen in a logical sequence and people don't think in a logical sequence. . . . I think it is possible to create multilevel events and characters that a reader could comprehend with his entire organic being.

William Burroughs, in Odier, The Job: Interviews with William Burroughs

The word of course is one of the most powerful instruments of control as exercised by the newspaper and images as well; there are both words and images in newspapers. . . . Now if you start cutting these up and rearranging them you are breaking down the control system.
          William Burroughs, in Odier, The Job: Interviews with William Burroughs

All out of time and into space. Come out of the time word "the" forever. Come out of the body word "thee" forever. There is nothing to fear. There is no thing in space. There is no word to fear. There is no word in space.
                                    William Burroughs, The Soft Machine

Cure is always: Let go! Jump!
                                    William Burroughs, Naked Lunch

In some ways William Burroughs's *Naked Lunch* is the ulti-mate paramodernist text, a fact that has contributed no little bit to its critical reception, I suspect. One critic has straightfor-wardly stated that, sordid subject matter not withstanding, he found the text simply boring and that "what most makes for boredom in this novel is its technical experiment."[60] Undeni-ably, the obscurity or "unreadability" of the text derives from its systematic utilization of the spectrum of paramodernist tech-niques designed to explode continuity in narrative fiction.

In this respect the very modality of the text should be noted. Like Dos Passos, to whom he admits an indebtedness, Bur-roughs has incorporated into the final text of *Naked Lunch* a number of separate and recognizable literary forms. On either side of the "narrative" of *Naked Lunch*—the Internal Fields of Reference that constitute the "fiction" proper—the reader en-counters texts that contribute to the texture and meaning of the macrotext. First, there are excerpts from the trial of *Naked Lunch;* the various statements by judges, prosecutors, and literati act as a factual and yet tongue-in-check testimonial to the value of the "fiction." A second preface consists in Bur-roughs's own "deposition" concerning addiction and the writ-ing of *Naked Lunch*. This section, in the form of a discursive personal essay, presents information about the source and meaning of the title, the metaphoric significance of Junk, and the objectives of the narrative proper. Appended to the deposi-tion is a postscript consisting of the fragmented and hallucina-tory prose that characterizes the body of the text, thus introducing readers to the method of "Bill's Naked Lunch Room." There follows the "fiction" proper of *Naked Lunch* (about which more later), which culminates in its own semi-discursive "Atrophied Preface." Finally, there is an appendix consisting of a scholarly article written by Burroughs on the subject of drug addiction and reprinted from a British medical journal. The addition of these extrafictional texts transforms the larger text by complicating its morphology. The text becomes a polymorphous constellation of diverse literary shapes: trial transcripts, personal depositions, fictional texts, and expository essays. The frame, which usually guarantees the hermeticism of fictional worlds, is shattered. Burroughs often reminds the reader of that fact when within his "fictional" text he refers readers to the extra-"fictional" sections.

The multiplication of shapes within the space of narrative serves to increase its intratextuality; there are necessarily gaps between the disparate shapes. In *Naked Lunch* the same principle radically infects the space of the heterocosmic fictional world, the NARRATIVAL SPACE generated around the actants and story of the "fiction." As in other paramodernist fictions, these two elements of narrative are transformed into radically discontinuous entities. In fact, the term STORY might be a misnomer when applied to the narrative of *Naked Lunch,* since it implies continuity, and what critics univocally single out in *Naked Lunch* is the complete absence of continuity.[61] In the "atrophied preface" of the text, the speaker addresses this aspect of textuality: "Why all this waste paper getting The People from one place to another? Perhaps to spare The Reader stress of sudden space shifts and keep him Gentle?"[62] There is no wasting of paper or sparing of the reader in the STORY of *Naked Lunch.* The STORY is completely pulverized, its motifs uniformly distributed rather than successively developed. The principle of composition here is parataxis; relatively autonomous narrative segments are simply juxtaposed, without benefit of coordination, subordination, chronology, or sequence. There are twenty-two separate sections in the text, twenty-one with separate boldface titles. The titles serve as points of intersection and the speaker of the "atrophied preface" tells the reader, "you can cut into *Naked Lunch* at any intersection point" (p. 224). The "space" of the intersection invariably transports the reader from a locale and set of actants that are only vaguely familiar to a totally unfamiliar topos and scenario. For example, the gap between sections two and three ("BENWAY" and "JOSELITO") carries the befuddled reader from a first-person satirical sketch of a control addict's operation in Annexia to a highly obscure scene at a sanitarium involving characters named Carl and Joselito. Confronted by the discontinuity, the reader's only alternative is to "jump."

As the above example indicates, the principle of discontinuity "contaminates" the system of actants as well as the system of STORY. There is no "logic" at all to the appearance, disappearance, and reappearance of "The People" of the fiction. Characters who "die" in one section return in others (Vigilante, Sailor); they "fade out" within sections and then pop up unexpectedly in other circumstances; they become their social function (Party Leader, County Clerk). From section to section there is never any continuity of character; the nearest thing to a central character is probably the quasiautobiographical Lee, who figures prominently in only two sections (the opening section and "Hauser and O'Brien").[63]

To suggest that *Naked Lunch* consists of separate sections is perhaps to mislead the reader and to cause him to anticipate a text similar to *Collages* or even West's *Miss Lonelyhearts* or Chopin's *The Awakening*. Discontinuity in *Naked Lunch* is radical. Here is a sample taken from the section entitled "THE MARKET":

> A waste of raw pink shame to the pastel blue horizon where vast iron mesas crash into the shattered sky.
> "It's all right." The God screams through you three thousand year rusty load. . . .
> Hail of crystal skulls shattered the greenhouse to slivers in the winter moon. . . .
> The American woman has left a whiff of poison behind in the dank St. Louis garden party.
> Pool covered with green slime in a ruined French garden. Huge pathic frog rises slowly from the water on a mud platform playing the clavichord. (P. 118)

Much of the text is not so disjointed as the above, but this passage is not at all anomalous. From time to time the text lapses into what might be referred to as "junk visions," consisting of a discontinuous series of random and hallucinatory images,[64] which the reader must simply experience, for there is no possibility of naturalization or recuperation. In a way these sequences are models for the shape of the whole text. The NARRATIVAL SPACE of *Naked Lunch* is so fractured, its STORY so dismantled, its actants so fragmented and fragmentary, its topoi so multiplied, that the reader is quite literally confronted with a "continuous present," simply because of the immediacy and autonomy of narrative segments. As Burroughs suggests in his prefatory deposition, the reader must deal with "frozen moments" of *Naked Lunch* (p. xxxvii).

In texts like Nin's *Collages* and Hawkes's *The Cannibal*, the landscape of the fictional world is broken up into discrete, autonomous units and individual scenes are essentially self-contained and autotelic, and yet these fictions nonetheless "feel" unified, connected. The unity of these texts derives not from NARRATIVAL SPACE, but from NARRATIONAL SPACE. Behind (or, in the case of some of Hawkes's later fictions, in front of) the fragmented and disparate narrative sequences, the reader senses the presence of a singular speaking subject that acts as the principle of COHERENCE for the text. This speaker manifests itself in its distinctive idiolect, which informs the lexicon and syntax of the fiction. This speaking subject further manifests itself in the consistency in the point of view and the tone (which is, of course, a product of point of view, pattern of diction, and syntactic pattern). This speaker to a certain extent guarantees the COHERENCE of the fragmented text.

Naked Lunch, by way of contrast, does not offer the consolations of a single speaker, or for that matter, of a single type of narrative situation. Types of speakers and narrative situations are so proliferated as to destroy almost the promise of unity in the text. Here is a sample of some of the narrational modes that the reader finds in *Naked Lunch:*

(1) conventional first-person actantial: "I can feel the heat closing in" (p. 1).
(2) editorial: "(Note: Grass is English thief slang for inform)" (p. 2).
(3) (Victorian) authorial: "Gentle reader, the ugliness of that spectacle buggers description" (p. 39).
(4) first-person confessional (à la diary): "*Disintoxication notes. Paranoia of early withdrawal* . . . . Everything looks blue. . . . Flesh dead, doughy, toneless" (p. 55).
(5) the satirical skit: "Party Leader" and friends (pp. 121ff.).
(6) the polemical essay: "Bureaucracy is wrong as cancer, a

turning away from the human evolutionary direction of
infinite potentials and differentiation and independent
spontaneous action, to the complete parasitism of a virus"
(p. 134).
(7) dramatic monologue: "I run into Ted Spigot the other
day . . . a good old boy, too. Not a finer man in the Zone
than Ted Spigot" (pp. 172ff.).

The above list suggests the range and variety of the points of
view and types of discourse in *Naked Lunch* without exhausting
the text at all. In this respect one might describe the text as
cacographic. Tony Tanner has said that *"Naked Lunch* is a book
with no narrative continuity, and with no sustained point of
view; the separate episodes are not interrelated, they co-exist in
a particular field of force."[65] The field-of-force metaphor is
appropriate, as is Mary McCarthy's comparison of the text to a
carnival or a circus.[66] The reader has an arena before him or
her—the fabulous Interzone—but he or she has no idea what
kind of acts will appear, who will perform, or how long the act
will last.
    If both the NARRATIVAL and NARRATIONAL SPACES are de-
formed, dilated, or disrupted beyond recognition, is there any
reason to think that unity or coherence is a quality of this text?
And, lacking these qualities, is it appropriate to speak of the
"meaning" of the text? These are by no means easy questions,
even if critical consensus does suggest that the text is meaningful.[67] The transformations worked upon NARRATIVAL and NAR-
RATIONAL SPACE are, after all, profound: Burroughs presents
the reader with a fiction whose actants possess neither duration,
identity, nor personality; whose topoi are neither recognizable
nor contiguous; whose STORY violates expectations of movement, irreversibility, and teleology; whose speaker is not singular; and whose mode of discourse is not uniform. The text is
literally "polymorphously perverse." In the atrophied preface
the speaker describes the text as follows:

The Word is divided into units which be all in one piece and should
be so taken, but the pieces can be had in any order being tied up
back and forth, in and out fore and aft like an innaresting sex
arrangement. This book spill off the page in all directions, kaleido-
scope of vistas, medley of tunes and street noises, farts and riot
yipes and the slamming steel shutters of commerce." (P. 229)

The description, which continues the blazon of images for about ten more lines, is appropriate, but what is more interesting is Burroughs's suggestion that the Word should be taken as of a piece, as unitary, as a totality. Elsewhere in the text, Burroughs puts these words in the mouth of an ancient called Prophet: "The word cannot be expressed direct. . . . It can perhaps be indicated by mosaic of juxtaposition like articles abandoned in a hotel drawer, defined by negatives and absence . . ." (p. 116). In *Naked Lunch* the word is to be "defined by absence," the vacuum to be filled by the athletic reader, who must learn somehow to "jump." The unity of the text rests simply in "totality of vision," this totality being neatly summarized by Burroughs as "the Word," the term intimating the religious nature of the vision.

And the Word for Burroughs seems intimately bound up with (if not identified with) an absolute freedom from all forces of control. Burroughs's revelation consists in the realization that what we accept as "reality" has been imposed upon us by an infernal and clandestine group of "control addicts," bent on feeding their habit by extending and consolidating their control. One way to resist this monolithic reality imposed from without is to fragment it, to fracture it and to juggle the pieces. Burroughs intuits that the domain of the control addicts extends into the realm of literature and that conventional narrative is merely one more form of control. As one critic says, "Conventional narrative is an act of domestication, one that enables us to integrate revelation into our established associative channels. It offers the 'White Junk' fix for readers who cannot bear violence and outrage in discrete, total encounters."[68]

If conventional narrative acts as a tranquilizer prescribed to render readers "Gentle," then *Naked Lunch* is designed specifically to counteract that sedative, by providing relief in two different ways. First, it diagnoses the "virus" that has infected all of America and reduced the entire populace to junkies of one kind or another. But since this diagnosis is nowhere spelled out, it is available only to readers who can master or possess the chaotic narrative surface of the text. The reader understands the ubiquity and the insidiousness of the control virus only after bringing the disparate pieces of his naked lunch into a single, coherent "Word." What becomes of particular importance for the rehabilitation of the reader is less the content of *Naked Lunch* than its method and the process that method catalyzes in the reader. To read the text is to learn the art and necessity of jumping and thus to take a step in the direction of personal freedom. One learns not to expect consecutiveness, "logic," continuity, connections, or common sense, and one experiences the exhilaration of liberation from these sets of controls.

There is, of course, a bit of a contradiction in method and message here. The reader is in effect told that to have certain expectations about the continuity of narrative literature is to be controlled and that to be rid of those expectations is to be free, a consummation devoutly to be wished. But the text as a whole does have a Word to pass on, a message to be decoded, pertaining to the perniciousness of control systems. That message in itself constitutes a kind of "control system," in that it purports to be true. As a matter of fact any act of semiosis, taken on faith and meant to be deciphered, reveals itself as a reifible truth system. And the sanctity of this Word that threatens to become Law is implicit in the laws that surround and mystify textuality, in particular, the law that dictates the inviolability of the text and the conventionality of its syntactic articulations. After *Naked Lunch* Burroughs comes to understand that the most dangerous control system might well be language and its inherent laws.[69] His 1960 text *The Exterminator,* written in collaboration with Brion Gysin, specifically addresses itself to this uncomfortable fact. The text begins with the warning that "The Human Being are strung lines of word associates that control 'thoughts feelings and *apparent* sensory impressions.' . . . See and hear what they expect to see and hear because The Word Lines keep Thee In Slots."[70] The solution to this dilemma is to perform violence upon the "word lines," and this is what the text prescribes: "Cut the Word Lines with scissors or switch blade as preferred The Word Lines keep you in Time . . . Cut the Lines . . . Make out lines to Space" (p. 5).

Another method Burroughs advocates is that of fold-in— folding the page of one text in half and superimposing it on the page of another text and then reading straight across the page. He argues that these methods afford the reader new perceptions and insights: "Cut-ups establish new connections between images, and one's range of vision consequently expands."[71] It is this assertion that critics who speak of the technique of cut-up most frequently contend with. Noting that much of *The Exterminator*, by Burroughs's admission, was composed by cut-up, critics then critique the novel on these terms; for example, "Many passages in his books can catch something of the atmosphere of dreams in which vivid fragments of hallucinatory vividness rise and fade in utter silence. . . . But to what extent [cut-up] can secure genuinely new ways of 'reading' reality I am not sure."[72] This type of critique I think misses the point. What is important here is the technique (the method of composition) and not the product (the actual "text" of *The Exterminators*). Burroughs implicitly demands that readers cut up his texts as well as the texts of others (by the way, cutting up pages of *The Exterminator* often yields interesting—and quasi-coherent—results), his objective being not to name a meaning but to instigate a process. In the first place, "the new techniques, such as cutup, will involve much more of the total capacity of the observer."[73] As I have noted throughout this section, paramodernist techniques implicate the reader in narrative management in new ways. In particular, the reader's activities are channeled less and less into tasks of interpretation and more and more into acts of composition. The reader is asked to discover principles of coherence that can invest the discontinuous or hermetically sealed narrative with unity or totality. Confronted by a text whose meaning and structure are both undetermined, the reader is compelled to determine the semantic dimensions of the work by shoring fragments together into a "totality of vision." The space of the reader changes ontologically from HERMENEUTIC to COMPOSITIONAL. Much of this activity of composition takes place in the imagination of the reader, who mentally juggles disparate scenes, motifs, actants, and discursive forms. The technique of cut-up can then be seen as the logical extension of the reader's compositional activities; the reader is directed literally to "compose" her or his own text. If one literally makes one's own text, one can be sure that the "truths" discovered therein are not imposed from without but come from within. The reader "rubs out the Word" from without in order to "write your own message that is you" (*The Exterminator*, p. 15). And, as will be seen, the paramodernist technique of cut-up, with the heavy burden it lays upon the reader, leads logically to postmodernist "cut-up" and its ironic treatment of the *response*-ible reader.

Prologue to Chapter 4

KLINKOWITZ: *In Richard Schickel's* New York Times Magazine *piece last year, you were reported as saying that "The principle of collage is the central principle of all art in the twentieth century in all media." Would you care to expand and perhaps tell me how it specifically applies to fiction?*
BARTHELME: *I was probably wrong.*
> *Jerome Klinkowitz, Barthelme interview in* The New Fiction

But however beautiful it may be, one literary form can become fatally monotonous, particularly for those whose only concern is with literature, who make it from morning till night and live by it. Then a strange need for change grows in us; even the greatest of the wonders which we so passionately admire turn us against them, because we know only too well how they are produced: we belong, as they say, to that fraternity. So we look out for something else, or, rather, we turn back to something else; but we seize on this "something else," recast it, add to it, and make it our own.
> *Guy de Maupassant, "Emile Zola"*

I am afraid that we are not rid of God because we still have grammar.
> *Friedrich Nietzsche, in Josipovici,* The Lessons of Modernism

The end of linear writing is indeed the end of the book, even if, even today, it is within the form of the book that new writings—literary or theoretical—allow themselves to be, for better or worse, encased. It is less a question of confiding new writings to the envelope of the book than of finally reading what wrote itself between the lines in the volumes. That is why, beginning to write without the line, one begins to reread past writing according to a different organization of space. If today the problem of reading occupies the forefront of science, it is because of this suspense between two ages of writing. Because we are beginning to write, to write differently, we must reread differently.
> *Jacques Derrida,* Of Grammatology

If an author really does not care whether his works leave his readers in some sense better for having read them, if he feels no connection at all between his artistic motives and some improvement in the quality of the lives led by his readers, attempts to prove such a connection will be futile. And it is quite conceivable that a society might become so demoralized that most artists would feel driven to use their art for destructive ends.
> *Wayne Booth,* The Rhetoric of Fiction

157

The more accelerated our life becomes, the more we have to learn to select only the essential, to create our own repose and meditation islands within an uncluttered mental space.

Anaïs Nin, The Novel of the Future

In fact, no one ever really witnesses cases of total radical invention, *nor indeed of total moderate invention, since texts are maze like structures combining inventions, replicas, stylizations, ostentions, and so on. Semiosis never rises* ex novo *and* ex nihilo. *No new culture can ever come into being except against the background of an old one.*

Umberto Eco, A Theory of Semiotics

4

Dis-Easy Peace
Postmodernist Reoccupation of Fictional Space

The authorial minds that in Tom Jones *and* Tristram Shandy *play with events and the reader in so nearly divine a way become the great and strangely effective symbols of liberty operating in a world of necessity and this is more or less true of all the novelists who* contrive *and* invent.
　　　　　Lionel Trilling in Samet, "The Modulated Vision: Lionel Trilling's 'Larger Naturalism'"

The tamed world, the controlled world, the world whose ground rules are no longer confining, these are the worlds that help us to overcome too much reality.
　　　　　Eric S. Rabkin, The Fantastic in Literature

1. TEXT SPACE *and the Reader*

As postulated above, there are two basic areas of signification within the TEXT SPACE of a fiction, NARRATIVAL space and NARRATIONAL space, the former generated by the signs that particularize the fictional world, the latter by the signs particularizing the speaker who recounts the story of that world. Previous chapters have described the radical changes in the nature and form of this fictional space precipitated by the modernist retreat of the Author from her or his prerogated space as "authorial persona." This evacuation, catalyzed by cultural pressures that make "totalization" more and more difficult, transfers the responsibility of interpretation to the reader. Paramodernist fictions compel the reader to occupy more and more "space" in the narrative by leaving sizable gaps in it. And there exists a kind of postmodernist fiction—which I

159

shall term METAFICTION, borrowing the word from Scholes, who attributes it to William Gass[1]—that presents itself as the logical outcome of this process. Acknowledging the fact that the reader has secured a place within the narrative ontology, the metafictional author reenters ironically the traditional space of the author and, in effect, contends with the reader for occupation of fictional space. The author returns, but flaunting his or her *author*-ial mask, thus foregrounding notions of fictional space and fictionality in general. The dynamics of this process can best be described by returning to a consideration of the space of the speaker, the NARRATIONAL SPACE of a fiction.

1.1. *The Model*

NARRATIONAL SPACE can be divided into two major systems of subspaces—the space generated by the fact that the narrative exists by virtue of some sort of speech act by a speaking subject (DISCURSIVE SPACE), and the space attendant upon the fact that this speech act is transcribed on some kind of physical medium (ICONIC SPACE). These two subspaces may be further particularized, as has been done in chapter 1. What should be emphasized is the fact that these two subspaces textually indicate that the narrative proper is mediated and metatextually remind the reader that what he or she is experiencing is not unadulterated "reality." Following the example of Brooke-Rose, we can, in fact, apply the notions of text and metatext to our map of NARRATIONAL SPACE in order to distinguish between TEXT SPACE and PARASPACE (the space of the reader), and to define more clearly the metafictional potential of NARRATIONAL SPACE.

In her extended consideration of "The Turn of the Screw," Brooke-Rose distinguishes between the text and the metatext for any narrative unit.[2] The text consists in the denotative signification (the simple textual meaning) of the words in the unit in question. The full signification of a narrative unit is not limited to its denotative value, however; necessarily adhering to a narreme, there are the unstated connotations that are generated in the reader's mind. The reader brings a metatext (something "beyond" the text), derived from cultural conventions that govern and direct understanding, to every bit of text that he or she consumes. As Brooke-Rose says, "metatext is always essentially the reader's text."[3] For example, Brooke-Rose analyzes the text and metatext of the famous first sentence of the governess's account ("I remember the whole beginning as a succession of flights and drops, a little see-saw of the right throbs and the wrong") as follows:

> *The whole beginning* connotes (AM)* a tendency to dramatise ("the beginning" would have been enough for denotation), and, by the same token, the narrator's type of talent, for the fact that any narrator must have at least the talent to keep us interested (a talent lent by the author) is of great importance. . . . *As a succession of little flights and drops* denotes her alternating impressions, connotes the above *plus* a certain instability of the narrator (AM). *A little see-saw of the right throbs and the wrong* (adding to the talent-metatext with a telling metaphor) connotes (AM) all the above *plus* a tendency to see things in Manichean and moralistic terms (up/down//right/wrong).[4]

The analysis here captures quite well the dynamics of the text/metatext reading process. In it Brooke-Rose works from the pattern of diction and elements of style to infer certain qualities or characteristics of the speaker. Clearly this might be done for any narreme from any first-person narrative since every word and phrase the speaker uses acts as an index of his or her character.

The same logic obtains for narratives in which the speaking subject is not quite so foregrounded as in first-person; in particularly, to "authorial" and "impersonal" enunciations (regardless of the visibility of the speaker). Any narreme can be analyzed stylistically and rhetorically for indexical information about the nature of the speaking subject (this is just what Wayne Booth does to several impersonal enunciations in the first chapter of *The Rhetoric of Fiction*). It follows that authorial narratives, ones that make substantial use of components of DISCURSIVE SPACE, offer relatively more information about the speaking subject; as critics have noted, the histor of Fielding's fictions and the persona in Austen's fictions are in some ways the most important characters in their respective works.

As the diagram on page 162 indicates, the reader "reads" elements of DISCURSIVE SPACE as indexical signs for the speaker and for the culture that produced the enunciation. Similarly, the reader confronted by a text that occupies portions of ICONIC

---

*(AM) is Brooke-Rose's abbreviation for Author's Metatext.

Diagram 4: Text Space and Metatext

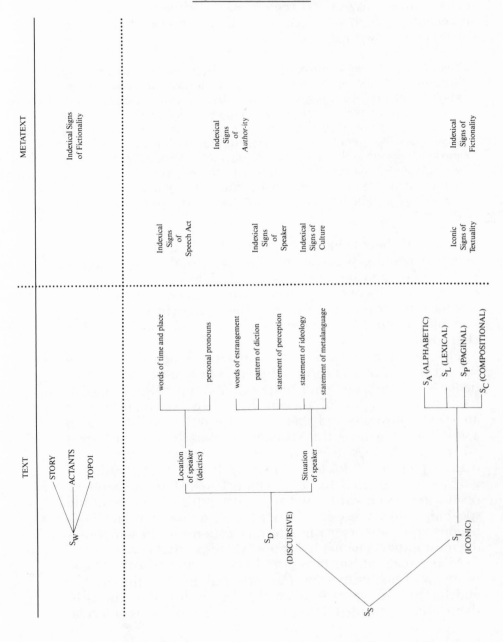

SPACE is encouraged to read those signs metatextually as an index to the nature of textuality. The iconic configuration explores the notion of what it is to be a text. It should be noted finally that both DISCURSIVE and ICONIC SPACE give rise to (at several removes) a metatextual reading tht ponders and then explores the nature and fact of fictionality, the former by reminding the reader again and again that the STORY has been mediated and is therefore *only* a version, the latter by foregrounding the fact that the STORY consists *only* in so many words on so many pages, not reality after all.

As Brooke-Rose has noted, metatext is essentially the reader's text. An author may, however, preempt readerly prerogatives in this regard simply by incorporating metatextual commentary into his or her own discourse, by occupying or manipulating its DISCURSIVE and ICONIC SPACES. Or an author might so manage its WORLD and STORY as to call attention to the "made-up-ness" of these components and thus to foreground the fraudulence or fictionality of the narrative enterprise. Any narrative that deploys its NARRATIVAL and NARRATIONAL SPACES in such a way as to foreground its own fictionality is a METAFIC-TION.

1.2 *The Battle for Fictional Space*

The strength of "fictional space" as a narratological tool rests both in its metaphorical aptness and in its capacity to encompass all three centers of the act and experience of literature: the culture-specific author, the realized text, and the recreating and responding reader. It should be clear that this dynamic is implicit in the very nature of narrative, which presupposes a teller, a tale, and a told. In traditional narrative, the nature and temper of this interrelationship is serene, cooperative, mutually satisfying. As the instigator of the contact, the author assumes control and "creates . . . an image of himself and another image of his reader; he makes his reader, as he makes his second self, and the most successful reading is one in which the created selves, author and reader, can find complete agreement"; there exists during the reading experience "an implied dialogue among author, narrator, the other characters, and the reader."[5]

Some postmodernist authors have, in recent years, realized that this sort of "ideal" relationship is no longer available to

them. The modernist author abdicated certain authorial privileges, and other writers and critics put their stamp of approval
upon this practice; "showing" was elevated above "telling."
Paramodernist authors contributed to the debunking of *author*-
ity by forcing upon the reader compositional as well as interpretive responsibilities; the reader became part of the
formal furniture of the house of fiction. What, then, are the
alternatives for the author who wishes, for reasons having to do
with the culturological situation, to reassume some of the prerogatives of authorial narration? Clearly, the author cannot act
as though the twentieth century has not happened and reassume the magisterial privileges that Victorian authors accepted
as part of their birthright. For one thing, some readers might
object to the anachronism as self-righteousness, as a usurpation
of readerly prerogatives, as an act of patronization, as pre-
sumptuous posturing. For another thing, postmodernist authors, aware of the arbitrary nature of language, of the gap
between sign and referent, between signified and signifier, can
no longer accept what the Victorian author took for granted—a
belief in the reciprocity or interplay between language and the
world (whether that world be conceived as located in empirical
or in psychological "reality"). Victorian authors for the most
part assume automatically a relationship of correspondence between the "real world" and its components, and the WORLD of
the fiction and its components; for them language is mainly a
tool for *re*-presentation. Postmodernist authors are aware that
fiction is at least twice removed from "reality": in the first place,
it is "made up"; in the second place, it is made up of words,
signifying entities whose relation to the signified actuality is
arbitrary—words are merely substitutes for the "real thing."
For them, *re*-presentation becomes problematical at best.

"WHAT RECOURSE" asks one of Barthelme's texts in huge
block type, as if to play up the predicament of the well-read and
self-conscious postmodernist author. The author may reoccupy
previously evacuated portions of his or her fictional space, but
without the innocence of Victorian predecessors. The author
reoccupies ironically, blatantly sporting an Authorial mask, and
addressing questions of Fictionality, *Author*-ity, Textuality, and
the *Response*-ibility of the Reader. In effect, the whole notion of
the space of the fiction is foregrounded as the author/speaker
announces an intention to reclaim the imaginal terrain, if only
so that he or she might finally go silent. The fiction feeds on its
own processes, like the phoenix rising out of its ashes.

1.3 *Self-Conscious and Self-Reflexive Texts*

There is, of course, nothing new about self-conscious authors, or fictions about writers, or stories about the desire to tell stories; Sterne's *Tristram Shandy* can serve as the prototype for this narrative subgenre. What is "new" about postmodernist metafictions—and it makes a radical difference—is the motivation behind the foregrounding of the processes of fiction. About earlier examples of metafictional art, one critic has said:

> the Greeks were concerned with metafiction, but not as a self-consciousness problematic about the "meaning" of one's interpretations. For them one's way of interpreting expressed the qualities of a person, and only secondarily reflected the possible intelligibility of events.[6]

In other words, metafictional devices were employed as a means of characterizing the speaking subject. Or, in other circumstances, the speaker might call attention to himself in order to promote the fictional illusion, a technique William Empson refers to as "pseudo-parody to disarm criticism."[7] The text reveals its own artificiality, but only to demonstrate an awareness that there might be other versions of the story and to suggest that this version will therefore give the reader the unadulterated "truth." And last, metafictional techniques may be employed, as in the case of *Don Quixote* and *Tristram Shandy*, in order to make fun of other literary genres, conventions, or texts. Common to all these functions is an assumption about the relation of fiction and reality—a belief in the "explicable and intersubjective nature of the world."[8] It is thus the responsibility of narrative fiction to reproduce or to lay bare the underlying order, to give the reader a "totalized" vision.

As argued above, belief in some rational order of reality is not available to postmodernist authors; in fact, the very notion of such an order is ludicrous. In these circumstances it is equally ludicrous to demand of fiction that it discover the "deep structure" of reality, perhaps even ludicrous for fiction to undertake to *re*-present reality, especially given the Protean quality of contemporary reality. Metafictional techniques in postmodernist fictions are founded on a different epistemology, one unconvinced of the knowability of the world. For these reasons it is appropriate to refer to these texts as self-reflexive and not simply self-conscious. The self-conscious text broods on its own processes and components in a thoughtful and considered (if frequently comical) fashion. The self-reflexive text regurgitates the elements of fiction only to make fun of them, to explode them, to deconstruct them. As one critic notes, postmodernist fiction evinces the "activist faith that discourse, become self-conscious and self-reflexive, can raise the writer's and reader's awareness of the properties and operations of language and social discourse and of their own problematic placement within them."[9] These fictions constitute a deliberate and measured assault upon the fact of fiction, the need for fiction, the form of fiction; they expose the fraudulence of the lofty cognitive ends that some people ascribe to fictions.

In certain postmodernist fictions, then, which I shall term METAFICTIONS, the authors occupy ironically their fictional space, calling attention to themselves as authors and to their works as fiction and at the same time belittling the seriousness and importance of their enterprise. In particular, metafictionists mock the reader's desire for "meaning," for a totalized vision of reality. Their works strive for a "systematic exemption of meaning"[10] by thwarting the "meaning-mongering" process in a number of ways (a situation that raises a number of problems with traditional forms of interpretive criticism, another subject entirely). Despite the nihilism upon which this practice is founded, there is real exuberance and infectious energy about much of this fiction, attributable perhaps to the freedom that the postmodernist author experiences within his or her fictional space. To play with elements of contemporary reality, to mock readerly expectations, to parodize forms of fiction is, in a sense, to be free of them, and ironic reoccupation of fictional space enables the author to accomplish just those ends. Tony Tanner has used a very telling phrase to account for the length of Barth's *Giles Goat-Boy:* "The length of his book is the tenure of his freedom."[11] The space of a metafiction is patently under the control of its omnipotent and omnipresent Author. If, like Nabokov's Humbert Humbert, he has only words to play with, and if even words are counterfeit currency, he is nonetheless free to play. We must imagine the metafictionist as happy.

2. *NARRATIVAL SPACE and Metafiction*

I have argued above that one of the primary characteristics of contemporary METAFICTION is the ironic reoccupation of areas of NARRATIONAL SPACE. This is not to say that all metafictions are necessarily characterized by a discourse that ponders its enabling codes or its processes. A fiction may foreground its fictionality in a number of ways. It may, for example, present itself as a member of a literary genre whose WORLD does not correspond to our experiential world. In this way it abrogates the mimetic contract, establishing itself as something "made-up." This is the case for genres of romance like fantasy and science fiction. Or a fiction may so manage its NARRATIVAL SPACE as to expose its fraudulence at the same time as it seems to be telling a rather conventional story. Any description of META-FICTION must begin with its deployment of elements of NARRATIVAL SPACE.

2.1 *The Overdetermination of* NARRATIVAL SPACE

But the possibility of constructing a fantastically baroque plot appealed to me most: the idea of turning vigorously against the modernist notion that plot is an anachronistic element in contemporary fiction.

John Barth, in Bellamy, The New Fiction

The two most recognizable components of any NARRATIVAL SPACE are its STORY and its ACTANTS, a fact reflected in the preoccupation of traditional criticism with plot and characterization. Not surprisingly then, some contemporary metafiction transforms these components in such a way as to expose their conventionality at the same time that it "exploits" them in order to bring the fiction into existence. The basic technique utilized for this purpose can be referred to as overdetermination. An overdetermined literary device is one that serves several functions at once (an effect with several causes) and which thus draws attention to itself as a device. Barth uses the term *escalation* in an interview, a word more interesting than appropriate in that it suggests the adversary role of the author *vis-à-vis* his text and his audience.

Speaking of the necessary tension between fiction and reality, Barth has said, "A different way to come to terms with the discrepancy between art and the Real Thing is to affirm the artificial element in art (you can't get rid of it anyhow) and make the artifice part of the point."[12] One affirms the artificial element by defamiliarizing it, by bringing the literary convention to the foreground. For example, Barth foregrounds the

STORY of *Giles Goat-Boy* by so emphasizing the "plottiness" of the tale that the reader is constantly reminded that he or she is in a fiction. The full title of the text, with its biblical overtones, reminds the reader that George's life recapitulates Christ's; George's ambition to become a mythic hero and his exposure to various mythical texts underscore the STORY's scrupulous adherence to Joseph Campbell's monomyth of the hero with 1,000 faces. Added to fidelity to ur-textual models is the tendency of the STORY to repeat obsessively and predictably certain motifs (George must pass through the belly of WESCAC three times, learning a new lesson each time) and to proliferate coincidences to the point of absurdity. Whatever else the text is, it is thickly *plotted*.

In *V.*, Thomas Pynchon draws attention to the human pattern-making instinct, our need to conceive or contrive plots, by making a central character, Herbert Stencil, obsessed with the enigmatic character V., a woman somehow connected with the "Plot Which Has No Name." Stencil is "quite purely He Who Looks for V.," and by treating his obsession with the magic initial ironically, Pynchon is able to explore the absurdity and values of the human need to invent plots.

In similar fashion, the metafictionist can emphasize characterliness (or the lack of this quality) by working some simple transformations upon his or her system of ACTANTS. Donald Barthelme and Robert Coover make traditional figures from literary folklore (Snow White, Little Red Riding Hood, Hansel and Gretel) primary ACTANTS in their fictions, but assign to them a contemporary idiom or life style that serves to mock readerly expectations about their identities. An even more disconcerting example of actantial transformation might be the appearance within the fiction of the (as it were) flesh-and-blood author himself. A character uncannily like John Barth appears magically to rescue Sheherazade in a moment of distress in *Chimera.* And the hero of the majority of Ronald Sukenick's fictions is a character variously identified as Ron, Ronnie, Sukenick, or Ronald Sukenick, who teaches English at a university and writes novels.

Yet another way to foreground NARRATIVAL SPACE involves making the narrative act itself the subject of the STORY by making the primary actant a fictionist struggling with his or her own narrative. Raymond Federman's *Double or Nothing* recounts the elaborate plans of a would-be novelist who intends to lock himself up in a room, subsist entirely on noodles, and write his experience of America. Several of the stories in Barth's *Lost in the Funhouse* deal with self-conscious fiction-makers or tale-spinners whose self-consciousness results in writer's block or outlandishly contrived fictions. And Gilbert Sorrentino's *Mulligen Stew* incorporates a novel-in-progress; the diaries and letters of the novel's author, Tony Lamont; excerpts from the fiction of rival novelists; and the diary of one of the characters in Lamont's novel, who happens to be aware of his "job" as a character and is dissatisfied with his "role."

Preoccupation with "plottiness" and plots, characters stolen from "real life" or the literary tradition, and narratives about the trials and "triumphs" of frustrated fictionists—these narrative ploys and strategies call attention to the artifice and conventionality of fiction—its *fiction*-ality—at the same time as they compound the strangeness of fictional space. Overdetermination of elements of NARRATIVAL SPACE enables metafictionists "to acknowledge what [they're] doing while [they're] doing it."[13]

2.2 *NARRATIVAL SPACE and the "Real World"*

The notion of using personal facts within a fictional construct in such a way as to emphasize the artifice of life and of the novel instead of using the representational mimesis of the traditional autobiography is essential to Sukenick's theory of fiction.
Timothy Dow Adams, "Obscuring the Muse: The Mock Autobiographies of Ronald Sukenick"

In chapter 3 I noted how certain paramodernist authors, in an attempt to deal with the ever-increasing amount of "reality" in the twentieth century, incorporated the unprocessed "stuff" of history—facts, events, personages—in a separate but equal portion of fictional space. Readers were subsequently obliged to assemble the disparate pieces of the fiction into a coherent whole. This process of assimilation of undigested and untransformed historical fact continues in forms of postmodernist narrative like the nonfiction novel. This contemporary narrative subgenre has been dealt with satisfactorily elsewhere,[14] so we need not say more than that it can be seen as a logical extension of certain paramodernist strategies for accommodating the fiction/reality tension.

We do need, however, to distinguish another form of post-

modernist narrative—Federman and Sukenick refer to it as
surfiction—which has devised its own strategies for the fiction/
reality polarity. In a statement that recalls Barth's famous jest
about God's not being a bad novelist for a "realist," Sukenick
has said, "God was the omniscient author, but he died; now no
one knows the plot, and since our reality lacks the sanction of a
creator, there's no guarantee as to the authenticity of the received version."[15] Convinced, like the metafictionist, that "reality" is just another fiction, that we make up our lives much as a
fictionist invents a fictional world, the surfictionist contrives
narrative situations that highlight the fictionality of reality and
the reality of fiction. Rejecting the hermetically sealed fictions
of metafictionists like Barth and Nabokov, the surfictionist
opens his or her narrative to the pressures of reality, often by
making the central speaker a character whose life style and
vocation match that of the "real-life" author. In Sukenick's *UP*
the real-life models for the invented characters of the novel
show up at "Sukenick's" place to celebrate the completion of his
novel: "Now Sukenick is holding a champagne glass in the air
and doing his own crazy dance to Greek bouzouki music. He
must be drunk already. Live it up Ron boy, the book's almost
over."[16] By conflating the once distinct realms of reality and
fiction, the surfictionist replicates the discontinuous and absurd
feel of "real" experience while at the same time asserting its
problematic status as fictional construct. And, as one critic argues, "Part of the joy comes about because the mock-
autobiographer, by writing his own life as fiction, can
simultaneously tell his story and comment on the process."[17]
The surfictionist "masters" reality by playing with it within the
fictional space.

A similar motive links other contemporary metafictions that
deal more directly with the stuff of history—fictions like Pynchon's *V.* and *Gravity's Rainbow,* Doctorow's *Ragtime,* and Coover's *The Public Burning.* These fictions deliberately convert
history into fiction, by assuming the privilege of rewriting entire historical epochs or events in a way that satisfies the needs
of the imagination. In *The Public Burning,* for example, Coover
reinvents the "true" history behind the scenes of the Rosenberg
trial and execution, turning the event into a ritualized (and
totally ludicrous) mass public catharsis, engineered by none
other than Nixon (who narrates about half the novel),
Eisenhower, and other "real-life" witch-hunters. In this novel

and others like it, history is not a nightmare from which to escape but just another narrative or meaning system to make over. The fictionist expropriates history and refashions or over-determines it according to imaginative caprice. It is as if the fictionist intends to "eat" history—consume, digest, and regurgitate it—before history eats him. In this way the fictionist demonstrates a mastery of history; to play with or deconstruct history is in effect to be free of it while at the same time acknowledging its existence as an experiential pressure.

3. NARRATIONAL SPACE and Metafiction

NARRATIONAL SPACE, generated by those sign vehicles which situate and particularize the speaking subject or the text's materiality, consists of two signifying subspaces—DISCURSIVE and ICONIC SPACE. A basic metafictional strategy involves deploying these subspaces in such a way as to foreground either the speaking subject or the text's materiality. In the former case the fiction calls into question notions of *author*-ity; in the latter case, notions of textuality.

3.1 Overdetermination of DISCURSIVE SPACE

No climax. There's the story. Finished? Not quite. Story of our lives. The last word in fiction, in fact. I chose the first-person narrative viewpoint in order to reflect interest from the peculiarities of the technique (such as the normally unbearable self-consciousness, the abstraction, and the blank) to the nature and situation of the narrator and his companion, despite the obvious possibility that the narrator and his companion might be mistaken for the narrator and his companion. Occupational hazard.

John Barth, "Title," Lost in the Funhouse

The most obvious way to incorporate metafictional elements within a fictional space is to place them in the enunciation of the speaker, in the form of "metalingual" community. That is, the speaker interrupts the STORY to interpose statements that address the medium, the codes, or the conventions of the narrative act. A speaker may, for example, pause to consider the medium through which contact is made with the receiver; the paradigm for this type might be Humbert Humbert's cry from within the pages of his text: "Oh, my Lolita. I have only words to play with!"[18] This cry has been echoed in various ways in a number of contemporary metafictions:

—Oh I wish there were some words in the world that were not the
words that I always hear![19]

—In fact there can always be more words   words![20]

—I'm going to finish this today, the hell with it. I've had enough of
this. I'm just playing with words anyway, what did you think I was
doing? Just playing with words ga-ga-ga-ga-ga-ga-goo-goo-gig-
geg-gug-gack.[21]

A speaker can make a similarly "phatic" statement by discussing
the syntax his message conforms to or the page on which it
appears. This is particularly the narrative focus of much of
Federman's "Pretext" to *Take It or Leave It.*

A second kind of metalingual remarks consists in references
by the speaker to the literary codes that govern and direct the
understanding of the literary message. Barthelme addresses
the whole notion of a symbolic field or symbol-hunting in "The
Glass Mountain," a story designed "simply to disenchant a symbol."[22] And in a story in the same volume, "Kierkegaard Unfair
to Schlegel," he examines the Code of Irony: "Now I suppose
that I am suddenly curious about this amazing magical power.
Suppose I become curious about how my irony actually
works—how it functions" (*City Life,* p. 94). The metalinguistic
operation in this story enables the respondent, who is being
quizzed by some sort of computer, to have his irony and eat it at
the same time. In the companion story to this piece, "The Explanation," the "computer" and the respondent question the
very method of their story and accordingly tend to belittle it.
John Barth's recent fictions, *Lost in the Funhouse* (1968) and
Chimera (1972), contain lengthy and frequently profound
enunciative disquisitions on the code that insists that the very
impulse to narrate is predicated upon innate mythopoeic pro-
clivities. And the enumeration of metalinguistic motifs could be
extended.

It should be noted at this point that ironic reoccupation of
DISCURSIVE SPACE does not appear solely in contemporary
metafiction; one can find similar metalingual commentary in
texts by Sterne, Faulkner, Gide, or Mann, for example. What is
particularly postmodernist about contemporary instances of
this device is their tendency to treat the stuff of fiction and its
enabling codes in a flippant or parodic manner. An examination of the author's treatment of DISCURSIVE SPACE and the relation he or she posits with the reader helps to locate the

pervasive (and some would say, corrosive) irony that "contaminates" this *text*-ure.

3.2 *Metafiction and* ICONIC SPACE

A thoroughgoing poetics must confront literature as an inscribed object and recognize that it can be engaged only through an act of reading. *Proper attention to the nature of writing will be concerned not simply with isolated experiments, but with the role that vision plays in all reading and the effect of print on signification in all works.*
      Stephen Ross, " 'Voice' in Narrative Texts: The Example of* As I Lay Dying"

Overdetermination in the deployment of elements of NAR-RATIVAL SPACE and discursive metalingual statements of a parodic intent remind readers of the fictionality—and ultimately the fraudulence—of that which they read. An important aspect of fictionality in the Western world is textuality, and a fiction that deploys its latent ICONIC SPACE undertakes to explore and perhaps comprehend what it is to be a Text, especially a fictional text. The ICONIC SPACE of a fiction evolves out of the ineluctable fact of the text's physicality—its existence primarily as a number of letters, grouped according to convention into recognizable words, which are deployed across a number of pages, these pages to be received in a certain order. Any fiction that systematically foregrounds one or another of these aspects may be said to utilize ICONIC SPACE and thus metatextually to call itself into question as a text. The sections that follow enumerate the subspaces of ICONIC SPACE and describe individual texts that tend to foreground these subspaces. It should be noted that the fictions cited for exemplary deployment of a particular ICONIC subspace may also deploy other subspaces; the subspace in question serves in my opinion as the dominant system of the fiction.

3.2.1. ALPHABETIC SPACE *and* Alphabetical Africa

Although the letters of the alphabet are independent of each other, people tend to ingest or read them, as the case may be, in small and large clusters that are called words. No matter what people say to each other, they are using words, not letters, When a word is not understood, the person using it is obliged to spell it aloud. This entails breaking the word into letters. However, if one is careful, one can speak for hours on end, even months sometimes without being compelled to spell a word. In the more rural sections of the U.S. people do not resort to spelling difficult words . . . instead they plunge a V-shaped knife into the other fella, who moans, "Ohhh." O also happens to be the fifteenth letter in the alphabet. For some reason it is often used by insecure people.

Walter Abish, Minds Meet

In Nabokov's *Lolita* the reader is presented with a list of Lolita's schoolmates, upon which there appears the name Vivian Darkbloom; the reader aware of Nabokov's penchant for lexical sport recognizes the name as an anagram of Vladimir Nabokov. And in his *Ada* some of the characters amuse themselves during an outing by thinking of anagrams for the word "insect" (they come up with incest, scient, and nicest, all words with heavy metatextual resonance). In this way Nabokov foregrounds the almost magical power of letters to generate different semantic spaces through the smallest change in configuration. In Nabokov's fictions, the deployment of AL-PHABETIC SPACE is minimal, but other fictions make this signifying subsystem more instrumental. For example, Gilbert Sorrentino's *Splendide-Hotel* and Richard Horn's *Encyclopedia* both rely on the alphabet as the "shaping principle." The latter has a conventional story to tell but chooses to order its materials in the way of an encyclopedia; on the first few pages the reader can consult entries entitled "ABORTION," "AKTEDRON," "ANDERSON, LANE," "ANDERSON, VALERIE," AND "ANGRIE, EUGENE," each entry supplying but a part of a STORY that must be pieced together.[23] *Splendide-Hotel* consists of an alphabetically ordered series of meditations on the letters of the alphabet, and Sorrentino, who writes, for example, that "It is my opinion as well as that of others that the word *grey* spelled with a e is 'grey-er' than the same word spelled with an a: *gray,*" admits that he employs this principle of organization out of desperation—"One must find some structure, even if it be this haphazard one of the alphabet."[24]

But the "ultimate" in this type of fiction must surely be Abish's *Alphabetical Africa,* in which the letters of the alphabet are at once the ordering principle, a formal constraint, and metatextually the subject of the composition. The text is divided into fifty-two sections, each assigned a letter of the alphabet from A to Z and then from Z to A. The letters not only order the text, they impose a "constrictive form" upon it;[25] in the first section the author limits himself to words beginning with the letter A, in the second to words beginning A or B, in the third to words beginning A or B or C, and so on, ultimately creating a text that in the first half expands its vocabulary and diversity only to begin a process of regular diminishment at the midway point as the range of the text contracts from Z back through A again. One critic describes the book as like "taking a deep breath and letting it out."[26] Below is a sample of the texture of the fiction, drawn from sections A_1, F_1, L_2:[27]

> Africa again: Albert arrives, alive and arguing about African art, about African angst, and also, alas, attacking Ashanti architecture, as author again attempts an agonizing alphabetical appraisal. (Pp. 1–2)

> Downcast, feeling dejected after first frustrating African experience, Ferdinand flies back. Flies first class Eastern. Enjoys fried frogs for dinner. Fabulous dinner. Fabulous frogs, author decides. But erases Ferdinance. Feeble fucker. (P. 13)

> Like everyone else deeply interested in letters I got a hand-engraved invitation for a Letter Auction in late July. Daily I had been complaining how I had been losing a few letters each day. I couldn't explain it. At first I didn't inform anyone about it, but after I contacted a few friends in early June I discovered how everyone else also interested in language and letters had been burglarized, chiefly and almost exclusively losing letters concerning Africa. . . . In losing letter after letter I had lost an entire African legacy. . . . How could I ever complete a book about Alva. (P. 121)

The excerpts above should demonstrate that the text *does* have a *STORY,* involving the quest by the "author" for an alphabet, Africa, and attractive Alva, an undertaking jeopardized, among other things, by an army ant attack. The selection should also indicate how frequently this "author," through puns or direct metalingual statements, makes it clear that his subject is his alphabet and what he can do with it, as well as his Alva and his Africa.

Abish has said in the interview cited above, "I was fascinated to discover the extent to which a system could impose on the contents of a work a meaning that was fashioned by the form, and then to see the degree to which the form, because of the conspicuous obstacles, undermined that very meaning. For example, I could not introduce the first person singular until I had reached the ninth section. Frequently I intended to follow one direction and was compelled to follow another." We can say, then, that Abish extends the metafictional exploration of narrative to the hyposemiotic stuff in order to explore both its constrictive *and* generative properties. Clearly, he is concerned with the restrictions that signifying systems impose upon human communication and understanding; he notes that the first person is unavailable to him until its ninth section, which characteristically begins "I haven't been herebefore. . ." (p. 21). Section S₁ commences with the statement "Summarizing Africa: I can speak more freely. I find fewer and fewer impediments" (p. 47), and the reader is reminded that the "author" can use the word *speak* now and that the bulk of the alphabet is at his disposal. The notion of the restrictions inherent in signification is reflected also in the STORY of the text, which is predicated on the fact that Africa is shrinking. Africa shrinks throughout the first half of the text because the "author's" ability to describe the continent (capture it with his vocabulary) is constantly growing. That it keeps shrinking in the second half serves to remind the reader that the word-hoard is shrinking and the text *Alphabetical Africa* is dwindling to Absence.

Perhaps more interesting than the limitations of hyposemiotic stuff is its generative property. Abish has said that he was intrigued by the choices he found he could make once he accepted the alphabetical gambit. The entire process tended to "illuminate the formation of thought,"[28] which Abish regards as art's most important function. The reader of *Alphabetical Africa* constantly feels the foregrounding of this process of thought's formation. The reader is continually amazed at what the author *can* do within the stringent alphabetical constraints, and, more important, senses the residual magic of signifying systems—their very strange ability to generate new thought, new ideas, new content.

3.2.2 *LEXICAL SPACE and* Lost in the Funhouse

Is this what we're going to talk about, our obscene verbal problem? It'll be our last conversation. Why talk at all? Are you paying attention? I dare you to quit now! Never dare a desperate person. On with it, calmly, one sentence after another, like a recidivist. A what? A common noun. Or another common noun. Hold tight. Or a chronic forger, let's say; committed to the pen for life. Which is to say, death. The point, for pity's sake! Not yet. Forge on.

John Barth, "Title," Lost in the Funhouse

John Barth's *Lost in the Funhouse,* a serial collection of short fictions "meant to be received 'all at once'" (p. ix), may be seen as an exhaustive compendium of all the metafictional tactics and graphotechnics that I have described thus far. Without too much trouble we can identify at least the following metafictional strategies:

(1) overdetermination of motifs of STORY: in "Night-Sea Journey" and "Menelaiad"
(2) interpolation of ironic metalingual statements: "Lost in the Funhouse" and "Life-Story"
(4) parody of narrative conventions: the tale-within-a-tale in "Menelaiad"; the history of fiction in "Anonymiad"
(5) ALPHABETIC space: especially the letters A, B, C, D in "Frame-Tale," "Night-Sea Journey," and the Ambrose stories[29]
(6) parody of the notion of fictional space: "Frame-Tale."

And this is not to mention that the text taken as a novelistic whole can be read as the conception and birth of a narrative voice, its coming of age, and then its exhaustion of the entire genre of prose fiction. The text can be almost endlessly plumbed for its systematic foregrounding of its fictionality.

Here I would like to look at two stories in particular— "AUTOBIOGRAPHY: A Self-Recorded Fiction" and "Title" (the titles themselves are indicative of the archness of the stories)— because of their systematic exploitation of what I have termed LEXICAL SPACE. By LEXICAL SPACE I mean those narrative strategies which foreground the "wordiness" of a fiction. One way to accomplish this end is to make the language of the discourse so abstract, opaque, or obscure that the reader is unable to work from the signifier to the signified; meanings keep evaporating or canceling out. John Ashbery creates this kind of space in *Three Poems,* a text that is intended to promote "reading without comprehension."[30] There is another way to forground the individual words of the fiction, one that better "makes the artifice part of the point." It consists in selecting words that have several meanings that fit the narrative context, creating what might be termed an overdetermined semantic space. "AUTOBIOGRAPHY: A Self-Recorded Fiction" is a good example of a text that systematically overdetermines its language so as to draw the reader's attention to the "wordiness" of fiction.

Barth's story begins with the following words:

You who   listen   give me life   in a manner of speaking.

I won't hold you responsible.

My first words weren't my first words. I wish I'd begun differently (p. 33; this last paragraph foreshadows the last paragraph of
the story which reads: "Nonsense, I'll mutter to the end, one word
after another, string the rascals out, mad or not, heard or not, my
last words will be my last words").

Having been informed by the "seven Additional Author's
Notes" that the speaker of this "self-composition" is the story,
speaking of itself, the reader initially understands this passage
as a form of reader address; an acknowledgment of the
reader's role in constituting a fiction. But the spacing of the first
sentence reminds the reader that the whole sentence might also
be read as a plea; this realization transforms the entire semantic
import of these first few phrases and makes the reader wonder
at the remarkable semantic properties of language.

The rest of the story keeps the semantic properties of language at the surface of the story with such overdetermined
enunciative units as:

> I see I see myself as a halt narrative: first person, tiresome. Pro-
> noun sans ante or precedent, warrant or respite. Surrogate for the
> substantive; contentless form, Who am I. A little *crise d'identité* for
> you.
> I must compose myself.
>
> Look, I'm writing. No, listen, I'm nothing but talk. (P. 33)

Unhappily, things get clearer as we go along. I perceive that I have
no body. What's less, I've been speaking of myself without delight
or alternative as self-consciousness pure and sour; I declare now
that even that isn't true. I'm not aware of myself at all, as far as I
know. I don't think . . . I know what I'm talking about. (P. 35)

The locus of narrative action in this story becomes purely the
limited space that "lexical playfields" (the phrase is Nabokov's)
afford, as Barth reminds us again and again of the lexical
confines that hold for all fictions.

Of the story "Title," the author says, "In the stereophonic
version of the story, the two 'sides' debate—in identical authorial voice, as it is after all *monologue interieur*—across the twin
channels of stereotape, while the live author supplies such self-
interrupting and self-censoring passages as 'Title' and 'fill in
the blank'—relinquishing his role to the auditor at the" (p. xi).
This description indicates at once the form, tone, and method

of the story. Two characters debate the situation of fiction, their dialogue interrupted by authorial intrusions that single out the words of the fiction by identifying their part of speech and thus parody the reader's role in fiction. The opening paragraphs read as follows:

> I think she comes. The story of our life. This is the final test. Try to fill the blank. Only hope is to fill the blank. Efface what can't be faced or else fill the blank. With words or more words, otherwise I'll fill the blank with this noun here in my prepositional object. . . .
> . . . Can't we start over? What's past is past. On the contrary, what's forever past is eternally present.
> The future? Blank. All this is just fill in. Hang on.
> Still around. In what sense? Among the gerundive. What's that supposed to mean? Do you think I meant to fill in the blank? Why should I? On the other hand, why not? What makes you think I wouldn't fill in the blank instead? (Pp.102–3)

As one can see from these excerpts, the phrase *fill in the blank* becomes at once a reminder of the fact that fiction is made of words, a description of what the speakers in the story are trying to do (fill in the blank of their story) and a command to the reader. As the story progresses, the single word *blank* comes to be substituted for the phrase, and the reader is reminded that words are blanks, that the story (and, by extension, fiction) is a blank, and that readers' attempts to rectify this situation are absurd if not ridiculous. This movement culminates in the penultimate passage of the story:

> And that my dear is what writers have got to find ways to write about in this adjective adjective hour of the ditto ditto same noun as above, or their, that is to say our, accursed self-consciousness will lead them, that is to say us, to here it comes, say it straight out, I'm going to, say it in plain English for once, that's what I'm leading up to, me and my bloody anticlimactic noun, we're pushing each other to fill in the blank.
> Goodbye. Is it over? Can't you read between the lines? One more step. Goodbye suspense goodbye.
> Blank.

There is one more paragraph to the story, a tirade against self-consciousness. This paragraph, and the story, end appropriately with an incomplete sentence as the text iconically reminds us that we must fill in the

3.2.3 *PAGINAL SPACE* and **Double or Nothing**

The objects which occur at every given moment of composition (of recognition we can call it) are, can be, must be treated exactly as they occur therein and not by any ideas or preconceptions from outside the poem, must be handled as a series of objects in field. . . . Which brings us up, immediately, bang, against grammar generally, that is, as we have inherited it. Do not tenses, must they not also be kicked around anew, in order that time, that other governing absolute, may be kept, as must the space-tensions of a poem, immediate, contemporary to the acting-on-you of the poem? . . . The LAW OF THE LINE, *which projective verse creates, must be hewn to, obeyed and the conventions which logic has forced on syntax must be broken open.*

Charles Olson, Selected Writings

The "Pretext" of Raymond Federman's *Take It or Leave It*, sub-titled "a spatial displacement of words," speaks of traditional syntax in somewhat derogatory terms: syntax is "the unity, the continuity of words, the law which dominates them. It reduces their multiplicity, controls their violence. It fixes them into a place, a space, prescribes an order to them. It prevents them from wandering. Even if it is hidden, it reigns always on the horizon of words which buckle under its mute exigency" (no page). The "Pretext" thus addresses self-consciously issues that Federman's earlier novel, *Double or Nothing*, had dealt with more *im*-mediately: the restraints inherent in conventional syntax and the possibilities of the page.

Unlike the pages of conventional fiction, no two pages of *Double or Nothing* look quite alike. On each page Federman takes major or minor typographic liberties, any one of which serves to remind the reader of the blank space of the page, a space as inviting as an unblemished snow-covered field. Most fictions conceive this space as able to accommodate only a traditional syntax with its linear, sequential, left-to-right articulations. Federman's fictions reconceive that space as a field of action in which change and spontaneity reign. Although almost each page of *Double or Nothing* presents the reader with an idosyn-cratic typographical experiment, it is possible to identify two main types of paginal strategies.

One strategy consists in quite literally turning the page into an iconic sign of its content,[31] a strategy that I shall term *concret-ism* because of its equivalence to the technique of concrete poetry. The page becomes a sign of its semantic content and a sign of its "page-ness." As Ferdinand Kriwet has pointed out, the resulting "visually perceptible literature" tends to collapse *reading* and *seeing* into a single act.[32] The *im*-mediate visual force of the page counteracts the more intellective process of reading; the tension between perception and intellection becomes a source of energy (not to mention further reflection) for the text. The figure at the bottom of p. 85 can serve as an interesting example of this seeing/reading dynamic. The reader sees the word-arrow at the bottom of the page, an arrow that acts as an iconic sign of the fact that the page is to be turned at this point. Reading the words themselves for their semantic value, the reader is reminded how far this text departs from "straight prose," which has, for one thing, no ———————— in the middle (cf. the hole in the middle of the arrow). Further reflection yields the realization that straight prose tends to use its language indexically, as *arrows* that point to some extratextual reality; by way of comparison, the iconicity of Federman's prose points nowhere but to the next page.

The next major transformation of PAGINAL SPACE consists in waging war with conventional syntax. The words on the page are arranged in such a way as to emphasize the ways in which they depart from normal syntactic articulations. For example, on one page the reader is advised to start at the bottom of the page and read up from it proceeding from left to right (p. 127); the very next page has to be read from bottom to top *and* right to left. Some pages employ a syntax that can only be described as paginal, with words scattered all over (e.g., p. 38), while others employ double and triple columns of writing, some to be read up and down, some side-to-side, some either way (pp. 25, 166). The point is that traditional syntax carries with it metaphysical baggage, which the fictionist wishes to unload. One critic writes, "every sentence takes on a metaphysical direction implying, in subordination, for example, causality and a rational universe—a syntax of reality made apparent by a syntax of language."[33] The battle against syntax seeks to explode those metaphysical monsters.

For a metaphysic, like a literary form or any other institutionalized system, tends eventually to turn on its master or creator; in terms of fiction, it tends to channel narrative energies into the conventional, the acceptable, another adjectival noun. And so Federman hopes through the utilization of PAGINAL SPACE to re-energize a moribund literary form: "Variety that's the spice of life Though after a while it gets repetitious A guy must vary if he wants to survive. Must invent Let it happen by itself Let the damn thing shape itself by itself Create new forms New Noodles Improvise anything Improvise on a puff of smoke QUICKLY And keep going" (p. 6).

3.2.4 *COMPOSITIONAL SPACE and* Pale Fire

> *But all at once it dawned on me that* this
> *Was the real point, the contrapuntal theme;*
> *Just this: not text, but texture; not the dream*
> *But topsy-turvical coincidence,*
> *Not flimsy nonsense, but a web of sense.*
> *Yes! It sufficed that I in life could find*
> *Some kind of link-and-bobolink, some kind*
> *Of correlated pattern in the game.*
> *Plexed artistry, and something of the same*
> *Pleasure in it as they who played it found.*
> *Vladimir Nabokov,* Pale Fire

The reader is informed in the table of contents that the "Pre-text" of Federman's *Take It or Leave It* may be inserted anywhere in the text, instructions that single out an aspect of textuality— its existence as *ordered* narrative sections—and at the same time emphasize the reader's instrumentality in creating that order. Any fiction that calls attention to its existence as these pages in this (or that) order may be said to activate its latent COMPOSITIONAL SPACE (so named because of its etymology: "to put together") and to implicate the reader in narrative management. A novel in a box foregrounds its COMPOSITIONAL SPACE because it wishes to raise the reader's consciousness about his or her importance within any narrative ontology. There exists a yet more radical deployment of COMPOSITIONAL SPACE, namely, one that makes fun of the reader's compositional activities at the same time as it necessitates those activities. A text that does this double duty is Nabokov's *Pale Fire*.[34]

The text of *Pale Fire* contains, among other things, an index that faithfully and alphabetically records the what and the where of the main texts. In that index one finds an entry entitled "Word Golf," which directs one to both the poem and the commentary but also adds "see Lass." Under Lass one finds the instructions "see Mass"; under "Mass, Mars, Mare," the instructions "see Male"; under Male, the instructions "see Word Golf."

This circuitous route has given the reader lass-to-male in four (an accomplishment Kinbote boasts of), has taken the reader on a tour through the index, but never once has it allowed him to go *beyond the text.* The little excursion with Word Golf might stand as a paradigm for the larger text.

Ever since Mary McCarthy's influential analysis of *Pale Fire* as composed of separate but parallel planes in fictive space,[35] critics have spoken of the various parallel worlds/spaces/motifs that exist in the text, singling out the text's mingling of different orders of "reality" as its distinctive feature. In this they tend to dwell on the *content* of the planes rather than the *form,* and thus neglect or overlook the very peculiar relation the text establishes with the reader.[36]

As has been noted but not pursued, the text consists of four very different kinds of discourse—an editor's foreword, an extended poem called "Pale Fire," a commentary by the editor, and an index for both poem and commentary. In the foreword of the text, the editor, Kinbote, suggests that the reader manage the text as follows: "Although these notes [the Commentary], in comformity with custom, come after the poem, the reader is advised to consult them first and then study the poem with their help, rereading them of course as he goes through its text, and perhaps, after having done with the poem, consulting them a third time so as to complete the picture" (p. 18). Kinbote's advice here singles out a possible problem for the reader: in what order is she or he to read the texts that follow? Assuming that the reader reads the foreword first (highly probable), it would seem that there are three main ways to approach the text. First, one could follow Kinbote's advice and read commentary, then poem, then commentary again (C–P–C). Or one could read as the literary convention of annotated poetry suggests, moving from poem to commentary to poem to commentary in a continuous dynamic (P↔C). Or one may read in the order dictated by conventions of textuality, from left to right, start to finish (P–C). All these options are open to the reader, and the option he chooses substantially *determines* the text that he reads; there are as many versions of *Pale Fire* as there are ways to read it!

Let us look at our three primary reading possibilities with this idea in mind. If we read the novel in Kinbote's preferred order, we experience first an exotic tale about a "distant northern land." This text approximates the condition of a novel despite the editor's protest to the contrary: "I have no desire to twist and batter an unambiguous *apparatus criticus* into the monstrous semblance of a novel" (p. 62). And as a novel, it makes for lively reading. Certainly, when we turn from Zemblan intrigue to Shade's meditation on mortality, the latter suffers by way of contrast; Kinbote's assessment of the poem as an "autobiographical, eminently Appalachian, rather old-fashioned narrative in a Neo-Popian prosodic style" (p. 209) strikes me as not far from the mark. In this reading order, the poem truly seems but a "pale fire" of the commentary, "void of Kinbote's magic, of that special rich streak of magical madness" that we found in the Zemblan text.

If we read poem and commentary simultaneously, what particularly strikes us is the incredible disparity between the planes of the text (I suspect that this is the way most of us read the text originally), between the substance of the poem and the substance of the commentary. Perhaps we are also delighted with the small congruences we find between the texts. But our overriding impression probably fixes on the madness of Kinbote's commentary. We read the text as, among other things, an extended parody on critics and criticism (see 4.2).

If we read the text linearly, beginning with Shade's poem and then moving through the commentary, we get a third reading. In the first place, the poem gains in stature when our measured reading reveals the elements of self-parody that balance its sententiousness. We consider its allusions more seriously and are amused at its playfulness with language. In this reading the commentary strikes us as primarily Other and therefore strange. We tend perhaps to deprecate its significance and therefore its importance.

These analyses of the responses produced by the possible reading orders are clearly rather subjective, but my method coincides with Nabokov's point. *Pale Fire* so manages its COMPOSITIONAL SPACE that the reader is physically inserted into the fictional space, and in a number of combinatorial ways. The reader, flipping back and forth between pages and sections as per the instructions of the editor or discovering new reading orders through use of the index, struggles with the "bookness" of the book in an attempt to find something besides or beyond in the maze, but it turns out to be only various incarnations of himself. The poem opens with a mirror image, as if to warn the reader that in the space of *Pale Fire* he will see nothing but a dim reflection of himself.

3.3 *The Collapse of Narrative into Discourse*

The writer invents a space (a fictitious, fraudulent space, even) into which he inserts the language of his fiction. That space is the distance that always exists between a certain moment (place also) in the past (the far past) and another moment in the past (the near past)—or the present itself—into which the narrative unfolds. In traditional fiction that space is made as narrow as possible (as short as possible)—though it can never be abolished even if such writers as Beckett or Calvino have managed to close it almost to lessnessness—in order to prevent linearity and sequentiality. The wider the spatial/temporal space is the more coherent the narrative, and the narrower it is the more fragmented, incoherent, simultaneous, etc., the narrative (or what's left of it).
Raymond Federman, in a letter to the author of October 21, 1976

Between the two TEXT SPACES of a fiction—NARRATIVAL and NARRATIONAL—there normally exists a distance, temporal and frequently spatial, that serves to guarantee the reader that the experience being recounted is both managed and pregnant with significance. The use of the epic preterit as the primary verb tense constitutes the formal sign of this guarantee. In addition, in what have been termed "authorial" narrations, the space of the DISCOURSE exists as it were "above" the space of the fictional world, at a position of privilege. From a position above the world in which the characters live, the authorial persona is free to comment on their behavior, to pass judgment, to confide in his readership, and so on. In previous chapters of this text, I have discussed a number of possible transformations that can be worked upon this distance and the relationship of privilege.

A simple way to deprive DISCURSIVE SPACE of its inherent position of privilege is to make the speaker of the discourse one of the ACTANTS in the fictional field. This strategy in effect drops DISCURSIVE SPACE into the space of the fictional world. All discursive units belong not to an authorial persona but to one of the characters, and the enunciation partakes of the same degree of fictiveness as the other components of the narrative. In some instances of first-person narrative situation (see above, chapter 3), the enunciation of the actantial speaking subject takes precedence over the narrative that brings that enunciation into being (S_D-dominated first-person narratives as in some of Hawkes's recent fictions). It should be noted that in both of these transformations, there remains a distance (temporal/spatial) between the moment of the STORY and the moment of the DISCOURSE; the speaker speaks of events that have occurred sometime in the past, and the fact of "past-ness" guarantees to some extent their significance.

Clearly there remains another way to manage the distance between NARRATIVAL and NARRATIONAL space, and that consists in attempting to eliminate it, the story of the STORY becoming the story of the DISCOURSE.

Here is a sample of the way in which this sort of discourse generates itself in one of Federman's recent fictions:

> But in case you guys get confused in the course of this
> twin recitation with the me and the he
>   & the I and the He
>   & the me now and the he then
>   & the he past and the me present (he past in the hole
>   me present on the platform
> let me make it quite clear once and for all lest WE forget it
> (here & there & everywhere)
> I am here alone
>   He is there together we are
> as one are we not / multiple though single / I + HE = WE or
> WE - I = HE pluralized in our singularity
>   me telling him
>   him telling me   etc.
> thus again should you guys confuse me for him as I confuse
> myself with him and in him and vice versa let me assure you
> you may be confused or you may not even care.[37]

Federman's speaker eventually "resolves" the problem of the I and the HE by inventing a character named *Moinous*. Federman's point obviously has to do with the fact that the teller and the "hero" of first-person narratives are at once the same (they are, after all, the same character) and different (the former is presumably older and wiser than the latter).

A more dramatic example might be the ending of Sukenick's *98.6;* it consists in an extended litany built around the author's activity at that moment:

> AT THE SAME TIME my life is unravelling AT THE SAME TIME the novel
> is bundled fragments stitched together AT THE SAME TIME every-
> thing is seamless perfect not because because because but AT THE

SAME TIME playing the blues letting it go it is as it is. Another failure.[38]

In both instances the moment of the STORY gives way to the moment of the DISCOURSE as the fictionist in effect exposes the fraudulence of the illusion that anything exists beyond the act of enunciation. In this way he or she is able to explode the pretense of realism and in a sense to erase the world. The moment of the discourse is liberated from its subservience to an *a priori* "reality," and the fictionist is free to make it up as he goes; Frederick Barthelme discovers in this way that "writing a novel is easy" in *War and War.* Sukenick closes his novel *UP* with these words:

> I just make it up as I go along, the hell with it, I'm finishing today. Though it's all true what I've written, every word of it, I insist on that. . . . Maybe I better keep it up a while longer, what am I going to do when I'm done? No, impossible. It's dissolving into words, script on paper. (P. 329)

Not surprisingly, despite the fact that the speaker vows to finish, his words tend to proliferate themselves, and he mutters on for about a page. As one critic has noticed, "these writers demonstrate not, as do the fictions of the Flaubertians, how difficult it is to give rise to a single sentence, but rather how difficult it is to keep a torrent of sentences from giving rise to themselves."[39] The collapse of the narrative into the discourse, NARRATIVAL into NARRATIONAL SPACE, liberates the fictionist from the constrictions of mimesis and relieves him or her of the responsibilities that pertain to that asthetic code. The net result is a discourse that sprawls all over the page and reproduces itself almost endlessly, finding in its own articulations and processes a movable feast for the narrative imagination.

4. *Metafiction and the Reader*

The foregoing discussion of metafiction's treatment of TEXT SPACE reveals that metafiction establishes new relations with readers, that readers looking for a cooperative relation with the narrative speakers may well have their expectations frustrated. In traditional fiction, either authorial or first-person, the relation between speaker and reader is friendly and mutually satisfying; the speaker attempts to create a fictional community, welcoming readers into the domain of the narrative. In contemporary metafiction, the speaker sometimes treats the reader as an adversary and frequently preempts readerly activities. The speaker accomplishes this by occupying or overdetermining areas of signification that in traditional fiction "belong" to the reader. In so doing, the contemporary metafictionist calls into question or parodies the good intentions of the responsible reader.

4.1 *Speaker/Reader Dynamics in Contemporary Metafiction*

The reader! You, dogged, uninsultable print-oriented bastard, it's you I'm addressing, who else, from inside this monstrous fiction. You've read me this far, then? Even this far? For what discreditable motive? How is it you don't go to a movie, watch TV, stare at a wall, play tennis with a friend, make amorous advances to the person who comes to your mind when I speak of amorous advances? Can nothing surfeit, saturate you, turn you off? Where's your shame?

John Barth, "Life-Story," Lost in the Funhouse

From time to time the speaker of *Tristram Shandy* turns from the matter at hand to address the members of his reading audience personally. On occasion he even puts words in their mouths. "— How could you, Madam, be so inattentive in reading the last chapter? I told you in it, *That my mother was not a Papist.* —Papist! You told me no such thing, Sir. —Madam, I beg leave to repeat it over again, That I told you as plain, at least, as words, by direct inference, could tell you such a thing. —Then, Sir, I must have miss'd a page."[40] This kind of address establishes a certain type of relation between the speaker and the reader at the same time that it serves to enlarge the DISCURSIVE SPACE of the fiction. Although Tristram occasionally berates or castigates his readers, it is only in order that they might perform their readerly responsibilities more efficiently and promptly. Tristram tries to make his readers contributing members of a fictional community. This is the type of relation that all traditional fiction tries to establish between its readers and its texts, even when it does not address them personally. The fiction introduces its actants severally and gracefully, it situates and particularizes its milieus and settings, it provides adequate transitions from its narrative kernels; in these ways the reader is made to feel welcome within the boundaries of the text. Contemporary metafiction, like *Tristram Shandy* and other metafictions, similarly demonstrates its awareness of the reading audience by making discursive statements to them. But the relation it posits with its readers is not necessarily an amicable one, and frequently proves to be adversarial, as in the Barth passage excerpted above. The author reveals his awareness of the reader's culturally sanctioned role as receiver and interpreter of the fiction but seems to resent these responsibilities or at least the "space" that consequently devolves to the reader. The author thus resorts to a number of discursive devices to make fun of the reader and in effect to usurp the latter's prerogatives.

For one thing, the author resents the fact that the reader assumes the privilege of taking the words, kernels, and motifs of the text and assigning to them an extratextual meaning. Barthelme incorporates into his fiction *Snow White* (pp. 82–83) a questionnaire for his readers that parodies their hermeneutic activities. The questionnaire poses questions like "Has the work, for you, a metaphysical dimension?" and "Have you understood, in reading to this point, that Paul is the prince figure?"—questions that poke fun at the reader's search for significance at the same time as they preempt readerly responsibilities. In a bit of deliberate "play-giarism" Federman steals Barthelme's idea and inserts a questionnaire of his own in *Take It or Leave It* (no page); his questionnaire, which he invites the reader to clip out and mail to the publisher, includes questions like "Have you understood up to now that Moinous dead or alive is only a symbolic figure?" and "Is it clear that the journey is a metaphor for something else?" and closes with a series of questions that make fun of the notion of intertextuality:

P.S. Do you think all books should have such a QUESTIONNAIRE?

YES ( )   No ( )

And furthermore have you ever seen such a QUESTIONNAIRE?

YES ( )   No ( )

If so where?_____

The cumulative effect of such strategies is to jolt the reader out of his or her complacency and reinforce the postmodernist notion that the truth of the reading activity lies less in the "meaning" which the reader decodes than in the *jouissance* that he or she experiences. The pleasure is to be had not "by reading between the lines themselves (for there is nothing there, in

those white spaces) but by reading the lines themselves—
looking at them and so arriving at a feeling not of satisfaction
exactly, that is too much to expect, but of having read them, of
having 'completed' them" (Barthelme, *Snow White,* p. 106).

As noted above in chapter 3, paramodernist fictions tend to
demand from their readers slightly different activities from
modernist fictions; in particular, these fictions de-emphasize
hermeneutic activities in favor of a quest for a totality of vision.
The reader is invited to discover a principle of coherence for
the text, to assemble the text's disparate narrative segments.
The reader becomes the text's chief gap-filler and connection-
maker, a role especially to be valued because of its relevance to
the discontinuous nature of extratextual reality. Contemporary
metafiction makes fun of this readerly activity at the same time
as it makes the activity impossible. For example, George Chambers's *The Bonnyclabber* opens with a perfectly blank page
marked only by footnotes numbered 12 through 15 at the bottom.[41] The reader's first inclination is to attempt to reconstruct
the text that generated these (frequently interesting) footnotes,
and he or she might even underake the process of reconstruction before realizing how absurd the proposition is. Even when
the text proper begins, the reader is at a loss to discover any
kind of correspondence between the text and its footnotes. In
this way Chambers is able to ridicule the reader's pretensions to
gap-filling and to mock the convention of learned annotation.

Ronald Sukenick's novel *Out* (1973) consists entirely in relatively dissociated and distinct narrative segments. A reader
familiar with paramodernist literary techniques automatically
seeks out the underlying or informing shaping principle for the
fragmented narrative. The reader's enterprise becomes progressively more difficult as the fragments themselves tend to
dwindle and disappear. By the end of the text, the narrative
consists in a meager two or three lines of type that struggle
haltingly across the page. As the text dwindles away to silence,
the reader has no alternative but to follow suit. With texts as
fragmented and fragmentary as these, the reader has no recourse but to obey the "Mosaic Law" because the "novel is based
on the Mosaic Law the law of mosaics or how to deal with parts
in the absence of wholes" (Sukenick, 98.6, p. 167). Abandoning
obsolete notions to teleology, closure, and coherence, the
reader can "take greater pleasure in the fragment, revel in its
stupidity, its inconsequentiality, its mocking recalcitrance."[42]

"What reigns here is an indefinite addition but also no summation" (Federman, *Take It or Leave It,* "Pretext").

It should be clear from the foregoing that the various assaults on readerly prerogatives are predicated on a hyperawareness of the reader's presence within any narrative ontology. A narrative can come into full existence only if there is someone to receive it. Concomitantly, we can argue that the simple existence of a reader may precipitate a narrative from a storyteller. And if one reviles his or her tendency to fabricate stories, to narrate, because to narrate is to lie, then that reader may be held responsible for the narrative act, for the act could not exist, would not exist, if the reader did not exist (no narrative comes into full existence until the reader cooperates and *realizes* its language). Thus Barth pleads from within his fictions for the reader to put an end to the farce:

> Why has the author as it were ruthlessly set about not to win you over but to turn you away? Because your own author bless and damn you his life is in your hands! He writes and reads himself; don't you think he knows who gives his creatures their lives and deaths? Do they exist except as he or others read their words? Age except we turn their pages? And can he die until you have no more of him? . . . But as he longs to die and can't without your help you force him on, force him on. Will you deny you've read this sentence? This? . . . As if he'd know you killed him! Come on. He dares you.
> In vain. You haven't: the burden of his knowledge. That he continues means that he continues, a fortiori you too. Suicide's impossible: he can't kill himself without your help." (*Lost in the Funhouse,* p. 124)

If the terrible dilemma of our lives consists in knowing too much and living too little, in a paralyzing self-consciousness that makes unreflective and adjective existence impossible, then the root of the problem may be laid at the foot of the Other as *pour-soi,* and one solution might be the obliteration of the Other. Tongue firmly in cheek, contemporary metafiction carries out successive pogroms against its readers while spinning stories out of that program.

4.2 *Metafiction, Meaning, and the Critic*

If, as some maintain, ours is an age of criticism, then the first echelon of readers is made up of those professional interpreters, the critics. Contemporary metafiction is aware of the prestige accorded the critical activity and devotes some of its energies to debunking critical authority. One way to accomplish this end may be termed overinterpretation. The metafictionist incorporates within his fictional space so much evidence pointing at a particular reading that the reading is paradoxically invalidated; it becomes gratuitous, superfluous, or too easy. In Nabokov's *Lolita,* for example, the narrator, Humbert Humbert, dwells at such length on a traumatic childhood experience with obvious potential for psychic repercussions that the psychoanalytic reading of Humbert's unusual biography is preempted. That particular interpretation is at one and the same time too appropriate and inappropriate (perhaps because that reading is too available and the critical tradition prefers its meanings partially hidden.) Another overinterpretive technique of the metafictionist consists of the inclusion within the text of a number of possible readings and their variants. An example might be Barth's *Giles Goat-Boy,* in which the author makes good use of the fact that the story is predicated upon a pun that equates universe and university. In the course of his quest, Giles continually runs into academic types only too willing to subject his history and ambitions to the most pedantic forms of analysis. In this way a plenitude of possible critical readings work their way into the text as Barth attempts to eat the critics before they eat him. In either case, the author overinterprets the text beforehand and thus preempts the potential space of the critic.

Another technique designed to foil the critical activity consists in overt parody of the conventions or processes of criticism. Rovert Coover, for example, cleverly parodies the search for hidden significance in a short fiction entitled "Panel Game."[43] The central figure on a panel show is fed obscure clues that he feels he must decipher:

> So think. Stickleback. Freshwater fish. Freshwater fish: green sea man. Seaman: semen. Yes, but green: raw? spoiled? vigorous? Stickle: stubble. Or maybe scruple. Back: Bach: Bacchus: baccate: berry. Raw berry? Strawberry? Maybe. Sticky berry in the raw? In the raw: bare. Bare berry: beriberi. Also bearberry, the dog rose, dogberry. Dogberry: the constable, yes, right, the constable in . . . what? *Comedy of Errors!* Yes! No.

A similarly absurd concatenation of free associations for each of the other "clues" brings the contestant back again to Dogberry the constable, but he can never remember the correct play. And of course his convoluted acts of "reasoning" bring him to the correct "solution," even if he is unable to name it— *Much Ado About Nothing,* a phrase certainly meant to summarize Coover's opinion of the critical enterprise in general. The contestant fails to come up with the answer and swings from a rope at the end of the fiction.

A metafiction may also incorporate any number of *textes critiques,* drawn from real life or invented. In one of the latter sections of *Take It or Leave It* the present of the fiction (sometime in the early fifties) is invaded by a critic/hitchhiker from the 1970s (patterned after the "real-life" literary critic Campbell Tatham) who carries under his arm a dissertation on a literary figure named Hombre de la Plume (Feather Man), whose career just coincidentally recapitulates that of Raymond Federman. When the critic takes his leave, he just happens to steal the protagonist's wallet, but only after they have had a long conversation about the future of criticism and *écriture.* And Barth's *Chimera* contains a learned lecture that summarizes the course of his career and suggests the direction his future fiction will take. Perhaps the most notorious of the metafictions that incorporate *textes critiques* is Nabokov's *Pale Fire,* a novel consisting of a "definitive" edition of an extended poem about mortality in Wordsworthian style. The editor, a paranoid pedant named Kinbote who fancies himself the deposed king of a kingdom named Zembla, exploits the poem as an occasion to dwell on his ignominious and exotic past. In this way Nabokov exposes in a single stroke the pedantries and pretensions of the critical profession as well as its necessary parasitism and lack of objectivity (see also 3.2.4).

Confronted (insulted) by texts that in this way nullify, preempt, or ridicule the critical quest for meaning, the critic is forced to reexamine his assumptions and procedures. The texts demand other kinds of activities, other kinds of readings. In the end a metafiction attempts to establish new relations with "reality" and to create readers able to accommodate those new relations.

5. Posttext

The most important and insidious legacy of the New Criticism is the widespread and unquestioning acceptance of the notion that the critic's job is to interpret literary works.
  Jonathan Culler, "Beyond Interpretation: The Prospects of Contemporary Criticism"

A number of recent critical works have addressed the instrumentality of interpretation to critical practice. Even reader-response-oriented criticism tends to accept that the production of "readings" is the function of the processes it describes. Wolfgang Iser in *The Act of Reading*, for example, demonstrates the way in which a text's "perspectives" structure the reader's obligatory participation in the dynamics of meaning production.[44] Steven Mailloux, rejecting Iser's model as too text-centered, locates interpretive constraints in social reading models based on "traditional," "regulative," or "constitutive" conventions.[45] The debate revolves about the *how* and *where* of interpretation, the locus of interpretive constraints, rather than upon the possibility of interpretation.

Postmodernist texts, however, tend to call in question the very possibility of interpretation. They accomplish this end, in the main, by a systematic overdetermination of conventional narrative elements like plot, character, point of view, structure, and language, elements traditionally drawn upon to produce and substantiate interpretation. An overdetermined element has more than one determining narrative function, value, or factor, thus drawing attention to itself as a literary device while at the same time preempting at least one way to "read" it. It points to other signifiers rather than to structures of signifieds. The systematic deployment of such elements makes for a text that resists, defies, or ridicules interpretive activity.

In chapter 6 of *Interpretive Conventions*, Mailloux argues that "all interpretation is translation":

> we translate one meaning into another
> > one text into another
> > one phenomenon into another
> > one interpretation into another
> > one translation into another.[46]

He also notes that the word *interpretation* derives from the Latin *interpres*, meaning an agent who passes back and forth between two parties, an intermediary. Viewed in this light, interpretation can be seen as the ongoing activity of filling the gap between one text and another. In chapter 3, I showed how paramodernist works similarly required readers to fill in gaps in order to invest radically discontinuous texts with coherence. Reading a paramodernist text, then, can be seen as a variation of conventional interpretive practice; the gaps in this case infect the text itself, and the reading process involves not so much a search for a valid translation (the text of the real) as the creation of a seamless texture. Such is not the case with the postmodernist overdetermined text, which questions all models of *vraisemblance* and calls for novel readings. Mailloux notes that current literary theorists agree "that the reading conventions which constitute the 'set of acceptable or plausible readings' are always evolving."[47] That evolution is not dictated or directed by the reader but by culture-specific texts, which subvert or undermine regular conventions (interpretation as translation, gap-filling, assemblage) and therefore force new conventions to emerge. The conventions for "reading" a postmodernist text have yet to be codified or determined.

Notes

Pretext: The Relation of Fiction and Reality

1. W. J. Harvey summarizes the differences in the aesthetic assumptions and prac-
tices of the two critical theories in the first chapter and second appendix of his *Character
and the Novel* (Ithaca, N.Y.: Cornell University Press, 1965). Harvey, incidentally, admits
candidly in his first chapter that "in the last analysis I find myself firmly on the side of
mimesis" (p. 13). The term *basic narrative world* is borrowed from Lubomir Dolezel,
"Narrative Modalities," *Journal of Literary Semantics* 5 (April 1976):5–14.

2. Ortega y Gasset, *The Dehumanization of Art* (1925; reprint, Princeton, N.J.: Princeton University Press, 1948), p. 31.

3. "Sterne's *Tristram Shandy:* Stylistic Commentary," in *Russian Formalist Criticism: Four
Essays,* ed. Lemon and Reis (Lincoln: University of Nebraska Press, 1965), p. 57.

4. Raymond Federman, "Surfiction—Four Propositions in the Form of an Introduction," in *Surfiction,* ed. Raymond Federman (Chicago: Swallow Press, 1975), p. 8.

5. John Fowles, *The French Lieutenant's Woman* (1969; reprint, New York: New American Library, 1970), p. 81.

6. William Gass, *Fiction and the Figures of Life* (1971; reprint, New York: Vintage,
1972), p. 25.

7. Cited by Raymond Federman in "Surfiction—Four Propositions in the Form of an
Introduction," p. 5.

8. Cited by Robert Scholes in *The Fabulators* (New York: Oxford University Press,
1967), p. 137.

9. Robert M. Davis, ed., *The Novel: Modern Essays in Criticism* (Englewood Cliffs, N.J.:
Prentice-Hall, 1969), p. 140. See also Walter L. Reed, "The Problem with a Poetics of
the Novel," *Novel* 9 (Winter 1976): 101–13.

10. "Introduction to Reception Aesthetics," *New German Critique* 10 (Winter 1977):
62, 53, 56. See also David Bathrick, "The Politics of Reception Theory in the GDR,"
Minnesota Review 5 (Fall 1975): 125–33; Dieter Richter, "Teachers and Readers: Reading
Attitudes As a Problem in Teaching Literature," *New German Critique* 7 (Winter 1976):
21–43; and Robert Weimann, "French Structuralism and Literary History," *New Literary
History* 6 (Spring 1973): 437–69.

11. Vladimir Nabokov admits that he finds this word troublesome and insists that it
should always appear in quotation marks in "Vladimir Nabokov on a book entitled
Lolita," included as an afterword to *Lolita* (1955; reprint, New York: Berkley Medallion,
1966), p. 283.

12. Harvey, *Character and the Novel,* pp. 16ff.

13. Ibid., p. 24.

14. Ortega y Gasset, *Dehumanization of Art,* p. 171.

15. For an extended discussion of the literary process of foregrounding, see Jan
Mukarovsky, "Standard Language and Poetic Language," in *A Prague School Reader on*

196

Esthetics, Literary Structure, and Style, ed. Paul Garvin (Washington, D.C.: Georgetown University Press, 1964), pp. 17–30.

16. Georg Lukacs, *Realism in Our Time,* trans. John Necke Mander (New York: Harper and Row, 1962), pp. 24–26.

17. "The Novel Again," in Davis, ed., *The Novel: Modern Essays in Criticism,* p. 284.

18. Charles Aukema, from the bibliographical appendix to *Cutting Edges: Young American Fiction for the '70s,* ed. Jack Hicks (New York: Holt, Rinehart, and Winston, 1973), pp. 518–19.

19. Excerpts from Reeve's argument can be found in *Novelists on the Novel,* ed. Miriam Allott (New York: Columbia University Press, 1959), pp. 45, 47, 86–87.

20. Lukacs, *Realism in Our Time,* p. 19.

21. "Fiction, History, and Empirical Reality," *Critical Inquiry* 1 (December 1974), 336.

22. Federman, "Surfiction—Four Propositions in the Form of an Introduction," pp. 8–10.

23. Ronald Sukenick "The New Tradition in Fiction," in Ibid., p. 40.

24. The phrase is John Barth's, from *Lost in the Funhouse* (1968; reprint, New York: Bantam Books, 1969).

25. See, for example, Mas'ud Zavarzadeh, *The Mythopoeic Reality: The Postwar American Nonfiction Novel* (Urbana: University of Illinois Press, 1976), especially chap. 1.

26. Reprinted in *The American Novel Since World War II,* ed. Marcus Klein (Greenwich, Conn.: Fawcett, 1969), pp. 267–79.

27. Zavarzadeh, *Mythopoeic Reality,* chap. 2.

Chapter 1. A Theory of Fictional Space

1. Nathaniel Hawthorne, *The Scarlet Letter,* ed. Sculley Bradley et al. (New York: W. W. Norton, 1962), pp. 30–31. In the elaboration of this metaphor I am indebted to Terence Martin's discussions of Hawthorne's poetics. See, in particular, his "The Method of Hawthorne's Tales," in *Hawthorne Centenary Essays,* ed. R. H. Pearce (Columbus: Ohio State University Press, 1964), pp. 7–30; and his *Nathaniel Hawthorne* (New York: Twayne, 1965), especially chap. 2.

2. Cited by Martin, "The Method of Hawthorne's Tales," p. 17.

3. I am indebted in this paragraph to Joseph Kestner, *The Spatiality of the Novel* (Detroit, Mich.: Wayne State Univ. Press, 1978), pp. 113ff.; and W. J. J. Mitchell, "Spatial Form in Literature: Toward a General Theory," *Critical Inquiry* 6 (Spring 1980): 551ff. The quote from Genette can be found in Joseph Frank, "Spatial Form: Some Further Reflections," *Critical Inquiry* 5 (Winter 1978): 290.

4. Adam Smith, *Powers of Mind* (New York: Random, 1975), pp. 220–21.

5. Teun A. van Dijk, *Some Aspects of Text Grammars,* (The Hague: Mouton, 1972), p. 290. I am indebted here and in the analysis that follows to this text and to Benjamin Hrushovski, "The Structure of Semiotic Objects: A Three-Dimensional Model," *Poetics Today* 1, nos. 1–2 (Autumn 1979): 363–76; and Zavarzadeh, *Mythopoeic Reality,* chap. 2.

6. The discrimination here is clearly a matter of degree. Indeed, one can imagine constructing a typology of factual/counterfactual prose narratives based upon a description of the nature and kind of out-referential *FRs.*

7. Roger Fowler, *Linguistics and the Novel* (London: Methuen, 1977), p. 80.

8. Umberto Eco, *A Theory of Semiotics* (Bloomington: Indiana University Press, 1976), chap. 1.

9. Ibid., p. 62. One of the inherent weaknesses of criticism privileging the conventions of realism is that it sometimes falls prey to the referential fallacy.

10. Wayne Booth, *The Rhetoric of Fiction* (1961; reprint, Chicago: University of Chicago Press, 1964).

11. See, for example, Maurice Z. Shroder, "The Novel as a Genre," *Massachusetts Review* 4 (1963): 291–308.

12. Ralph Freedman, "The Possibility of a Theory of the Novel," in *The Disciplines of Criticism: Essays in Literary Theory, Interpretation and History,* ed. Peter DeMetz et al. (New Haven, Conn.: Yale University Press, 1968), pp. 57–77.

13. For summaries of the way in which Greimas uses the term *actant,* see Jonathan Culler, *Structuralist Poetics: Structuralism, Linguistics and the Study of Literature* (Ithaca, N.Y.: Cornell University Press, 1975), and Robert Scholes, *Structuralism in Literature: An Introduction* (New Haven, Conn.: Yale University Press, 1974). Mas'ud Zavarzadeh adopts the same term in *The Mythopoeic Reality.* Lotman uses the term *topoi* in a manner similar to mine in *The Structure of the Artistic Text,* trans. Ronald Vroon, Michigan Slavic Contributions no. 7 (Ann Arbor: University of Michigan Press, 1977), pp. 231ff.

14. Seymour Chatman, *Story and Discourse* (Ithaca, N.Y.: Cornell University Press, 1978), pp. 107ff. For an attempt at such an analysis, see Fernando Ferrara, "Theory and Model for the Structural Analysis of Fiction," *New Literary History* 5 (Winter 1974): 245–68. Joel Weinsheimer also deals with this problem in "Theory of Character: *Emma,*" *Poetics Today* 1, nos. 1–2 (Autumn 1979): 185–211.

15. Roland Barthes, *S/Z,* trans. Richard Miller (New York: Hill & Wang, 1974), p. 191.

16. Chatman, *Story and Discourse,* p. 46.

17. Chatman, although he adopts a structuralist methodology, rejects the possibility of a grammar of stories; "For the present, the notion that all narratives can be successfully grouped according to a few forms of plot-content seems to me highly questionable. Work should proceed genre by genre, for much is to be learned in comparing narratives from a content-formal point of view. We are not ready yet for a massive assault on the question of plot macrostructure and typology" (*Story and Discourse,* p. 95).

18. Claude Bremond, "The Logic of Narrative Possibilities," *New Literary History* 11 (Spring 1980): 390.

19. See, especially, Victor Shklovsky, "Sterne's *Tristram Shandy,*" in Lemon and Reis, pp. 25–57.

20. For "functional" analyses, see V. Propp, *Morphology of the Folktale,* trans. Lawrence Scott (Austin: University of Texas Press, 1968); A. J. Greimas, "Narrative Grammar: Units and Levels," *Modern Language Notes* 86 (December 1971): 793–806; and Bremond, "The Logic of Narrative Possibilities." See also Gerald Prince, *A Grammar of Stories* (The Hague: Mouton, 1973), and "Aspects of a Grammar of Narrative," *Poetics Today* 1, no. 3 (Spring 1980): 49–63; Lubomir Dolezel, "Narrative Modalities," *Journal of Literary Semantics* 5 (April 1976): 5–14, "Narrative Semantics," *PTL: A Journal of Descriptive Poetics and Theory of Literature* 1 (January 1976): 129–152, and "Narrative Worlds," in *Sound, Sign,* and *Meaning: Quinquagenary of the Prague Linguistic Circle,* ed. Ladislav Matejka, Michigan Slavic Contributions (Ann Arbor: University of Michigan Press, 1976), pp. 542–52; and Edward Kahn, "Finite-State Models of Plot Complexity," *Poetics* 9 (1973): 5–20. Kieran Egan attempts to define plot rigorously and explores its effects in "What Is Plot?" *New Literary History* 9 (Spring 1978): 455–73. See also Lotman, *The Structure of the Artistic Text,* pp. 231–34, and Teun van Dijik, *Some Aspects of Text Grammars* (The Hague: Mouton, 1972), pp. 293ff.

21. Barthes, *S/Z,* p. 30.

22. Egan, pp. 464ff. Scholes's argument can be found in *Structural Fabulation* (South Bend, Ind.: University of Notre Dame Press, 1975), esp. chaps. 1 and 2.

23. Steven Marcus, "The Novel Again," in *The Novel: Modern Essays in Criticism,* ed. Robert Murray Davis, p. 284.

24. For a brief summary of Benveniste's work and Todorov's and Barthes's appropriation thereof, see Culler, *Structuralist Poetics,* pp. 197–200. Seymour Chatman adopts the same terminology in *Story and Discourse.* Todorov gives his view of discourse in "Language and Literature" in *The Structuralist Controversy: The Languages of Criticism and the Sciences of Man,* ed. R. Macksey and E. Donato (Baltimore, Md.: Johns Hopkins University Press, 1970), pp. 125–133. And Roger Fowler provides a comprehensive overview of discourse in narrative in *Linguistics and the Novel,* chap. 4.

25. Barthes, *S/Z,* p. 156.

26. *A Poetics of Composition,* trans. V. Savarin and S. Wittig (Berkeley: University of California Press, 1973), pp. 85ff.

27. Barthes, *S/Z,* pp. 97–98. Roger Fowler examines this code in detail, especially the ways in which it conjoins textual and extratextual realities, in "Referential Code and Narrative Authority," *Language and Style* 10 (Summer 1977): 129–61.

28. Roland Barthes, "To Write: An Intransitive Verb?" in *The Structuralist Controversy,* p. 144.

29. Michael Holquist and Walter Reed, "Six Theses on the Novel—and Some Metaphors," *New Literary History* 11 (Spring 1980): 419.

30. Eco, *A Theory of Semiotics,* p. 268.

31. This passage is taken from a personal letter to me, dated October 21, 1976.

32. Edward Marcotte, "Intersticed Prose," *Chicago Review* 26, no. 4 (1975): 33.

33. Ibid., p. 34.

34. Roman Jakobson, "The Dominant," in *Readings in Russian Poetics,* ed. L. Matejka and K. Pomorsk (Cambridge, Mass.: MIT Press, 1971), p. 83.

35. Lubomir Dolezel, "The Typology of the Narrator: Point of View in Fiction," in *To Honor Roman Jakobson: Essays on the Occasion of His Seventieth Birthday* (The Hague: Mouton, 1967), 1:541–53. Gerard Genette takes a similar position in this regard. One critic summarizes Genette as follows: "The customary classification of narrators according to 'person' (first person, third person) is inadequate, since it makes variation depend on an element which is in fact invariant. In a nongrammatical sense, the presence of the narrator in his narrative, like the presence of any subject of the *énonciation* in his *énoncé,* can only be 'in the first person' "; Shlomith Rimmon, "A Comprehensive Theory of Narrative: Genette's *Figures III* and the Structuralist Study of Fiction," *PTL* 1 (1976): 54.

36. Jonathan Culler, "Making Sense," *Twentieth Century Studies* 12 (1974): 27–36.

37. The phrase is Menakhem Perry's, from "Literary Dynamics: How the Order of a Text Creates Its Meanings," *Poetics Today* 1, nos. 1-2 (Autumn 1979): 43. Cf. Todorov: "The image of the narrator is not a solitary image: when it appears on the first page, it is accompanied by what can be called 'the image of the reader' "; cited by Kestner, *The Spatiality of the Novel,* p. 154. Peter Rabinowitz examines the types of audience presupposed by a literary narrative in "Truth in Fiction: A Reexamination of Audiences," *Critical Inquiry* 4 (Autumn 1977): 121–41. I speak in my own discussion of what he calls the "authorial audience" (pp. 125ff.). This audience consists, not simply of a set of knowledge, beliefs, and familiarity with conventions as he argues, but also of a set of mental operations dictated by the horizon of expectations.

38. Culler, *Structuralist Poetics,* pp. 140–60.

39. Umberto Eco describes the process of recuperation in theoretical terms ("extensional operations" in a "still-bracketed possible world") in *The Role of the Reader: Explorations in the Semiotics of Texts* (Bloomington: Indiana University Press, 1979), esp. pp. 21ff.

Perry's essay (mentioned above) contains an exhaustive description of the process of reading Faulkner's "A Rose for Emily."

40. See Culler, *Structuralist Poetics*, pp. 79–95, for a summary of Greimas's work on structural semantics.

41. One can find all of these readings, and others, elaborated in *Twentieth Century Interpretations of* The Castle, ed. Peter F. Neumeyer (Englewood Cliffs, N.J.: Prentice Hall, 1969).

42. One might cite as examples the endings to "The Birthmark," "The Minister's Black Veil," and "Wakefield."

43. Wolfgang Iser, *The Implied Reader: Patterns of Communication in Prose Fiction from Bunyan to Beckett* (Baltimore, Md.: Johns Hopkins University Press, 1974), p. 32. The first two chapters, in particular, describe the new kinds of activities demanded from the reader by the Novel.

44. Culler, *Structuralist Poetics*, p. 143.

45. Both phrases are borrowed from Culler's "Making Sense," p. 35.

46. Barthes, *S/Z*, pp. 3–4.

47. For a thorough examination of totalization and the evolution of non-totalizing narrative, see Zavarzadeh, *Mythopoeic Reality*, chap. 1.

Chapter 2. The Evacuation of Fictional Space

1. Mas'ud Zavarzadeh, *Mythopoeic Reality*, p. vii.

2. For a helpful survey of various definitions of modernism, see the first three chapters of Monroe K. Spears, *Dionysus and the City* (New York: Oxford University Press, 1970).

3. These particular arguments are articulated, respectively, in the following texts: Leon Edel, *The Modern Psychological Novel* (1955; reprint, New York: Grosset & Dunlop, 1964); Percy Lubbock, *The Craft of Fiction* (1921; reprint, New York: Viking, 1957); Alan Friedman, *The Turn of the Novel* (London: Oxford University Press, 1966); David Daiches, *The Novel and the Modern World* (Chicago: University of Chicago Press, 1960); Irving Howe, "The Idea of the Modern," in *Literary Modernism*, ed. Irving Howe (Greenwich, Conn.: Fawcett, 1967), pp. 11–40; and Ortega y Gasset, *The Dehumanization of Art*.

4. See Victor Ehrlich, "Literary Dynamics," in *Russian Formalism: History—Doctrine*, pp. 251–71; and Jurij Tynjanov, "On Literary Evolution," in *Readings in Russian Poetics: Formalist and Structuralist Views*, pp. 66–78.

5. Cf. David Daiches in "What Was the Modern Novel?" *Critical Inquiry* 1 (June 1975): 819: "I think the ways in which the modern novel was related to the society of its time is a fascinating, complex, and challenging subject, on which much work still remains to be done."

6. The quote is, of course, from her famous essay "Mr. Bennet and Mrs. Brown," reprinted in any number of places. In the light of the notion that the observer interferes with the observed, it is interesting to note that Woolf is sometimes misquoted as saying "human *nature* changed." The statements are obviously not identical.

7. Cited in Daiches, *The Novel and the Modern World*, p. 3.

8. Robert Scholes, "The Illiberal Imagination," *New Literary History* 4 (Spring 1973): 526. For a similar view, see Stanislaw Eile, "The Novel as an Expression of the Writer's Vision of the World," trans. Teresa Halikowska-Smith, *New Literary History* 9 (Autumn 1977): 115–28.

9. "The Referential Code and Narrative Authority," p. 134.

10. Gustave Flaubert, in a letter to George Sand dated August 10, 1868, excerpted in *Novelists on the Novel,* ed. Miriam Allott (1959; reprint, New York: Columbia University Press, 1966), pp. 94, 274.

11. Daiches, *The Novel and the Modern World,* p. 4.

12. *The Rhetoric of Fiction,* p. 45.

13. "I feel myself show [ghosts] best by showing almost exclusively the way they are felt, by recognizing as their *main interest* some *impression strongly made by them* and intensely perceived." Preface to "Altar of the Dead," in *The Art of the Novel: Critical Prefaces,* ed. R. P. Blackmur (New York: Charles Scribner's Sons, 1962), p. 256.

14. Percy Lubbock, *The Craft of Fiction,* esp. pp. 156–71.

15. Christine Brooke-Rose, "The Squirm of the True: An Essay in Non-Methodology," *PTL: A Journal for Descriptive Poetics and Theory of Literature* 1 (1976): 265–94; "The Squirm of the True: A Structural Analysis of Henry James's *The Turn of the Screw*," *PTL* 1 (1976), 513–46; "Surface Structure in Narrative: The Squirm of the True, Part III," *PTL* 3 (1977): 517–62. Brooke-Rose addresses related matters in "Historical Genres/Theoretical Genres: A Discussion of Todorov on the Fantastic," *New Literary History* 8 (Autumn 1976): 145–58.

16. Brooke-Rose, "The Squirm of the True, Part I," 291–92. Shoshana Felman makes a similar argument in "Turning the Screw of Interpretation," *Yale French Studies* 55/56 (1977): 94–207.

17. Brooke-Rose, "The Squirm of the True, Part I," p. 268.

18. The following texts explicitly or implicitly discuss the text as fundamentally duplicitous: Shlomith Rimmon, *The Concept of Ambiguity—The Example of James* (Chicago: University of Chicago Press, 1977), chap. 5; H. Robert Huntley, "James' *The Turn of the Screw:* 'Its Fine Machinery,' " *American Imago* 34 (Fall 1977): 224–37; Peter Obuchowski, "Technique and Meaning in *The Turn of the Screw*," *College Language Association Journal* 21 (March 1978): 380–89; and Anthony J. Mazzella, "An Answer to the Mystery of *The Turn of the Screw*," *Studies in Short Fiction* 17 (Summer 1980): 327–34.

19. Cf. Uspensky's definition of a panchronic narrator in chapter 2 of *The Poetics of Composition.* A synchronic narrator is one who has evacuated portions of DISCURSIVE SPACE.

20. Richard Gullon, "On Space in the Novel," *Critical Inquiry* 2 (1975): 12.

21. Henry James, The Norton Critical Edition of *The Turn of the Screw,* ed. Robert Kimbrough (New York: Norton, 1966), p. 6. All further references will be to this edition and will be inserted parenthetically in the text.

22. For an interesting discussion of narrator's and author's metatext in *The Turn of the Screw,* see Brooke-Rose, "The Squirm of the True, Part III."

23. Interpretations of the governess as "author" can be found in E. C. Curtsinger, "*The Turn of the Screw* as Writer's Parable," *Studies in the Novel* 12 (Winter 1980): 344–58; and Edwin Fussell, "The Ontology of *The Turn of the Screw*," *Journal of Modern Literature* 8 (1980): 118–28.

24. Compare, for example, the ending to another tale with a framing device written at about the same time, Conrad's "Heart of Darkness." Here the nameless narrator returns at the end of Marlow's story for this brief authenticating coda: "The offing was barred by a blank bank of clouds, and the tranquil waterway leading to the uttermost ends of the earth flowed under an overcast sky—seemed to lead into the heart of an immense darkness."

25. Obuchowski, "Technique and Meaning in *The Turn of the Screw*," p. 384.

26. Preface to *The Awkward Age* (1899; reprinted, Middlesex, Eng.: Penguin, 1972), p. 18. All subsequent references will be to this edition. The analysis that follows de-

scribes the "shape" of *The Awkward Age.* An exemplary interpretation of the novel can be found in Tzvetan Todorov, "The Verbal Age," *Critical Inquiry* 4 (Winter 1977): 351–71.

27. The letter, dated August 14, 1912, is excerpted in the Norton Critical Edition of *The Ambassadors,* ed. S. P. Rosenbaum (New York: W. W. Norton, 1964), p. 409. This edition of the text will be used in the analysis that follows. The phrase *stuff of drama* is taken from the preface to the novel, Norton Critical Edition, p. 12.

28. Henry James, "Preface to *The Golden Bowl,*" in *Novelists on the Novel,* ed. Miriam Allot, p. 265. James's prefaces and critical writings have been reprinted and excerpted in numerous places. A handy collection of his critical texts, noteworthy both for its organizational principle (arranged according to subject matter) and for its completeness, is *Theory of Fiction: Henry James,* ed. James E. Miller (Lincoln: University of Nebraska Press, 1972).

29. Many critics have commented on this aspect of the novel. Cf. "Nothing in the scene has any importance, any value in itself; what Strether sees in it—that is the whole of its meaning. . . . Strether's mind is dramatized," Percy Lubbock, *The Craft of Fiction,* pp. 161–2. "What Strether *sees* is the entire content, and James thus perfected a device both for framing and for interpreting experience," F. O. Mathieson, *Henry James: The Major Phase* (New York: Oxford University Press, 1944), p. 22. "It is the *seeing* that is the subject of the novel, perception at the pitch of awareness," Leon Edel, from an "Introduction," rpt. in the Norton Critical Edition, p. 441. The use of vision as a recurrent motif in the novel, one signifying at once the act of perception and the process of interpretation, has often been noticed by critics.

30. See Percy Lubbock, *The Craft of Fiction,* p. 40; John E. Tilford, Jr., "James the Old Intruder," *Modern Fiction Studies,* 4 (Summer 1958): 157–64; and William Thomas, "The Author's Voice in *The Ambassadors,*" *Journal of Narrative Technique* 1 (1971): 108–21.

31. Franz Stanzel, *Narrative Situations in the Novel,* trans. James P. Pusack (Bloomington: Indiana University Press, 1971). Stanislaw Eile refers to this type of narrational situation as "personal" in "The Novel as an Expression of the Writer's Vision of the World," *New Literary History* 9 (Autumn 1977): 115–28. Such nomenclature is preferable to an oxymoron like "limited omniscience."

32. Christof Wegelin, "The Lesson of Social Beauty," in the Norton Critical Edition, p. 455.

33. For a sample of various critical readings and a summary of major areas of controversy (for example, the "meaning" of Paris, or Strether's "retreat" at the end of the novel), see *Twentieth-Century Interpretations of* The Ambassadors, ed. Albert E. Stone (Englewood Cliffs, N.J.: Prentice Hall, 1969).

34. Cf. James's comment in the preface, p. 3: "he would have . . . imagination galore. . . . It was immeasurable, the opportunity to 'do' a man of imagination." And at several places in the novel (e.g., pp. 290, 299), Strether's wealth of imagination is made much of.

35. James describes the experience as follows in the "Project" for the novel, Norton Critical Edition, p. 389: "Well, he finds himself sinking, as I say, up to the middle in the Difference—difference from what he expected, difference in Chad, difference in everything, and the Difference . . . is what I give."

36. Several critics have offered readings similar to this, if not quite expressed in the same terms. See William Veeder, "Strether and the Transcendence of Language," *Modern Philology* 69 (1971): 116–32; Ronald Wallace, "Comic Form in *The Ambassadors,*" *Genre* 5, 1 (March 1972): 31–50; and Joseph Warren Beach, *The Method of Henry James,* excerpted in the Norton Critical Edition, pp. 439–40.

37. This reading of the novel—the novel as a series of "readings"—is supported by

certain metatextual references within the text. Strether at one point realizes that the "facts" of Paris might not suit his own book (p. 107). Bilham refers to Chad as a book to be read (p. 111), and Strether at one point fancies Mme. de Vionnet to be the "heroine of an old story." The climax of the book, the chance meeting with Chad and Mme. de Vionnet in the countryside, is loaded with metatextual references (e.g., the episode is "queer as fiction, as farce.")

38. Cf. James's comments in his "Project," p. 384: "His judgments, conclusions, discriminations are more or less in solution—in the pot, on the fire, stewing and simmering again, waiting to come up with what will be doubtless new combinations." And, p. 388, "everything is altered for him by the fact that nothing, damn it, is as simple as his scheme."

39. At one point he feels that he has made a breakthrough in that he has identified the true object of Chad's affections: "It's the child!" he exclaims to Maria Gostrey (p. 136). Her ironic rejoinder consists in the announcement that she is leaving town.

40. Cf. E. M. Forster, *Aspects of the Novel* (1927; reprinted, New York: Harcourt Brace, 1955), p. 159: "[Strether] has gone on. The Paris [that Chad and Mme. de Vionnet] revealed to him—he could reveal it to them now, if they had eyes to see, for it is something finer than they could ever notice themselves, and his imagination has more spiritual value than their youth."

41. T. S. Eliot, "from 'Henry James,'" in *Selected Prose of T. S. Eliot,* ed. Frank Kermode (New York: Harcourt Brace Jovanovich, 1975), pp. 151–2.

42. William Gass, "Gertrude Stein: Her Escape from Protective Language," in *Fiction and the Figures of Life*, pp. 79–96; "Gertrude Stein and the Geography of the Sentence," in *The World within the Word* (New York: Alfred A. Knopf, 1978), pp. 63–123.

43. Gass, *Fiction and the Figures of Life*, p. 92.

44. There has been some critical disagreement as to "voice" in "Melanctha," disagreement as to the presence or absence of a speaking subject. Copeland, perhaps misled by Stein's admission that she had been reading and admiring Flaubert, argues that *Three Lives* employs narrators who are not at all "obtrusive"; who refuse to focus on the inner life of any central intelligence; and who have not the unlimited knowledge of human behavior of the narrator of *Q. E. D.* Critics like Michael Hoffman and Norman Weinstein, on the other hand, are impressed by the overweening presence of the narrator in the enunciation of the story. Weinstein speaks of the "active author intervention in the narrative flow." Even a casual perusal of the text reveals that Copeland is making it over into something that adheres to her understanding of the modernist aesthetic. See Carolyn Copeland, *Language and Time and Gertrude Stein,* pp. 19ff.; Michael Hoffman, *Gertrude Stein* (London: Twayne, 1976); and Norman Weinstein, *Gertrude Stein and the Literature of Modern Consciousness* (New York: Frederick Ungar, 1970), p. 18.

45. All page references are to Gertrude Stein, *Three Lives* (1909; reprinted, New York: Vintage Books, 1936).

46. Other than the reiterated statements about black culture and personality, one finds only two other instances of ideological intrusion—a summary statement about the need for young girls to "escape" (p. 96), and a somewhat disconcerting "essay" of two paragraphs contrasting "tenderhearted" and "passionate" natures (pp. 186–7). One should compare the number of "truth statements" in "Melanctha" with the number in "The Gentle Anna," where the narrator speaks confidently about the effects of spring air (p. 28), the ways in which the passions show themselves (p. 29), the nature of large women (p. 29), and the complexion of working women (p. 31), all in the space of a few pages.

47. The test consists almost entirely of dialogue, reported dialogue, and perceptual

statements. Event statements are kept to a minimum, as reflected in the relative plot-lessness of the story.

48. Marjorie Perloff makes a similar point in "Poetry as Word-System: The Art of Gertrude Stein," *American Poetry Review* 8, no. 5 (1979): 37–8.

49. Reid Maynard, "Abstractionism in *Three Lives*," *Ball State University Forum* 13, no. 1 (1972): 69.

50. Donald Sutherland, *Gertrude Stein: A Biography of Her Work* (New Haven, Conn.: Yale University Press, 1951), p. 11.

51. Gertrude Stein, *Narration* (Chicago: University of Chicago Press, 1935), p. 25.

52. Ibid.

53. Stein, cited in Tony Tanner, *The Reign of Wonder: Naivety and Reality in American Literature* (1965; reprinted, Cambridge: Cambridge University Press, 1977), p. 193. Tanner provides a good general overview of the purposes behind the creation of a "complete and actual present," pp. 187–204.

54. In *Gertrude Stein: Writings and Lectures, 1911–1945,* ed. Patricia Meyerowitz (London: Peter Owen, 1967), pp. 21–30.

55. Stein, *Narration*, p. 22.

56. Stein, cited in Tanner, *The Reign of Wonder*, p. 193.

57. Gass, *The World within the Word*, p. 69.

58. Stein, *Narration*, p. vi.

59. Both quotes are from Perloff, pp. 35, 40.

60. For a helpful collection of Faulkner's disparate remarks on the novel, see "Faulkner Discusses *The Sound and the Fury*," in *Twentieth Century Interpretations of* The Sound and the Fury, ed. Michael H. Cowan (Englewood Cliffs, N.J.: Prentice-Hall, 1968), pp. 14–24.

61. See *Lion in the Garden: Interviews with William Faulkner, 1926–1962*, ed. James B. Meriwether and Michael Millgate (New York: Random House, 1968), pp. 146–7.

62. Cited in André Bleikasten, *The Most Splendid Failure: Faulkner's* The Sound and the Fury (Bloomington: Indiana University Press, 1976), p. 46. Bleikasten's book-length study is the most comprehensive work to date and contains a very helpful bibliography for the text. This book is particularly indebted to his analysis of the significance of Caddy for the novel.

63. Bleikasten, *Most Splendid Failure*, p. 53.

64. In *Twentieth Century Interpretations of* The Sound and the Fury, p. 18.

65. William Faulkner, *The Sound and the Fury* (1929; reprint, New York: Random House, 1946). All further references will be to this edition of the text.

66. Wolfgang Iser, *The Implied Reader* (Baltimore, Md.: Johns Hopkins University Press, 1974), p. 156.

67. The corresponding predicates for ordinary first person would be [+ DISCURSIVE] and [+ ULTERIOR]; the speaker knowingly discourses with someone about events that have happened sometime in the past.

68. The enunciation of Jason differs substantially from those of his brothers. His section introduces a degree of movement from the private heterocosm to the public arena, both in form and content. Giving readers the portrait of a "man of action" trying to make the world conform with his preconceived ideas, the section takes the form of a dramatic monologue, complete with awareness on Jason's part of the fact of speech ("Once a bitch always a bitch, *what I say. I says* you're lucky if . . ." p. 223, emphasis added). Since Jason is not addressing anyone in particular, it seems as if his discourse were aimed directly at the reader, as if Jason were attempting to create a community of himself and the reader.

69. Boris Uspensky, *A Poetics of Composition*, pp. 85ff.

70. For a similar argument, see Margaret Blanchard, "The Rhetoric of Communion: Voice in *The Sound and the Fury*," *American Literature* 41 (1970): 555–65.

71. Witness Edmund Volpe's reconstruction of *fabula* from *sujet* for Benjy's and Quentin's sections in *Twentieth Century Interpretations of* The Sound and the Fury, pp. 103–8.

72. Catherine B. Baum, " 'The Beautiful One': Caddy Compson as Heroine of *The Sound and the Fury*," *Modern Fiction Studies* 13 (Spring 1967): 33–44.

73. Interestingly enough, one may group the major sets of interpretations of the novel according to whether they emphasize the diachronic or the synchronic axis. The former group generally sees the novel as a negative Bildungsroman charting the psychological and social disintegration of a representative Southern family. The latter generally views it as an ironic quest (or *re*-quest) for that which is absent, the absence being defined in any number of ways.

74. See Carvel Collins, "Christian and Freudian Structures," excerpted in *Twentieth Century Interpretations of* The Sound and the Fury, pp. 71–74.

75. Iser, *The Implied Reader*, pp. 136–51.

76. Arnheim, "A Stricture on Space and Time," 654–55.

77. R. W. Franklin, "Narrative Management in *As I Lay Dying*," *Modern Fiction Studies* 13 (Spring 1967): 58.

78. The phrase belongs to André Bleikasten, *"Faulkner's* As I Lay Dying," trans. Roger Little with the author (Bloomington: Indiana University Press, 1973), p. 51. Bleikasten's full-length work, though now eight years old, is still the most comprehensive treatment of the novel, and this essay is indebted to it for insights and arguments. Calvin Bedient has also argued of *As I Lay Dying* that "it is essentially spectacle" in "Pride and Nakedness: *As I Lay Dying*," *Modern Language Quarterly* 29 (March 1968): 62.

79. The transformation of time into space is reflected in one of Darl's musings at the river crossing: "It is as though time, no longer running straight before us in a diminishing line, now runs parallel between us like a looping string, the distance being the doubling accretion of the thread and not the interval between" (p. 139). All references are to William Faulkner, *As I Lay Dying* (1930; reprint, New York: Vintage, 1964).

80. Bedient, p. 62. Bedient's insight into the novel does not prevent him from providing his own "explanation" of its meaning.

81. One might mention here the tendency of many of the characters, especially Darl, to render experience statically, as a series of framed snapshots. See, for example, Darl's description of the burning of Gillespie's barn (pp. 208–12).

Chapter 3. Making Room for the Reader

1. Remember Frederick Henry's words in Hemingway's *A Farewell to Arms:* "I was always embarrassed by the words sacred, glorious, sacrifice, and the expression in vain. . . . I had seen nothing sacred, and the things that were glorious had no glory and the sacrifices were like the stockyards at Chicago if nothing was done to the meat except bury it. There were many words that you could not stand to hear and finally only the names of places had dignity. Certain numbers were the same way and certain dates and these with the names of the places were all you could say and have them mean anything. Abstract words such as glory, honor, courage, or hallow were obscene beside the concrete names of villages, the numbers of roads, the names of rivers, the numbers of regiments and the dates."

2. Jean-Marie Benoist, "The Fictional Subject," *Twentieth Century Studies* 6 (1971): 92.

3. Zavarzadeh has coined the term *paramodernism* to refer to works that share the modernist aesthetic but modify or extend modernist technique or practice. See the first chapter of *The Mythopoeic Reality*.

4. Eco, "The Poetics of the Open Work," p. 9.

5. *The Structure of the Artistic Text*, pp. 229–30.

6. Quoted by Sharon Spencer in *Space, Time and Structure in the Modernist Novel* (Chicago: Swallow, 1971), p. 59.

7. For a discussion of Miss Lonelyhearts as cartoon, see Nancy W. Hard, "A Novel in the Form of a Comic Strip: Nathanael West's *Miss Lonelyhearts*," *Serif* 5 (1968): 14–21. See also Deborah Wyrick, "Dadaist Collage Structure and Nathanael West's *The Dream Life of Balso Snell*," *Studies in the Novel* 11 (Fall 1979): 349–59.

8. Quoted by Spencer in *Space, Time and Structure*, p. 56.

9. The ideas, terms, and some of the phrasing are borrowed from Zavarzadeh, *Mythopoeic Reality*, pp. 55ff.

10. Zavarzadeh, *Mythopoeic Reality*, p. 58.

11. Harold Rosenberg, *Art on the Edge* (London: Secker and Warburg, 1976), pp. 173–80.

12. Lotman, *The Structure of the Artistic Text*, p. 283.

13. Tzvetan Todorov, "The Verbal Age," *Critical Inquiry* 4 (Winter 1977): 351–71.

14. Ernest Hemingway, "Hills like White Elephants," in *The Short Stories of Ernest Hemingway* (New York: Charles Scribner's Sons, 1966), p. 273.

15. Henry James, *The Awkward Age* (1899; reprint, London: Penguin Books, 1972), p. 136.

16. Hemingway, "Hills like White Elephants," p. 273.

17. James, *The Awkward Age*, p. 285.

18. No title, *New York Times Book Review*, December 5, 1976, p. 102.

19. Susan Strehle Klemtner, "'For a Very Small Audience': The Fiction of William Gaddis," *Critique* 19, no. 3 (1978): 61.

20. William Gaddis, *JR* (New York: Alfred A. Knopf, 1975), p. 25. All further references will be to this edition of the text.

21. Jack Gibbs, liberal humanist and alcoholic, satirizes Mr. Whiteback's penchant for educational jargon as follows: "—In simple straightforward terms Dan, you might say that he structured the material in terms of the ongoing situation to tangibilitate the utilization potential of this one to one instructional medium in such a meaningful learning experience that those kids won't forget it for a hell of a long time, how's that Whiteback" (p. 47).

22. The places where the narrative skips over several days are frequently even trickier to decode. For example, the amount of time devoted to Norman Angel's business trip, an indeterminate period of about a week, is suggested by a series of interpolated weather reports, each of which announces the daily weather, and by the significant phrase *voices meeting and parting* (p. 155).

23. Cf. a comment by Jack Gibbs to Amy Joubert, p. 496: "—I mean sometimes there are situations that just don't seem to have any solution in their own context, do you see what I mean? And the only way to, the only way to do is to step in and change the whole context."

24. Klemtner summarizes some of the thematic import of those failures in "'For a Very Small Audience,'" pp. 61–73.

25. Coach Vogel's entire educational program consists in likening the human body to a machine, p. 29: "—that we call energy. Doing a regular day's work, this human machine needs enough fuel equal to about two pounds of sugar."

26. Oliver Evans, *Anaïs Nin* (Carbondale: Southern Illinois University Press, 1968),

p. 178. Bettina L. Knapp also refers to the text as "a collection of portraits, short stories, and novellas" in *Anaïs Nin* (New York: Frederick Ungar, 1978), pp. viii, 18.

27. Anaïs Nin, *Collages* (Chicago: Swallow, 1964), p. 7. All further references will be to this edition. This passage, by the way, introduces the motif of transformation, which is to become the major thematic chord of the text.

28. Cf. Jonathan Culler in *Structuralist Poetics*, p. 222: "The reader must organize the plot as a passage from one state to another and this passage or movement must be such that it serves as a representation of theme. The end must be made a transformation of the beginning so that meaning can be drawn from the perception of resemblance and difference."

29. Barbara Hernstein-Smith uses this term in a similar fashion in *Poetic Closure: A Study of How Poems End* (Chicago: University of Chicago Press, 1968), chap. 3.

30. Nin discusses the symbolic import of this quality in *The Novel of the Future* (New York: Collier, 1968), pp. 29–31.

31. Ibid., p. 130.

32. Ibid., p. 128.

33. Ibid., pp. 84–85.

34. Murray Krieger, "Fiction, History, and Reality," *Critical Inquiry* 1 (1974): 344.

35. For a more thorough discussion of modes of referentiality, see Zavarzadeh, *The Mythopoeic Reality*, pp. 54ff.

36. Alfred Kazin, "Introduction," to John Dos Passos, *U.S.A.* (1930; 1932; 1936; reprint, New York; New American Library, 1969), p. xv. All further references will be to this edition and will be identified parenthetically within the text by volume title and page number.

37. *John Dos Passos* (New York: Twayne, 1961), p. 154.

38. Cf. Charles Marz, "*U.S.A.*: Chronicle and Performance," *Modern Fiction Studies* 26 (Autumn 1980): 399: "The trilogy is not held together by any chain of events or 'storyline'; it must be apprehended spatially and not sequentially. Sequence yields to a structure characterized by the juxtaposition of disconnected and often incompatible word blocks."

39. Quoted by Sharon Spencer, *Space, Time and Structure in the Modern Novel*, p. 114.

40. Marz, "Dos Passos's Newsreels: The Noise of History," *Studies in the Novel* 11 (Summer 1979): 198.

41. For example, Blanche Gelfant, in "The Fulfillment of Form in *U.S.A.*," reprinted in *The Merrill Studies in* U.S.A., ed. David Sanders (Columbus, Ohio: Charles E. Merrill, 1972), writes: "Dos Passos's purpose is to achieve the highest degree of objectivity by withdrawing himself as narrator and allowing the characters to be the medium through which their stories achieve expression. . . . The evidence of the outside personality of the creator has been obliterated" (pp. 53–54).

42. Jean-Paul Sartre, "John Dos Passos and *1919*," reprinted in *Studies in* U.S.A., pp. 30–37.

43. Cf. Dos Passos's comments in the speech quoted by Chametzky, "Reflections on *U.S.A.*" in *Studies in* U.S.A., p. 62: "The novelist has to use all the little stories people tell about themselves, all the little dramas in other people's lives he gets glimpses of without knowing just what will come after, the fragments of talk he overhears on the subway or on the streetcar, the letter he picks up on the street addressed from one unknown character to another, the words on a scrap of paper found in a trashbasket, the occasional vistas of reality that flash from the mechanical diction of newspaper reports— these are the raw materials the *chronicles* of your own time are made up of" (emphasis added).

44. Barbara Foley, "From *U.S.A.* to *Ragtime:* Notes on the Form of Historical Con-

sciousness in Modern Fiction," *American Literature* 50 (March 1978): 93. She makes a similar point in "The Treatment of Time in *The Big Money:* An Examination of Ideology and Literary Form," *Modern Fiction Studies* 26 (Autumn 1980): 460ff.

45. One would suspect that Dos Passos is indebted to the example of Joyce's *A Portrait of the Artist as a Young Man* here. Donald Pizer analyzes the Camera Eye sections as a "story of maturation" in "The Camera Eye in *U.S.A.:* The Sexual Center," *Modern Fiction Studies* 26 (Autumn 1980): 417–30.

46. Harry Levin notes that in a letter to Malcolm Cowley Dos Passos promised "a certain amount of statement in the later Camera Eyes" in "Revisiting Dos Passos' *U.S.A.,*" *Massachusetts Review* 20 (Autumn 1979): 414.

47. See, for example, George Knox, "Voice in the *U.S.A.* Biographies," *Texas Studies in Language and Literature* 4 (1962): 109–16.

48. In the speech quoted by Chametzky, "Reflections on *U.S.A.,*" p. 62.

49. Malcolm Cowley says, in this respect, "I have heard Dos Passos violently attacked on the ground that all these devices—Newsreels and Biographies and the Camera Eye—were presented arbitrarily, without relation to the rest of the novel. The attack is partly justified as regards 'The 42nd Parallel.' . . . But when we come to '1919' connections . . . are so frequent and obvious that even a careless reader could not miss them; and in 'The Big Money' all the technical devices are used to enforce the same mood and the same leading ideas." In "The End of a Trilogy," reprinted in *Studies in* U.S.A., p. 6.

50. For a similar argument, see John P. Diggins, "Visions of Chaos and Visions of Order: Dos Passos as Historian," *American Literature* 46 (1974): 329–46.

51. Lois Hughson also locates the ultimate meaning of *U.S.A.* in the "community of readers" in "Dos Passos's World War: Narrative Technique and History," *Studies in the Novel* 12 (Spring 1980): 46–61.

52. *The Blood Oranges* and other Hawkes fictions also qualify here. I am working with *Second Skin* because it is probably Hawkes's best-known piece and because it is such a good example of S_S-dominated first-person narration.

53. Robert Scholes, "John Hawkes," an interview in *The New Fiction: Interviews with Innovative American Writers,* ed. Joe David Bellamy (Urbana: University of Illinois Press, 1974), pp. 98, 99.

54. Textual evidence would seem to indicate that, at least according to conventional models of *vraisemblance,* Skipper fabricates a considerable portion of his story, particularly the parts dealing with his tropical island. He says of this locale that "it *is* a wandering island, of course, unlocated in space and quite out of time," and that "apparently our wandering island has become quite invisible": *Second Skin* (New York: New Directions, 1963), pp. 46, 109. All further references will be to this edition of the text. Hawkes has also said of *Second Skin* that "the fiction becomes totally a world of the imagination toward the end of the novel"; in "Response to Ron Imhof," *Mosaic* 8, no. 1 (Fall 1974): 63.

55. "Response to Richard Yarborough," *Mosaic* 8, no. 1 (Fall 1974): 74.

56. Culler, *Structuralist Poetics,* pp. 140ff.

57. See John Hawkes, *"The Floating Opera* and *Second Skin," Mosaic* 8, no. 1 (Fall 1974): 17–18; and his "Response to Ron Imhof," same issue, p. 63.

58. John Kuehl and John Hawkes, "Interview," in John Kuehl, *John Hawkes and the Craft of Conflict* (New Brunswick, N.J.: Rutgers University Press, 1975), p. 181.

59. Tanner, *City of Words* (New York: Harper and Row, 1971), p. 228. In this regard, the "easy" symbolism of the book—the antithetical islands, the demonic figures, the mythographical names, the overt literary allusions—should be taken not as a sign of underlying meaning but as additional (ironic?) evidence of Skipper's mythographic and literary powers.

60. David Lodge, "Objections to William Burroughs," *Critical Quarterly* 8 (Autumn 1966): 208. Another critic has said of the text that *"Naked Lunch* could hardly be more obscure than it seems"; R. G. Peterson, "A Picture Is a Fact: Wittgenstein and *Naked Lunch,"* *Twentieth Century Literature* 12 (July 1966): 78.

61. For example, Lodge remarks of a passage taken from *Naked Lunch,* "What is signally lacking in the Burroughs passage is continuity" (p. 209). Lodge goes on to condemn *Naked Lunch* as meaningless because "in the verbal medium meaning *is* continuity: discrete particulars are meaningless." The identification of meaning and continuity is a common prejudice in the criticism of fiction.

62. William Burroughs, *Naked Lunch* (1959; reprint, New York: Grove, 1966), p. 218. All further references will be to this edition of the text.

63. It is useful to compare *Naked Lunch* with *Collages* in this regard. Incidentally, at least one critic relies on the Lee sections to construct for *Naked Lunch* something approaching a coherent plot, not surprisingly modeled on the mythic quest: William Shull, "The Quest and the Question: Cosmology and Myth in the Work of William Burroughs, 1953–1960," *Twentieth Century Literature* 24 (Summer 1978): 225–42.

64. Other examples of sustained "junk vision" can be found on pp. 53–54, 93–96, 198–99, 207–9.

65. Tanner, *City of Words,* p. 114.

66. Mary McCarthy, "Burroughs' *Naked Lunch,"* *Encounter* 20, no. 4 (April 1963): 92–98.

67. Frank D. McConnell's opinion in this regard is typical: "The leitmotif of our new youth may or may not be a euphoric celebration of no-content, but this is certainly not the message of *Naked Lunch,* which shouts from every page the horror of vacuity and the terrible necessity for the rebirth of the will"; in "William Burroughs and the Literature of Addiction," *Massachusetts Review* 8 (Autumn 1967): 666.

68. Cary Nelson, *The Incarnate Word: Literature as Verbal Space* (Urbana: University of Illinois Press, 1973), p. 222.

69. This realization is, of course, implicit in the method of *Naked Lunch.* Writing texts is a form of "sending" after all, and sending is the most pernicious addiction of all: "Some maudlin citizens will think that they can send something edifying, not realizing that sending *is* evil. Scientists will say, 'Sending is like atomic power. . . . If properly harnessed.' Artists will confuse sending with creation. They will camp around screeching 'A new medium' until their rating drops off. . . . Philosophers will bat around the ends and means hassle not knowing that *sending can never be a means to anything but more sending, like Junk"* (p. 168).

70. William Burroughs and Brion Gysin, *The Exterminator* (n. p.: Auerbahn Press, 1960), p. 5. All further references will be to this edition of the text.

71. In *The Paris Review Interviews,* 3d series, p. 157.

72. Tanner, *City of Words,* p. 130.

73. Burroughs, *The Paris Review Interviews,* 3d series, p. 157.

Chapter 4. Dis-Easy Peace

1. Robert Scholes, "Metafiction," *Iowa Review* 1 (1970): 100–115.

2. Christine Brooke-Rose, "The Squirm of the True, Part III," *PTL* 3 (1977): 517–62.

3. Ibid., p. 538.

4. Ibid., pp. 521–22.

5. Booth, *The Rhetoric of Fiction,* pp. 138, 155.

6. Charles Altieri, "The Qualities of Action: A Theory of Middles in Literature," *boundary 2* 5 (1977): 333.

7. Empson, *Some Versions of Pastoral* (London: Chatto and Windus, 1950), p. 52.

8. The phrase belongs to the Stanislaw Eile, "The Novel as an Expression of the Writer's Vision of the World," p. 119.

9. Charles Russell, "Individual Voice in the Collective Discourse: Literary Innovation in Postmodern American Fiction," *Sub-Stance* 27 (1980): 38.

10. Roland Barthes, "The Death of the Author," in *The Discontinuous Universe*, ed. Sallie Sears and Georgianna Lord (New York: Basic Books, 1972), p. 111.

11. Tony Tanner, *The City of Words*, p. 248.

12. Cited by Robert Scholes, *The Fabulators* (New York: Oxford University Press, 1967), p. 137.

13. John Barth, *Lost in the Funhouse* (1968; reprint, New York: Bantam, 1969), p. 107. Other references to this collection will be incorporated parenthetically in the text.

14. Mas'ud Zavarzadeh, *The Mythopoeic Reality: The Postwar American Nonfiction Novel* (Urbana: University of Illinois Press, 1976).

15. Ronald Sukenick, "The Death of the Novel," in *The Death of the Novel and Other Stories* (New York: Dial Press, 1969), p. 41.

16. Ronald Sukenick, *UP* (New York: Dell, 1968), p. 324.

17. Timothy Dow Adams, "Obscuring the Muse: The Mock-Autobiographies of Ronald Sukenick," *Critique* 20, no. 1 (1978): 29.

18. Vladimir Nabokov, *Lolita* (1955; reprint, New York: Berkley, 1966), p. 32.

19. Donald Barthelme, *Snow White* (1965; reprint, New York: Atheneum, 1967), p. 6. Other references to this novel will be incorporated parenthetically in the text.

20. Raymond Federman, *Take It or Leave It* (New York: Fiction Collective, 1976), n.p. Federman's novel is not paginated. Other references to this novel will be incorporated parenthetically in the text.

21. Ronald Sukenick, *UP*, p. 329. Other references to this novel will be incorporated parenthetically in the text.

22. In *City Life* (1970; reprint, New York: Bantam, 1971), p. 68. Other references to this collection will be incorporated parenthetically in the text.

23. Richard Horn, *Encyclopedia* (New York: Grove, 1969).

24. Gilbert Sorrentino, *Splendide-Hotel* (New York: New Directions, 1973), pp. 15, 14.

25. Walter Abish, from an interview with Klinkowitz, in Jerome Klinkowitz, *The Life of Fiction* (Urbana: University of Illinois Press, 1977), p. 68.

26. Lawrence Alloway, cited by Klinkowitz, *The Life of Fiction*, p. 59.

27. All page references are to *Alphabetical Africa* (New York: New Directions, 1974).

28. In Klinkowitz, *The Life of Fiction*, p. 43.

29. See Christopher Morris, "Barth and Lacan: The World of the Moebius Strip," *Critique* 17, no. 1 (1975): 69–77.

30. John Ashbery, *Three Poems* (1972; reprint, New York: Viking, 1975), p. 13.

31. Raymond Federman, *Double or Nothing* (Chicago: Swallow Press, 1971), see pp. 85, 97.1, 122. Other references to this novel will be incorporated parenthetically in the text.

32. Ferdinand Kriwet, "Decomposition of the Literary Unit: Notes on Visually Perceptible Literature," *Tri-Quarterly* 20 (1971): 209–52.

33. Stanley Fogel, "'And All the Little Typtopies': Notes on Language Theory in the Contemporary Experimental Novel," *Modern Fiction Studies* 20 (1974): 331.

34. Vladimir Nabokov, *Pale Fire* (1962; reprint, New York: Berkley, 1969). All other references to this novel will be incorporated parenthetically in the text.

35. Mary McCarthy, "A Bolt from the Blue," *The New Republic,* June 4, 1964, pp. 21–27.

36. An exception is H. Grabe, *Fictitious Biographies: Vladimir Nabokov's English Novels* (The Hague: Mouton, 1977), esp. pp. 56–59. I am indebted to Grabe's analysis.

37. Raymond Federman, *Take It or Leave It,* n.p. This passage appears in the section titled "The Masturbatory Gesture."

38. Ronald Sukenick, *98.6* (New York: Fiction Collective, 1975), p. 188. Other references to this novel will be incorporated parenthetically in the text.

39. James Rother, "Parafiction: The Adjacent Universe of Barth, Barthelme, Pynchon, and Nabokov," *boundary 2* 5 (1976): 25.

40. Laurence Sterne, *Tristram Shandy,* ed. J. A. Work (New York: Odyssey, 1940), p. 56.

41. George Chambers, *The Bonnyclabber* (n.p. Panache and December, 1972), p. 1.

42. Jonathan Culler, "Making Sense," p. 35.

43. In *Pricksongs and Descants* (1969; reprint, New York: New American Library, 1970), pp. 79–88.

44. Wolfgang Iser, *The Act of Reading* (Baltimore, Md.: The Johns Hopkins University Press, 1978).

45. Steven Mailloux, *Interpretive Conventions: The Reader in the Study of American Fiction* (Ithaca, N.Y.: Cornell University Press, 1982), esp. chaps. 1, 2, and 5.

46. Ibid., p. 144.

47. Ibid., p. 59.

Bibliography

I. Theory of Narrative

Abrams, M. H. "What's the Use of Theorizing about the Arts?" In *In Search of Literary Theory.* Edited by Morton Bloomfield. Ithaca, N.Y.: Cornell University Press, 1972. Pp. 1–54.

Allott, Miriam, ed. *Novelists on the Novel.* New York: Columbia University Press, 1959.

Altieri, Charles. "The Qualities of Action: A Theory of Middles in Literature." *boundary 2* 5 (Winter 1977): 323–50.

Auerbach, Erich. *The Representation of Reality in Western Literature.* Translated by Willard R. Trask. Princeton, N.J.: Princeton University Press, 1953.

Barthes, Roland. "The Death of the Author." Translated by Richard Howard. In *The Discontinuous Universe.* Edited by Sallie Sears and Georgiana Lord. New York: Basic Books, 1972. Pp. 7–12.

———. "An Introduction to the Structural Study of Narrative." *New Literary History* 6 (Winter 1975): 237–72.

———. *Elements of Semiology.* Translated by Annette Lavers and Colin Smith. New York: Hill and Wang, 1968.

———. *S/Z.* Translated by Richard Miller. New York: Hill and Wang, 1974.

Benoist, Jean-Marie. "The Fictional Subject." *Twentieth Century Studies* 6 (1971): 88–97.

Booth, Wayne. *The Rhetoric of Fiction.* 1961; reprint, Chicago: University of Chicago Press, 1964.

Bremond, Claude. "The Logic of Narrative Possibilities." Translated by Elaine D. Cancalon. *New Literary History* 11 (Spring 1980): 387–411.

Brooke-Rose, Christine. "The Evil Ring: Realism and the Marvelous." *Poetics Today* 1, no. 4 (Summer 1980): 67–90.

———. "Historical Genres/Theoretical Genres: A Discussion of Todorov on the Fantastic." *New Literary History* 8 (1976): 145–58.

Bruss, Elizabeth W. "Models and Metaphors for Narrative Analysis." *Centrum* 2, no. 1 (Spring 1974): 14–42.

Butor, Michel. *Inventory: Essays by Michel Butor.* Edited by Richard Howard. New York: Simon and Schuster, 1968.

Campbell, Norman R. "Definition of a Theory." In *Foundations of Science.* London: Cambridge University Press, 1920. Pp. 122–25.

Caserio, Robert L. *Plot, Story, and the Novel: From Dickens to the Modern Period.* Princeton, N.J.: Princeton University Press, 1979.

Chatman, Seymour. "The Rhetoric of Difficult Fiction: Cortazar's 'Blow-Up.'" *Poetics Today* 1, no. 4 (Summer 1980): 23–66.

―――. *Story and Discourse: Narrative Structure in Fiction and Film.* Ithaca, N.Y.: Cornell University Press, 1979.

―――. "The Structure of Narrative Transmission." In *Style and Structure in Literature: Essays in the New Stylistics.* Edited by Roger Fowler. Ithaca, N.Y.: Cornell University Press, 1975. Pp. 213–57.

―――. "Toward a Theory of Narrative." *New Literary History* 6 (Winter 1975): 295–318.

Corti, Maria. *An Introduction to Literary Semiotics.* Translated by Margherita Bogat and Allen Mandelbaum. Bloomington: Indiana University Press, 1978.

Culler, Jonathan. "Defining Narrative Units." In *Style and Structure in Literature: Essays in the New Stylistics.* Edited by Roger Fowler. Ithaca, N.Y.: Cornell University Press, 1975. Pp. 123–42.

―――. "Fabula and Sjuzhet in the Analysis of Narrative." *Poetics Today* 1, no. 3 (Spring 1980): 27–37.

―――. *Structuralist Poetics.* Ithaca, N.Y.: Cornell University Press, 1975.

―――. "Structure of Ideology and Ideology of Structure." *New Literary History* 4 (Spring 1973): 471–83.

Derrida, Jacques. *Of Grammatology.* Translated by Gayatri Spivak. Baltimore, Md.: John Hopkins University Press, 1974.

Dijk, Teun A. van. *Some Aspects of Text Grammars: A Study in Theoretical Linguistics and Poetics.* The Hague: Mouton, 1972.

Dolezel, Lubomir. "Narrative Modalities." *Journal of Literary Semantics* 5, no. 1 (April 1976): 5–14.

―――. "Narrative Semantics." *PTL: A Journal for Descriptive Poetics and Theory of Literature* 1 (1976): 129–52.

―――. "Narrative Worlds." In *Sound, Sign and Meaning: Quinquagenary of the Prague Linguistic Circle.* Edited by Ladislav Matejka. Michigan Slavic Contributions. Ann Arbor: University of Michigan Press, 1976. Pp. 542–52.

―――. "Truth and Authenticity in Narrative." *Poetics Today* 1, no. 3 (Spring 1980): 7–25.

————. "The Typology of the Narrator: Point of View in Fiction." In *To Honor Roman Jakobson: Essays on the Occasion of His 70th Birthday.* vol. 1. No editor. Paris: Mouton, 1967. Pp. 541–53.

Donato, Eugenio. "The Shape of Fiction: Notes toward a Possible Classification of Narrative Discourse." *Modern Language Notes* 86 (1973): 807–22.

Eco, Umberto. "Poetics of the Open Work." *Twentieth Century Studies* 12 (1974): 6–26.

————. *The Role of the Reader: Explorations in the Semiotics of Texts.* Bloomington: Indiana University Press, 1979.

————. *A Theory of Semiotics.* Bloomington: Indiana University Press, 1976.

Egan, Kieran. "What Is Plot?" *New Literary History* 9 (Spring 1978): 455–73.

Eile, Stanislaw. "The Novel as an Expression of the Writer's Vision of the World." Translated by Teresa Halikowska-Smith. *New Literary History* 9 (Autumn 1977): 115–28.

Erlich, Victor. *Russian Formalism: History—Doctrine.* The Hague: Mouton, 1969.

Even-Zohar, Itamer. "Constraints of Realeme Insertability in Narrative." *Poetics Today* 1, no. 3 (Spring 1980): 65–74.

Ferrara, Fernando. "Theory and Model for the Structural Analysis of Fiction." *New Literary History* 5 (Winter 1974): 245–68.

Fowler, Roger. *Linguistics and the Novel.* London: Methuen, 1977.

————. "Referential Code and Narrative Authority." *Language and Style* 10 (1977): 129–61.

Freedman, Ralph. "The Possibility of a Theory of the Novel." In *The Disciplines of Criticism: Essays in Literary Theory, Interpretation, and History.* Edited by Peter Demetz et al. New Haven, Conn.: Yale University Press, 1968. Pp. 57–77.

Friedman, Norman. *Form and Meaning in Fiction.* Athens: University of Georgia Press, 1975.

Garvin, Paul L., ed. *A Prague School Reader on Esthetics, Literary Structure, and Style.* Washington, D.C.: Georgetown University Press, 1964.

Gasparov, Boris. "The Narrative Text as an Act of Transmission." *New Literary History* 9 (Winter 1978): 245–61.

Gass, William. *Fiction and the Figures of Life.* New York: Random House, 1971.

Genette, Gerard. "Boundaries of Narrative." *New Literary History* 8 (1976): 1–15.

————. *Narrative Discourse: An Essay in Method.* Translated by Jane E. Lewin. Ithaca, N.Y.: Cornell University Press, 1979.

Glucksman, Miriam. *Structuralist Analysis in Contemporary Social Thought: A Comparison of the Theories of Claude Levi-Strauss and Louis Althusser.* London: Routledge & Kegan Paul, 1974.

Greimas, A. J. "Narrative Grammar: Units and Levels." *Modern Language Notes* 86 (December 1971): 793–806.

Greimas, A. J., and J. Courtes. "The Cognitive Dimension of Narrative Discourse." *New Literary History* 7 (Spring 1976): 433–37.

Guirard, Pierre. *Semiology.* Boston: Routledge & Kegan Paul, 1975.

Harvey, W. J. *Character and the Novel.* Ithaca, N.Y.: Cornell University Press, 1965.

Hawkes, Terence. *Structuralism and Semiotics.* London: Methuen, 1977.

Heath, Stephen. "Narrative Space." *Screen* 17, no. 3 (August 1976): 68–112.

Hernstein-Smith, Barbara. *Poetic Closure: A Study of How Poems End.* Chicago: University of Chicago Press, 1968.

Holloway, John. "Supposition and Supersession: A Model of Analysis for Narrative Structure." *Critical Inquiry* 3 (1976): 39–56.

Holquist, Michael, and Walter Reed. "Six Theses on the Novel—and Some Metaphors." *New Literary History* 11 (Spring 1980): 413–23.

Hrushovski, Benjamin. "The Structure of Semiotic Objects: A Three-Dimensional Model." *Poetics Today* 1, nos. 1–2 (Autumn 1979): 363–76.

Iser, Wolfgang. "The Current Situation of Literary Theory: Key Concepts and the Imaginary." *New Literary History* 11 (Autumn 1979): 1–20.

Jakobson, Roman. "The Dominant." In *Readings in Russian Poetics: Formalist and Structuralist Views,* edited by Ladislav Matejka and Krystyne Pomorsk. Cambridge, Mass.: MIT Press, 1971. Pp. 82–87.

Kermode, Frank. *The Sense of an Ending: Studies in the Theory of Fiction.* New York: Oxford University Press, 1967.

————. "The Use of the Codes." In *Approaches to Poetics.* Edited by Seymour Chatman. New York: Columbia University Press, 1973. Pp. 51–79.

Kloepfer, Rolf. "Dynamic Structures in Narrative Literature: 'The Dialogic Principle.'" *Poetics Today* 1, no. 4 (Summer 1980): 115–34.

Krieger, Murray. "Fiction, History, and Empirical Reality." *Critical Inquiry* 1 (1974): 335–60.

Lodge, David. "Analysis and Interpretation of the Realist Text: A

Pluralistic Approach to Hemingway's 'Cat in the Rain.'" *Poetics Today* 1, no. 4 (Summer 1980): 5–22.

———. *The Modes of Modern Writing: Metaphor, Metonymy, and the Typology of Modern Literature*. Ithaca, N.Y.: Cornell University Press, 1979.

Lotman, J. M. "The Discrete Text and the Iconic Text: Remarks on the Structure of Narrative." *New Literary History* 6 (Winter 1975): 333–38.

———. "The Origin of Plot in the Light of Typology." *Poetics Today* 1, no. 1–2 (Autumn 1979): 161–84.

———. "Point of View in a Text." *New Literary History* 6 (Winter 1975): 339–52.

———. *The Structure of the Artistic Text*. Translated by Ronald Vroon. Michigan Slavic Contributions No. 7. Ann Arbor: University of Michigan Press, 1977.

Lubbock, Percy. *The Craft of Fiction*. 1921; reprint, New York: Viking, 1957.

Lucid, Daniel P., ed. *Soviet Semiotics*. Baltimore, Md.: Johns Hopkins University Press, 1977.

Lukács, Georg. *The Theory of the Novel*. Translated by Anna Bostock. 1920; reprinted, Cambridge, Mass.: MIT Press, 1971.

Macksey, Richard, and Eugenio Donato, eds. *The Structuralist Controversy: The Language of Criticism and the Sciences of Man*. Baltimore, Md.: Johns Hopkins University Press, 1970.

———, eds. *Velocities of Change: Critical Essays from MLN*. Baltimore, Md.: Johns Hopkins University Press, 1974.

Marcotte, Edward. "Intersticed Prose." *Chicago Review* 26 (1975): 31–36.

Matejka, Ladislav, and Irwin Titunik. *Semiotics of Art: Prague School Contributions*. Cambridge, Mass.: MIT Press, 1976.

Miller, J. Hillis. "The Figure in the Carpet." *Poetics Today* 1, no. 3 (Spring 1980): 107–18.

Moles, Abraham. *Information Theory and Esthetic Perception*. Translated by Joel E. Cohen. Urbana: University of Illinois Press, 1966.

Mooij, J. J. A. "The Nature and Function of Literary Theories." *Poetics Today* 1, no. 1–2 (Autumn 1979): 111–35.

Muir, Edwin. *The Structure of the Novel*. London: Hogarth, 1928.

O'Toole, Lawrence. "Dimensions of Semiotic Space in Narrative." *Poetics Today* 1, no. 4 (Summer 1980): 135–49.

Prince, Gerald. "Aspects of a Grammar of Narrative." *Poetics Today* 1, no. 3 (Spring 1980): 49–63.

———. *A Grammar of Stories.* The Hague: Mouton, 1973.

———. "On Presuppositions and Narrative Strategy." *Centrum* 1, no. 1 (Spring 1973): 23–31.

Propp, V. *Morphology of the Folktale.* Translated by Lawrence Scott. Austin: University of Texas Press, 1968.

Rabkin, Eric S. *The Fantastic in Literature.* Princeton, N.J.: Princeton University Press, 1976.

Reed, Walter L. "The Problem with a Poetics of the Novel." *Novel* 9 (Winter 1976): 101–13.

Regnier, Paul. "The Convention of 'Realism' in the Novel." *Genre* 10 (1977): 103–14.

Rimmon, Shlomith. "A Comprehensive Theory of Narrative: Genette's *Figures III* and the Structuralist Study of Fiction." *PTL: A Journal for Descriptive Poetics and Theory of Literature* 1 (1976): 33–62.

Robbe-Grillet, Alain. *For a New Novel: Essays on Fiction.* Translated by Richard Howard. New York: Grove, 1965.

Scholes, Robert. *Fabulation and Metafiction.* Champagne: University of Illinois Press, 1979.

———. "Metafiction." *Iowa Review* 1 (1970): 100–115.

———. *Structural Fabulation: An Essay on Fiction of the Future.* Notre Dame, Ind.: University of Notre Dame Press, 1975.

———. *Structuralism in Literature: An Introduction.* New Haven, Conn.: Yale University Press, 1975.

Scholes, Robert, and Robert Kellogg. *The Nature of Narrative.* New York: Oxford University Press, 1966.

Segre, Cesare. *Semiotics and Literary Criticism.* Translated by John Meddemmen. The Hague: Mouton, 1973.

———. *Structures and Time: Narration, Poetry, Models.* Chicago: University of Chicago Press, 1979.

Shklovsky, Victor. "Art as Technique." In *Russian Formalist Criticism: Four Essays.* Edited by Lee Lemon and Marion Reis. Lincoln: University of Nebraska Press, 1965. Pp. 3–24.

Shroder, Maurice. "The Novel as a Genre." *Massachusetts Review* 4 (1963): 291–308.

Smarr, Janet Levarie. "Some Considerations on the Nature of Plot." *Poetics* 8 (June 1979): 339–49.

Spencer, Sharon. *Space, Time and Structure in the Modern Novel.* Chicago: Swallow, 1971.

Stanzel, Franz. *Narrative Situations in the Novel:* Tom Jones, Moby Dick,

The Ambassadors, Ulysses. Translated by James P. Pusack. Bloomington: Indiana University Press, 1971.

―――. "Second Thoughts on *Narrative Situations in the Novel:* Towards a Grammar of Fiction." *Novel* 11 (1978): 247–64.

Stevick, Philip. "Metaphors for the Novel." *Tri-Quarterly* 30 (1974): 127–38.

Suleiman, Susan Robin. "Redundancy and the 'Readable' Text." *Poetics Today* 1, no. 4 (Summer 1980): 119–42.

Tatham, Campbell. "Beyond Structuralism." *Genre* 10 (1977): 131–55.

Todorov, Tzvetan. *The Fantastic: A Structural Approach to Literary Genre.* Translated by Richard Howard. Cleveland, Ohio: Case Western Reserve University Press, 1973.

―――. "The Origin of Genres." *New Literary History* 8 (1976): 159–70.

―――. *The Poetics of Prose.* Ithaca, N.Y.: Cornell University Press, 1977.

―――. "Structuralism and Literature." In *Approaches to Poetics.* Edited by Seymour Chatman. New York: Columbia University Press, 1973. Pp. 153–70.

Uspensky, Boris. *A Poetics of Composition: The Structure of the Artistic Text and Typology of a Compositional Form.* Translated by V. Zavarin and S. Wittig. Berkeley: University of California Press, 1973.

Valdes, M. J., and O. J. Miller, eds. *Interpretation of Narrative.* Toronto: University of Toronto Press, 1979.

Walton, Kendall L. "How Remote Are Fictional Worlds from the Real World?" *Journal of Aesthetics and Art Criticism* 37 (1978): 11–23.

Weinsheimer, Joel. "Theory of Character: *Emma.*" *Poetics Today* 1, no. 1–2 (Autumn 1979): 185–211.

Wittig, Susan, ed. *Structuralism: An Interdisciplinary Study.* Pittsburgh, Pa.: Pickwick Press, 1975.

Zavarzadeh, Mas'ud. *The Mythopoeic Reality: The Postwar American Nonfiction Novel.* Urbana: University of Illinois Press, 1976.

II. Space and the Reader's Share

Altieri, Charles. "The Hermeneutics of Literary Indeterminacy: A Dissent from the New Orthodoxy." *New Literary History* 10 (Autumn 1978): 71–99.

Arnheim, Rudolf. "A Stricture on Space and Time." *Critical Inquiry* 4 (1978): 645–55.

Bachelard, Gaston. *The Poetics of Space.* Translated by Maria Jolas. Boston: Beacon Press, 1964.

Bleich, David. "The Logic of Interpretation." *Genre* 10 (1977): 363–94.

———. *Readings and Feelings: An Introduction to Subjective Criticism.* Urbana, Ill.: NCTE, 1975.

———. "The Subjective Character of Critical Interpretation." *College English* 36, no. 7 (March 1975): 739–55.

———. "The Subjective Paradigm in Science, Psychology, and Criticism." *New Literary History* 7 (Winter 1976): 313–34.

Bogel, Frederick V. "Synonymy and Literary Meaning." *College English* 40 (October 1978): 133–38.

Cohen, Gillian. "The Psychology of Reading." *New Literary History* 4 (Autumn 1972): 75–90.

Crews, Frederick. *Out of My System: Psychoanalysis, Ideology, and Literary Method.* New York: Oxford University Press, 1975.

Culler, Jonathan. "Making Sense." *Twentieth Century Studies* 12 (1974): 27–36.

DeMaria, Robert. "The Ideal Reader: A Critical Fiction." *PMLA* 93 (1978): 463–74.

Dilthey, Wilhelm. "The Rise of Hermeneutics." *New Literary History* 3 (Winter 1972): 229–44.

Eco, Umberto. "The Problem of Reception." *Gradiva* 1 (Winter 1977): 115–19.

Erlich, Victor. "Reading Conscious and Unconscious." *College English* 36 (March 1975): 766–75.

Fish, Stanley. "Literature in the Reader: Affective Stylistics." *New Literary History* 1 (Autumn 1970): 123–63.

———. "Normal Circumstances, Literal Language, Direct Speech Acts, the Ordinary, the Everyday, the Obvious, What Goes Without Saying, and Other Special Cases." *Critical Inquiry* 4 (1978): 625–44.

Frank, Joseph. "Spatial Form: An Answer to Critics." *Critical Inquiry* 4 (1978): 231–52.

———. "Spatial Form: Some Further Reflections." *Critical Inquiry* 5 (1978): 275–90.

———. *The Widening Gyre: Crisis and Mastery in Modern Literature.* New Brunswick, N.J.: Rutgers University Press, 1963.

Glowinski, Michal. "Reading, Interpretation, Reception." *New Literary History* 11 (Autumn 1979): 75–82.

Gombrich, E. H. *Art and Illusion: A Study in the Psychology of Pictorial Representation.* New York: Pantheon Books, 1961.

Gregor, Ian. "Criticism as an Individual Activity: An Approach through Reading." In *Contemporary Criticism.* Edited by Malcolm Bradbury. London: Edward Arnold, 1970. Pp. 195–214.

Gullon, Ricardo. "On Space in the Novel." *Critical Inquiry* 2 (1975): 11–28.

Hartman, Geoffrey H. *The Fate of Reading and Other Essays.* Chicago: University of Chicago Press, 1975.

Holland, Norman H. *The Dynamics of Literary Response.* New York: W. W. Norton, 1968.

———. "Human Identity." *Critical Inquiry* 4 (1978): 451–69.

———. *Poems in Persons: An Introduction to the Psychoanalysis of Literature.* New York: W. W. Norton, 1973.

Holtz, William. "Spatial Form in Modern Literature: A Reconsideration." *Critical Inquiry* 4 (1977): 271–84.

Iser, Wolfgang. *The Act of Reading: A Theory of Aesthetic Response.* Baltimore, Md.: Johns Hopkins University Press, 1978.

———. *The Implied Reader: Patterns of Communication in Prose Fiction from Bunyan to Beckett.* Baltimore, Md.: Johns Hopkins University Press, 1974.

———. "Indeterminacy and the Reader's Response in Prose Fiction." In *Aspects of Narrative: Selected Papers from the English Institute.* Edited by J. Hillis Miller. New York: Columbia University Press, 1971. Pp. 1–45.

Jauss, Hans Robert. "Literary History as a Challenge to Literary Theory." *New Literary History* 2 (1970): 7–37.

Kestner, Joseph. *The Spatiality of the Novel.* Detroit, Mich.: Wayne State University Press, 1978.

Kriwet, Ferdinand. "Decomposition of the Literary Unit: Notes on Visually Perceptible Literature." *Tri-Quarterly* 20 (1971): 209–52.

McHughes, Janet Larson. "The Poesis of Space: Prosodic Structures in Concrete Poetry." *Quarterly Journal of Speech* 63 (April 1977): 168–79.

Marcotte, Edward. "The Space of the Novel." *Partisan Review* 41 (1974): 263–72.

Martin, Terence. "The Method of Hawthorne's Tales." In *Hawthorne Centenary Essays.* Edited by R. H. Pearce. Columbus: Ohio State University Press, 1964. Pp. 7–30.

———. *Nathaniel Hawthorne.* New York: Twayne, 1965.

Merleau-Ponty, Maurice. *Phenomenology of Perception.* Translated by Colin Smith. New York: Humanities Press, 1962.

Mitchell, W. J. T. "Spatial Form in Literature: Toward a General Theory." *Critical Inquiry* 6 (Spring 1980): 537–67.

Natanson, Maurice. "Phenomenology and the Theory of Literature." In *Literature, Philosophy, and the Social Sciences.* The Hague: Martin Nijhoff, 1966. Pp. 86–100.

Nelson, Cary. *The Incarnate Word: Literature as Verbal Space.* Urbana: University of Illinois Press, 1973.

Nelson, Lowry. "The Fictive Reader and Literary Self-Reflexiveness." In *The Disciplines of Criticism: Essays in Literary Theory, Interpretation, and History.* Edited by Peter Demetz el al. New Haven, Conn.: Yale University Press, 1968. Pp. 173–91.

Nerlich, Graham. *The Shape of Space.* Cambridge: Cambridge University Press, 1976.

Perry, Menakhem. "Literary Dynamics: How the Order of a Text Creates Its Meanings." *Poetics Today* 1, nos. 1–2 (Autumn 1979): 35–64, 311–61.

Poulet, Georges. "The Phenomenology of Reading." *New Literary History* 1 (Autumn 1969): 53–68.

Prince, Gerald. "Notes toward a Categorization of Fictional Narratees." *Genre* 4 (1971): 100—115.

———. "On Readers and Listeners in Narrative." *Neophilogus* 4 (1971): 117–22.

Rabinowitz, Peter J. "Assertion and Assumption: Fictional Patterns and the External World." *PMLA* 96 (May 1981): 408–19.

———. "Truth in Fiction: A Reexamination of Audiences." *Critical Inquiry* 4 (1977): 121–42.

Rabkin, Eric S. "Spatial Form and Plot." *Critical Inquiry* 4 (1977): 253–70.

Rader, Ralph. "Fact, Theory, and Literary Explanation." *Critical Inquiry* 1 (1974): 245–72.

Ritchie, Benbow. "The Formal Structure of the Aesthetic Object." In *The Problems of Aesthetics.* Edited by E. Vivas and M. Krieger. New York: Rinehart, 1965. Pp. 225–33.

Rovatti, Pier Aldo. "Critical Theory and Phenomenology." *Telos* 15 (1973): 25–40.

Schwartz, Murray. "Where Is Literature?" *College English* 36 (March 1975): 756–65.

Segers, Rien T. "An Interview with Hans Robert Jauss." *New Literary History* 11 (Autumn 1979): 83–95.

Segre, Cesare. "Space and Time of the Text." *Twentieth Century Studies* 12 (December 1974): 37–41.

Slatoff, Walter J. *With Respect to Readers: Dimensions of Literary Response.* Ithaca, N.Y.: Cornell University Press, 1970.

Smitten, Jeffery. "Approaches to the Spatiality of Narrative." *Papers on Language and Literature* 14 (Summer 1978): 296–314.

Suleiman, Susan, and Inge Crosman. *The Reader in the Text: Essays on Audience and Interpretation.* Princeton, N.J.: Princeton University Press, 1979.

Tatham, Campbell. "High-Altitude Hermeneutics." *Diacritics* 3, no. 2 (Summer 1973): 22–31.

Timpe, Eugene F. "The Spatial Dimension: A Stylistic Typology." In *Patterns of Exposition.* Edited by Joseph Strelka. University Park, Pa.: Pennsylvania State University Press, 1971. Pp. 179–97.

Winnicott, D. W. *Playing and Reality.* London: Tavistock Publications, 1971.

III. Culture, Crisis, and Twentieth-Century Literature

Barth, John. "The Literaure of Exhaustion." *The Atlantic,* August 1967, pp. 29–34.

Bathrick, David. "The Politics of Reception Theory in the GDR." *Minnesota Review* 5 (Fall 1975): 125–33.

Benamou, Michel, and Charles Caramello, eds. *Performance in Post-modern Culture.* Madison, Wis.: Coda Press, 1977.

Bernheimer, Charles. "Grammacentricity and Modernism." *Mosaic* 11, no. 1 (1977): 103–16.

Bradbury, Malcolm. *Possibilities: Essays on the State of the Novel.* New York: Oxford University Press, 1973.

Bruss, Elizabeth. "The Game of Literature and Some Literary Games." *New Literary History* 9 (Autumn 1977): 153–72.

Culler, Jonathan. "Beyond Interpretation: The Prospects of Contemporary Criticism." *Comparative Literature* 28, no. 3 (1976): 244–56.

Daiches, David. *The Novel and the Modern World.* Chicago: University of Chicago Press, 1960.

———. "What Was the Modern Novel?" *Critical Inquiry* 1 (1975): 813–19.

Davidson, Michael. "The Languages of Postmodernism." *Chicago Review* 27, no. 1 (1975): 11–32.

Dickstein, Morris. "Fiction Hot and Kool: Dilemmas of the Experimental Writer." *Tri-Quarterly* 33 (Spring 1975): 257–72.

Ehrmann, Jacques. "The Death of Literature." *New Literary History* 3 (Autumn 1971): 31–48.

Federman, Raymond, ed. *Surfiction.* Chicago: Swallow, 1975.

———. "Tri(y)log." *Chicago Review* 28, no. 2 (1976): 93–109.

Fogel, Stanley. "'And All the Little Typtopies': Notes on Language Theory in the Contemporary Experimental Novel." *Modern Fiction Studies* 20 (Autumn 1974): 328–36.

Goldmann, Lucien. "Problems of a Sociology of the Novel." *Telos* 18 (1973–74): 122–35.

———. *Towards a Sociology of the Novel.* Translated by Alan Sheridan. London: Tavistock, 1964.

Graff, Gerald. "Fear and Trembling at Yale." *American Scholar* 4 (1977): 467–78.

———. "The Myth of the Postmodernist Breakthrough." *Tri-Quarterly* 26 (Winter 1973): 383–417.

———. "The Politics of Anti-Realism." *Salmagundi* 42 (Summer/Fall 1978): 4–30.

Greenman, Myron. "Understanding New Fiction." *Modern Fiction Studies* 20 (Autumn 1974): 307–16.

Guerard, Albert J. "Notes on the Rhetoric of Anti-Realist Fiction." *Tri-Quarterly* 30 (Spring 1974): 3–50.

Hassan, Ihab. *The Literature of Silence.* New York: Alfred A. Knopf, 1967.

———. "The New Gnosticism: Speculations on an Aspect of the Postmodern Mind." *boundary 2* 1 (1973): 547–70.

———. *Paracriticisms: Seven Speculations of the Times.* Urbana: University of Illinois Press, 1975.

———. "POSTmodernISM." *New Literary History* 3 (Autumn 1971): 5–30.

———. "A re-Vision of Literature." *New Literary History* 8 (1976): 127–44.

Hohendahl, Peter Uwe. "Introduction to Reception Aesthetics." *New German Critique* 10 (1977): 29–63.

Howe, Irving, ed. *The Idea of the Modern in Literature and the Arts.* New York: Horizon, 1967.

Jameson, Fredric. "Ideology of the Text." *Salmagundi* 31–32 (Fall 1975/Winter 1976): 204–46.

———. "Metacommentary." *PMLA* 86 (1971): 9–18.

———. *The Prison House of Language.* Princeton, N.J.: Princeton University Press, 1972.

Josipovici, Gabriel. *Lessons of Modernism.* London: MacMillan, 1977.

———. *The World and the Book.* Stanford, Calif.: Stanford University Press, 1971.

Kostelanetz, Richard. *The End of Intelligent Writing.* New York: Sheed and Ward, 1974.

Lukács, Georg. *Realism in Our Time: Literature and the Class Struggle.* Translated by John and Necke Mandar. New York: Harper and Row, 1962.

McLuhan, Marshall. *Understanding Media: The Extensions of Man.* New York: McGraw Hill, 1966.

Miller, J. Hillis. "Ariadne's Thread: Repetition and the Narrative Line." *Critical Inquiry* 3 (1976): 57–78.

Modern Literature 3 (1974): 1065–1264. (Special issue on "From Modernism to Postmodernism.")

Nin, Anaïs. *The Novel of the Future.* New York: Collier Books, 1968.

Olson, Charles. *Selected Writings.* Edited by Robert Creeley. New York: New Directions, 1966.

Ortega y Gasset, José. *The Dehumanization of Art.* Princeton, N.J.: Princeton University Press, 1968.

Popper, Frank. *Art—Action and Participation.* New York: New York University Press, 1975.

Richter, Dieter. "Teachers and Readers: Reading Attitudes as a Problem in Teaching Literature." *New German Critique* 7 (Winter 1976): 21–43.

Rosenberg, Harold. *The Tradition of the New.* New York: Horizon Press, 1959.

Said, Edward. "*Abecedarium Culturae:* Structuralism, Absence, Writing." *Tri-Quarterly* 20 (Winter 1971): 33–71.

———. *Beginnings: Intention and Method.* New York: Basic Books, 1975.

———. "The Problem of Textuality: Two Exemplary Positions." *Critical Inquiry* 4 (1978): 673–714.

Samet, Tom. "The Modulated Vision: Lionel Trilling's 'Larger Naturalism.'" *Critical Inquiry* 4 (1978): 539–57.

Slater, Philip. *The Pursuit of Loneliness: American Culture at the Breaking Point.* Boston: Beacon Press, 1970.

Spanos, William V. "The Detective and the Boundary: Some Notes on the Postmodern Literary Imagination." *boundary 2* 1 (1972): 147–68.

———, ed. *Casebook on Existentialism.* Vol. 2. New York: Thomas Y. Crowell, 1976.

Spears, Monroe K. *Dionysus and the City: Modernism in Twentieth-Century Poetry.* New York: Oxford University Press, 1970.

Sypher, Wylie. *Loss of Self in Modern Literature and Art.* New York: Random House, 1962.

Tatham, Campbell. "Correspondences/Notes/Etcetera." *Chicago Review* 26, no. 4 (1975): 112–32.

————. "Critical Investigations: Language Games: (Post)Modern-(Isms)." *Sub-Stance* 10 (1974): 67–80.

Vernon, John. *The Garden and the Map: Schizophrenia in Twentieth-Century Literature and Culture.* Urbana: University of Illinois Press, 1973.

Wasson, Richard. "Notes on a New Sensibility." *Partisan Review* 36 (1969): 460–77.

Weimann, Robert. "French Structuralism and Literary History." *New Literary History* 6 (Spring 1973): 437–69.

Wheelis, Allen. *The End of the Modern Age.* New York: Basic Books, 1971.

Wiener, Norbert. *The Human Use of Human Beings: Cybernetics and Society.* Boston: Houghton Mifflin, 1954.

Zimmerman, Marc. "Polarities and Contradictions: Theoretical Bases of the Marxist-Structuralist Encounter." *New German Critique* 7 (1976): 69–90.

IV. Critical Studies of American Fiction

Aldridge, John W. *Time to Murder and Create: The Contemporary Novel in Crisis.* New York: McKay, 1966.

Alter, Robert. *Partial Magic: The Novel as a Self-Conscious Genre.* Berkeley: University of California Press, 1975.

Baumbach, Jonathan. *The Landscape of Nightmare: Studies in the Contemporary American Novel.* New York: NYU Press, 1965.

Bellamy, Joe David, ed. *The New Fiction: Interviews with Innovative American Writers.* Urbana: University of Illinois Press, 1974.

Berthoff, Werner. "A Literature without Qualities: American Writing Since 1945." *Yale Review* 68 (1979): 235–54.

Bryant, Jerry H. *The Open Decision: The Contemporary American and Its Intellectual Background.* New York: Free Press, 1970.

Chase, Richard. *The American Novel and Its Tradition.* New York: Doubleday, 1957.

Cohn, Dorrit. *Transparent Minds: Narrative Modes for Presenting Consciousness in Fiction.* Princeton, N.J.: Princeton University Press, 1978.

Deer, Harriet, and Irving Deer. "Satire as Rhetorical Play." *boundary 2* 5 (1977): 711–21.

Edel, Leon. *The Modern Psychological Novel.* New York: Grosset and Dunlap, 1956.

Fiedler, Leslie. *Love and Death in the American Novel.* Rev. ed. New York: Criterion Books, 1966.

Friedman, Alan. *The Turn of the Novel: The Transition to Modern Fiction.* New York: Oxford University Press, 1966.

Galloway, David. *The Absurd Hero in American Fiction.* Austin: University of Texas Press, 1966.

Grossvogel, David. *Limits of the Novel: Evolution of a Form from Chaucer to Robbe-Grillet.* Ithaca, N.Y.: Cornell University Press, 1968.

Hardy, Barbara. *Tellers and Listeners:· The Narrative Imagination.* London: Athlone, 1975.

Harris, Charles B. *Contemporary American Novelists of the Absurd.* New Haven, Conn.: College and University Press, 1971.

Hassan, Ihab. *Radical Innocence: The Contemporary American Novel.* Princeton, N.J.: Princeton University Press, 1961.

Hauck, Richard Boyd. *A Cheerful Nihilism: Confidence and "The Absurd" in American Humorous Fiction.* Bloomington: Indiana University Press, 1971.

Hayman, David. "Double Distancing: An Attribute of the 'Post-Modern' Avant Garde." *Novel* 12 (1978): 33–47.

Hendin, Josephine. *Vulnerable People: A View of American Fiction Since 1945.* New York: Oxford University Press, 1978.

Kennard, Jean E. *Number and Nightmare: Forms of Fantasy in Contemporary Fiction.* Hamden, Conn.: Archon Books, 1975.

Klein, Marcus, ed. *The American Novel Since World War II.* Greenwich, Conn.: Fawcett, 1969.

Klinkowitz, Jerome. *The Life of Fiction.* Urbana: University of Illinois Press, 1977.

———. *Literary Disruptions: The Making of a Post-Contemporary American Fiction.* Urbana: University of Illinois Press, 1975.

Le Vot, Andre. "Disjunctive and Conjunctive Modes in Contemporary American Fiction." *Forum* 14, no. 1 (1976): 44–55.

McConnell, Frank D. *Four Postwar American Novelists: Bellow, Mailer, Barth and Pynchon.* Chicago: University of Chicago Press, 1977.

Martin, Richard. "Clio Bemused: The Uses of History in Contemporary American Fiction." *Sub-Stance* 27 (1980): 13–24.

Olderman, Raymond. *Beyond the Wasteland: The American Novel in the Nineteen-Sixties.* New Haven, Conn.: Yale University Press, 1972.

Pearce, Richard. *Stages of the Clown.* Carbondale: Southern Illinois University Press, 1970.

Rother, James. "Parafiction: The Adjacent Universe of Barth, Barthelme, Pynchon, and Nabokov." *boundary 2* 5 (1976): 21–43.

Rubin, Louis D., Jr. *The Teller in the Tale.* Seattle: University of Washington Press, 1967.

Rupp, Richard H. *Celebration in Postwar American Fiction.* Coral Gables, Fla.: University of Miami Press, 1970.

Russell, Charles. "The Vault of Language: Self-Reflective Artifice in Contemporary American Fiction." *Modern Fiction Studies* 20 (Autumn 1974): 349–59.

Schulz, Max F. *Black Humor Fiction of the Sixties: A Pluralistic Definition of Man and His World.* Athens: Ohio University Press, 1973.

Stark, John O. *The Literature of Exhaustion.* Durham, N.C.: Duke University Press, 1974.

Stevick, Philip. "Scheherezade Runs Out of Plots, Goes on Talking; The King, Puzzled, Listens: An Essay on 'New Fiction.'" *Tri-Quarterly* 26 (1973): 332–62.

Sukenick, Ronald. "Fiction in the Seventies: Ten Digressions on Ten Digressions." *Studies in American Fiction* 5, no. 1 (1977): 99–108.

Tanner, Tony. *City of Words: American Fiction, 1950–1970.* New York: Harper and Row, 1971.

———. "My Life in American Literature." *Tri-Quarterly* 30 (1974): 83–109.

———. *The Reign of Wonder: Naivety and Reality in American Literature.* 1965; reprint, Cambridge: Cambridge University Press, 1977.

Waldmeir, Joseph J., ed. *Recent American Fiction: Some Critical Views.* Boston: Houghton Mifflin, 1963.

Wallace, Ronald. *The Last Laugh: Form and Affirmation in the Contemporary American Comic Novel.* Columbia: University of Missouri Press, 1979.

Weinberg, Helen A. *The New Novel in America: The Kafkan Mode in Contemporary Fiction.* Ithaca, N.Y.: Cornell University Press, 1971.

West, Paul. "Sheer Fiction: Mind and the Fabulist's Mirage." *New Literary History* 7 (Spring 1976): 549–63.

Wilde, Alan. "Barthelme Unfair to Kierkegaard: Some Thoughts on Modern and Postmodern Irony." *boundary 2* 5 (Fall 1976): 45–70.

V. Works on Individual Authors

Adam, Ian W. "Society as Novelist." *Journal of Aesthetics and Art Criticism* 25 (1967): 375–86.

Adams, Timothy Dow. "Obscuring the Muse: The Mock-

Autobiographies of Ronald Sukenick." *Critique* 20, no. 1 (1978): 27–39.

Alldredge, Betty. "Spatial Form in Faulkner's *As I Lay Dying.*" *Southern Literary Journal* 11 (Fall 1978): 3–19.

Bader, Julia. *Crystal Land: Artifice in Nabokov's English Novels.* Berkeley: University of California Press, 1972.

Banning, Charles Leslie. "William Gaddis' *JR:* The Organization of Chaos and the Chaos of Organization." *Paunch* 42–43 (1975): 153–56.

Bassoff, Bruce. "Gertrude Stein's 'Composition as Explanation.'" *Twentieth Century Literature* 24 (1978): 76–80.

———. "Mythic Truth and Deception in *Second Skin.*" *Etudes Anglaises* 30 (1977): 337–42.

Baum, Catherine B. "'The Beautiful One': Caddy Compson as Heroine of *The Sound and the Fury.*" *Modern Fiction Studies* 13 (1967): 33–44.

Bedient, Calvin. "Pride and Nakedness: *As I Lay Dying.*" *Modern Language Quarterly* 29 (1968): 61–76.

Beml, Maxy. "William Burroughs and the Invisible Generation." *Telos* 13 (1972): 125–31.

Bienstock, Beverly Gray. "Lingering on the Autognostic Verge: John Barth's *Lost in the Funhouse.*" *Modern Fiction Studies* 19 (1973): 68–78.

Blanchard, Margaret. "The Rhetoric of Communion: Voice in *The Sound and the Fury.*" *American Literature* 41 (1970): 555–65.

Bleikasten, Andre. *Faulkner's* As I Lay Dying. Translated by Roger Little with the author. Bloomington: Indiana University Press, 1973.

———. *The Most Splendid Failure: Faulkner's* The Sound and the Fury. Bloomington: Indiana University Press, 1976.

Bradbury, Malcolm. "Hello, Dollar." *New Statesman* 91 (18 June 1976): 820–21.

Bradbury, Nicola. *Henry James: The Later Novels.* Oxford: Clarendon Press, 1979.

Bradford, M. E. "Addie Bundren and the Design of *As I Lay Dying.*" *Southern Review* 6 (1970): 1093–99.

Brantley, John D. *The Fiction of John Dos Passos.* The Hague: Mouton, 1968.

Bridgman, Richard. "Melanctha." *American Literature* 33 (1961): 350–59.

Brooke-Rose, Christine, "The Squirm of the True: An Essay in Non-

Methodology." *PTL: A Journal for Descriptive Poetics and Theory of Literature* 1 (1976): 265–94.

―――. "The Squirm of the True: A Structural Analysis of Henry James's *The Turn of the Screw.*" *PTL: A Journal for Descriptive Poetics and Theory of Literature* 1 (1976): 513–46.

―――. "Surface Structure in Narrative: The Squirm of the True, Part III." *PTL: A Journal for Descritive Poetics and Theory of Literature* 3 (1977): 517–62.

Burroughs, William. "William Burroughs." An interview in *Writers at Work: The Paris Review Interviews,* 3d series. Edited by George Plimpton. New York: Viking, 1967. Pp. 141–74.

Busch, Frederick. *Hawkes: A Guide to His Fictions.* Syracuse, N.Y.: Syracuse University Press, 1973.

Chatman, Seymour. *The Later Style of Henry James.* New York: Barnes and Noble, 1972.

Clark, E. W. "Ironic Effects of Multiple Perspectives in *As I Lay Dying.*" *Notes on Mississippi Writers* 5 (1972): 15–28.

Collins, Carvel. "The Interior Monologues of *The Sound and the Fury.*" In *English Institute Essays.* Edited by Alan S. Downer. New York: Columbia University Press, 1954. Pp. 29–56.

Copeland, Carolyn F. *Language and Time and Gertrude Stein.* Iowa City: University of Iowa Press, 1975.

Cordesse, Gerard. "The Science Fiction of William Burroughs." *Caliban* 12 (1975): 33–43.

Cowan, Michael H., ed. *Twentieth Century Interpretations of* The Sound and the Fury. Englewood Cliffs, N.J.: Prentice-Hall, 1968.

Cowley, Malcolm. "Dos Passos: Poet against the World." In *After the Genteel Tradition: American Writers, 1910–1930.* Edited by Malcolm Cowley. Carbondale: Southern Illinois University Press, 1965. Pp. 134–46.

Curtsinger, E. C. "*The Turn of the Screw* as Writer's Parable." *Studies in the Novel* 12 (Winter 1980): 344–58.

Davis, Robert Gorham. *John Dos Passos.* Minneapolis: University of Minnesota Press, 1962.

DeKoven, Marianne. "Gertrude Stein and Modern Painting: Beyond Literary Cubism." *Contemporary Literature* 22 (Winter 1981): 81–95.

Diggins, John P. "Visions of Chaos and Visions of Order: Dos Passos as Historian." *American Literature* 46 (1974): 329–46.

Eliot, T. S. "From 'Henry James.'" In *Selected Prose of T. S. Eliot.* Edited by Frank Kermode. New York: Harcourt Brace Jovanovich, 1975. Pp. 151–52.

Evans, Oliver. *Anaïs Nin.* Carbondale: Southern Illinois University Press, 1968.

Felman, Shoshana. "Turning the Screw of Interpretation." *Yale French Studies* 55/56 (1977): 94–207.

Ferguson, Suzanne. "The Face in the Mirror: Authorial Presence in the Multiple Vision of the Third-Person Impressionist Narrative." *Criticism* 21 (Summer 1979): 230–50.

Field, Andrew. *Nabokov: A Bibliography.* New York: McGraw Hill, 1973.

Fitz, L. T. "Gertrude Stein and Picasso: The Language of Surfaces." *American Literature* 45 (1973): 228–37.

Flower, Timothy F. "The Scientific Art of Nabokov's *Pale Fire.*" *Criticism* 17 (1975): 223–33.

Foley, Barbara. "From *U.S.A.* to *Ragtime:* Notes on the Forms of Historical Consciousness in Modern Fiction." *American Literature* 50 (March 1978): 85–105.

———. "History, Fiction, and Satirical Form: The Example of Dos Passos' *1919.*" *Genre* 12 (Fall 1979): 357–78.

———. "The Treatment of Time in *The Big Money:* An Examination of Ideology and Literary Form." *Modern Fiction Studies* 26 (Autumn 1980): 447–67.

Fox-Genovese, Elizabeth. "*JR* by William Gaddis." *New Republic,* February 7, 1976, pp. 29–30.

Franklin, Benjamin. *Anaïs Nin: A Bibliography.* Kent, Ohio: Kent State University Press, 1973.

Franklin, Benjamin, and Duane Schneider. *Anais Nin: An Introduction.* Athens, Ohio: Ohio University Press, 1979.

Franklin, R. W. "Narrative Management in *As I Lay Dying.*" *Modern Fiction Studies* 13 (1967): 57–66.

Fussell, Edwin. "The Ontology of *The Turn of the Screw.*" *Journal of Modern Literature* 8 (1980): 118–28.

Gardner, John. "Big Deals." *New York Review of Books,* June 10, 1976, pp. 35–40.

Garis, Robert. "The Two Lambert Strethers: A New Reading of *The Ambassadors.*" *Modern Fiction Studies* 7 (1961–62): 305–16.

Gass, William H. "Gertrude Stein and the Geography of the Sentence." In *The World within the Word.* New York: Alfred A. Knopf, 1978. Pp. 63–123.

Goldman, Arnold. "Dos Passos and His *U.S.A.*" *New Literary History* 1 (1970): 471–83.

Goodman, Michael. *William S. Burroughs: An Annotated Bibliography.* New York: Garland, 1975.

Grabes, H. *Fictitious Biographies: Vladimir Nabokov's English Novels.* The Hague: Mouton, 1977.

Greenstein, Susan M. *"The Ambassadors:* The Man of Imagination Encaged and Provided For." *Studies in the Novel* 9 (1977): 137–53.

Greiner, Donald J. *Comic Terror: The Novels of John Hawkes.* Memphis, Tenn.: Memphis State University Press, 1973.

Gwynn, Frederick L., and Joseph Blotner, eds. *Faulkner in the University.* New York: Vintage, 1965.

Haas, Robert Bartlett. *Gertrude Stein: A Primer for the Gradual Understanding of Gertrude Stein.* Santa Barbara, Calif.: Black Sparrow Press, 1976.

Hagopian, John V. "Nihilism in Faulkner's *The Sound and the Fury.*" *Modern Fiction Studies* 13 (1967): 45–56.

Hard, Nancy W. "A Novel in the Form of a Comic Strip: Nathanael West's *Miss Lonelyhearts.*" *Serif* 5 (1968): 14–21.

Harvey, W. J. "George Eliot and the Omniscient Author Convention." *Nineteenth Century Fiction* 13 (1958): 81–108.

Hassan, Ihab. "The Novel of Outrage: A Minority Voice in Postwar American Fiction." *The American Scholar* 34 (1965): 239–53.

———. "The Subtracting Machine: The Work of William S. Burroughs." *Critique* 6 (Spring 1963): 4–23.

Hawkes, John. *"The Floating Opera* and *Second Skin." Mosaic* 8, no. 1 (1974): 17–28.

———. "Response to Richard Yarborough." *Mosaic* 8, no. 1 (1974): 73–75.

———. "Response to Ron Imhof." *Mosaic* 8, no. 1 (1974): 61–63.

Higgins, Joanna A. "The Ambassadorial Motif in *The Ambassadors.*" *Journal of Narrative Technique* 8 (Fall 1978): 165–75.

Hinz, Evelyn. *A Woman Speaks: The Lectures, Seminars, and Interviews of Anaïs Nin.* Chicago: Swallow, 1975.

Hoffman, Frederick. *Gertrude Stein.* Minneapolis: University of Minnesota Press, 1961.

Hoffman, Michael J. *The Development of Abstractionism in the Writings of Gertrude Stein.* Philadelphia: University of Pennsylvania Press, 1965.

———. *Gertrude Stein.* London: Twayne, 1976.

Hughson, Lois. "Dos Passos's World War: Narrative Technique and History." *Studies in the Novel* 12 (Spring 1980): 46–61.

———. "In Search of the True America: Dos Passos' Debt to Whitman in *U.S.A.*" *Modern Fiction Studies* 19 (Summer 1973): 179–92.

Huntley, H. Robert. "James' *The Turn of the Screw:* 'Its Fine Machinery.'" *American Imago* 34 (Fall 1977): 224–37.

Imhof, Ron. "On *Second Skin.*" *Mosaic* 8, no. 1 (1974): 51–61.

Jason. Philip K. *Anaïs Nin Reader.* Chicago: Swallow, 1973.

Johnson, R. E., Jr. "'Bees Barking in the Night': The End and Beginning of Donald Bartheleme's Narrative." *boundary 2* 5 (Fall 1976): 71–83.

Kappeler, Susan. *Writing and Reading in Henry James.* New York: Columbia University Press, 1981.

Kartiganer, Donald M. *The Fragile Thread: The Meaning of Form in Faulkner's Novels.* Amherst: University of Massachusetts Press, 1979.

Kazin, Alfred. Introduction. In *The 42nd Parallel.* 1930; reprint, New York: New American Library, 1969, pp. v–xviii.

Kinney, Arthur F. *Faulkner's Narrative Poetics: Style as Vision.* Amherst: University of Massachusetts Press, 1979.

Klemtner, Susan Strehle. "'For a Very Small Audience': The Fiction of William Gaddis." *Critique* 19, no. 3 (1976): 61–73.

Knapp, Bettina L. *Anais Nin.* New York: Frederick Ungar, 1978.

Knox, George. "Voice in the *U.S.A.* Biographies." *Texas Studies in Literature and Language* 4 (1962): 109–16.

Kostelanetz, Richard. "From Nightmare to Serendipity: A Retrospective Look at William Burroughs." *Twentieth Century Literature* 11 (1965): 123–30.

Kozikowski, Stanley J. "Unreliable Narration in Henry James's 'The Two Faces' and Edith Wharton's 'The Dillettante.'" *Arizona Quarterly* 35 (1979): 357–71.

Krier, William J. "*Lost in the Funhouse:* 'A Continuing, Strange Love Letter.'" *boundary 2* 5 (Fall 1976): 103–16.

Kuehl, John. *John Hawkes and the Craft of Conflict.* New Brunswick, N.J.: Rutgers University Press, 1975.

Lavers, Norman. "The Structure of *Second Skin.*" *Novel* 5 (1972): 208–14.

LeClair, Thomas. "The Unreliability of Innocence: John Hawkes' *Second Skin.*" *Journal of Narrative Technique* 3 (1973): 32–39.

Lee, Brian. "History and John Dos Passos." In *The American Novel and the Nineteen Twenties.* Edited by Malcolm Cowley and David Palmer. London: Edward Arnold, 1971. Pp. 197–214.

Levin, Harry. "Revisiting Dos Passos' *U.S.A.*" *Massachusetts Review* 20 (Autumn 1979): 401–15.

Liston, Maureen. *Gertrude Stein: An Annotated Critical Bibliography.* Kent, Ohio: Kent State University Press, 1979.

Little, Matthew. "*As I Lay Dying* and 'Dementia Praecox' Humor." *Studies in American Humor* 2 (April 1975): 61–70.

Lodge, David. "Objections to William Burroughs." *Critical Quarterly* 8 (Autumn 1966): 203–12.

McBrien, William. "Anaïs Nin: An Interview." *Twentieth Century Literature* 20 (October 1974): 277–90.

McCaffery, Larry. "Donald Barthelme and the Metafictional Muse." *Sub-Stance* 27 (1980): 75–88.

———. "New Rules of the Game." *Chicago Review* 29, no. 1 (Summer 1977): 145–49.

McCarthy, Mary. "A Bolt from the Blue." *The New Republic,* June 4, 1964, pp. 21–27.

———. "Burroughs' *Naked Lunch.*" *Encounter* 20, no. 4 (1963): 92–98.

McConnell, Frank D. "William Burroughs and the Literature of Addiction." *Massachusetts Review* 8 (Autumn 1967): 665–80.

McLuhan, Herbert Marshall. "John Dos Passos: Technique vs. Sensibility." In *Modern American Fiction: Essays in Criticism.* Edited by A. Walton Litz. New York: Oxford University Press, 1963.

Marz, Charles. "Dos Passos's Newsreels: The Noise of History." *Studies in the Novel* 11 (Summer 1979): 194–200.

———. "*U.S.A.:* Chronicle and Performance." *Modern Fiction Studies* 26 (Autumn 1980): 398–415.

Maynard, Reid. "Abstractionism in Gertrude Stein's *Three Lives.*" *Ball State University Forum* 15, no. 1 (1973): 68–71.

Mazzella, Anthony J. "An Answer to the Mystery of *The Turn of the Screw.*" *Studies in Short Fiction* 17 (Summer 1980): 327–34.

Meriwether, James B., and Michael Millgate, eds. *Lion in the Garden: Interviews with William Faulkner.* New York: Random House, 1968.

Michelson, Peter. "Beardsley, Burroughs, Decadence and the Poetics of Obscenity." *Tri-Quarterly* 12 (1968): 139–55.

Miller, James E., ed. *Theory of Fiction: Henry James.* Lincoln: University of Nebraska Press, 1972.

Monaghan, David M. "The Single Narrator of *As I Lay Dying.*" *Modern Fiction Studies* 18 (1972): 213–20.

Moore, Steven. "Chronological Difficulties in the Novels of William Gaddis." *Critique* 22, no. 1 (1980): 79–91.

Morris, Christopher D. "Barth and Lacan: The World of the Moebius Strip." *Critique* 17, no. 1 (1975): 69–77.

Mosaic 2, no. 2 (1978): 1–212. (Entire issue devoted to Anaïs Nin.)

Mottram, Eric. *William Burroughs: The Algebra of Need.* New York: Intrepid Press, 1971.

Nardin, Jane. "*The Turn of the Screw:* The Victorian Background." *Mosaic* 12 (Fall 1978): 131–42.

Obuchowski, Peter. "Technique and Meaning in James's *The Turn of the Screw.*" *College Language Association Journal* 21 (March 1978): 380–89.

Odier, Daniel. *The Job: Interviews with William Burroughs.* New York: Grove, 1970.

O'Donnell, Patrick. "The Hero as Artist in John Hawkes's *Second Skin.*" *International Fiction Review* 4 (1977): 119–27.

O'Hara, J. D. "Boardwalk and Park Place vs. Chance and Peace of Mind." *Virginia Quarterly Review* 52 (Summer 1976): 523–26.

Pearce, Richard. "Enter the Frame." *Tri-Quarterly* 30 (Spring 1974): 71–82.

Perloff, Marjorie. "Poetry as Word-System: The Art of Gertrude Stein." *American Poetry Review* 8, no. 5 (1979): 33–43.

Peterson, R.G. "A Picture Is a Fact: Wittgenstein and *Naked Lunch.*" *Twentieth Century Literature* 12 (July 1966): 78–86.

Pierce, Constance. "Being, Knowing, and Saying in the 'Addie' Section of *As I Lay Dying.*" *Twentieth Century Literature* 26 (Fall 1980): 294–305.

Pifer, Ellen. *Nabokov and the Novel.* Cambridge, Mass.: Harvard University Press, 1981.

Pizer, Donald. "The Camera Eye in *U.S.A.*: The Sexual Center." *Modern Fiction Studies* 26 (Autumn 1980): 417–30.

Poulet, Georges. "Henry James." In his *The Metamorphoses of the Circle.* Translated by Carley Dawson and Elliot Coleman. Baltimore, Md.: Johns Hopkins University Press, 1966. Pp. 307–20.

Reilly, Charlie. "An Interview with John Barth." *Contemporary Literature* 22 (Winter 1981): 1–23.

Rimmon, Shlomith. *The Concept of Ambiguity—The Example of James.* Chicago: University of Chicago Press, 1977.

Rooks, George. "Vardaman's Journey in *As I Lay Dying.*" *Arizona Quarterly* 35 (Summer 1979): 114–28.

Rose, Marilyn Gaddis. "Gertrude Stein and Cubist Narrative." *Modern Fiction Studies* 22 (1976–1977): 543–55.

Ross, Stephen M. "'Voice' in Narrative Texts: The Example of *As I Lay Dying.*" *PMLA* 94 (March 1979): 300–310.

Roth, Phyllis A. "The Psychology of the Double in Nabokov's *Pale Fire.*" *Essays in Literature* 2 (1975): 209–29.

Rowe, William Woodin. *Nabokov's Deceptive World.* New York: New York University Press, 1971.

Russell, Charles. "Individual Voice in the Collective Discourse: Literary Innovation in Postmodern American Fiction." *Sub-Stance* 27 (1980): 29–39.

Sanders, David, ed. *The Merrill Studies in* U.S.A. Columbus, Ohio: Charles E. Merrill, 1972.

Schmitz, Neil. "Portrait, Patriarchy, Mythos: The Revenge of Gertrude Stein." *Salmagundi* 40 (1978): 69–91.

Schneider, Daniel. *The Crystal Cage: Adventures of the Imagination in the Fiction of Henry James.* Lawrence, Kan.: Regents Press of Kansas, 1978.

Shoemaker, Alice. "A Wheel within a Wheel: Fusion of Form and Content in Faulkner's *As I Lay Dying.*" *Arizona Quarterly* 35 (Summer 1979): 101–13.

Spencer, Sharon. *Collage of Dreams: The Writings of Anaïs Nin.* Chicago: Swallow, 1977.

Stegner, Page. *Escape into Aesthetics: The Art of Vladimir Nabokov.* New York: Dial Press, 1966.

Stein, Gertrude. *Narration.* Chicago: University of Chicago Press, 1935.

Steiner, George. "Books: Crossed Lines." *The New Yorker,* January 26, 1976, pp. 106–9.

Stewart, Allegra. "The Quality of Gertrude Stein's Creativity." *Bibliography of American Literature* 28 (1957): 488–506.

Stimpson, Catherine R. "The Mind, the Body, and Gertrude Stein." *Critical Inquiry* 3 (1977): 489–506.

Stone, Albert E., ed. *Twentieth Century Interpretations of* The Ambassadors. Englewood Cliffs, N.J.: Prentice-Hall, 1969.

Stubbs, John C. "John Hawkes and the Dream-World of *The Lime Twig* and *Second Skin.*" *Literature and Psychology* 21, no. 3 (1971): 149–60.

Stull, William. "The Quest and the Question: Cosmology and Myth in the Work of William S. Burroughs, 1953–1960." *Twentieth Century Literature* 24 (1978): 225–42.

Sutherland, Donald. *Gertrude Stein: A Biography of Her Work.* New Haven, Conn.: Yale University Press, 1951.

Tanner, James E. "Experimental Styles Compared: E. E. Cummings and William Burroughs." *Style* 10 (Winter 1976): 1–27.

Tatham, Campbell. "Message (Concerning the *FELT* Ultimacies of One John Barth)." *boundary 2* 3 (1975): 259–88.

Tharpe, Jac. *John Barth: The Comic Sublimity of Paradox.* Carbondale: Southern Illinois University Press, 1974.

Thomas, William. "The Author's Voice in *The Ambassadors.*" *Journal of Narrative Technique* 1 (1971): 108–21.

Tilford, John E. "James the Old Intruder." *Modern Fiction Studies* 4 (1958): 157–64.

Todorov, Tzvetan. "The Verbal Age." *Critical Inquiry* 4 (1977): 351–72.

Twentieth Century Literature 24 (1978): 1–134. (Gertrude Stein issue.)

Veeder, William. "Strether and the Transcendence of Language." *Modern Philology* 69 (1971): 116–32.

Vitanza, Victor J. "The Novelist as Topologist: John Barth's *Lost in the Funhouse.*" *Texas Studies in Language and Literature* 19 (Spring 1977): 83–97.

Wagner, Linda W. *Dos Passos: Artist as American.* Austin: University of Texas Press, 1979.

Wallace, Ronald. "Comic Form in *The Ambassadors.*" *Genre* 5 (1972): 31–50.

———. "The Rarer Action: Comedy in John Hawkes's *Second Skin.*" *Studies in the Novel* 9 (1977): 169–86.

Wasiolek, Edward. "*As I Lay Dying:* Distortion in the Slow Eddy of Current Opinion." *Critique* 3 (Spring/Fall 1959): 15–23.

Watt, Ian. "The First Paragraph of *The Ambassadors:* An Explication." *Essays in Criticism* 10 (1960): 250–74.

Weeks, Robert P. "The Novel as Poem: Whitman's Legacy to Dos Passos." *Modern Fiction Studies* 26 (Autumn 1980): 431–46.

Weinstein, Norman. *Gertrude Stein and the Literature of Modern Consciousness.* New York: Frederick Ungar, 1970.

Weisenburger, Steven. "Contra Naturam?: Usury in William Gaddis's *JR.*" *Genre* 13 (Spring 1980): 93–110.

Westervelt, Linda A. "Teller, Tale, Told: Relationships in John Barth's Latest Fictions." *Journal of Narrative Technique* 8 (Winter 1978): 42–55.

Wyrick, Deborah. "Dadaist Collage Structure and Nathanael West's *Dream Life of Balso Snell.*" *Studies in the Novel* 11 (Fall 1979): 349–59.

Yarborough, Richard. "Hawkes's *Second Skin.*" *Mosaic* 8, no. 1 (Fall 1974): 65–73.

Zaller, Robert, ed. *A Casebook on Anaïs Nin.* New York: New American Library, 1974.

VI. Novels Discussed

Abish, Walter. *Alphabetical Africa.* New York: New Directions, 1974.

Barth, John. *Lost in the Funhouse.* 1968; reprint, New York: Bantam, 1969.

Barthelme, Donald. *City Life.* 1970; reprint, New York: Bantam, 1971.

———. *Snow White.* 1965; reprint, New York: Atheneum, 1967.

Burroughs, William S. *Naked Lunch.* New York: Grove Press, 1959.

Chambers, George. *The Bonnyclabber.* n.p.: Panache and December, 1972.

Dos Passos, John. *The 42nd Parallel.* 1930; reprint, New York: New American Library, 1958.

———. *Nineteen Nineteen.* 1932; reprint, New York: New American Library, 1960.

———. *The Big Money.* 1933; reprint, New York: New American Library, 1964.

Faulkner, William. *As I Lay Dying.* 1930; reprint, New York: Random House, 1964.

———. *The Sound and the Fury.* 1929; reprint, New York: Random House, 1946.

Federman, Raymond. *Double or Nothing.* Chicago: Swallow Press, 1971.

———. *Take It or Leave It.* New York: Fiction Collective, 1976.

Gaddis, William. *JR.* New York: Alfred A. Knopf, 1975.

Hawkes, John. *Second Skin.* New York: New Directions, 1964.

Hawthorne, Nathaniel. *The Scarlet Letter.* Edited by Sculley Bradley et al. New York: W. W. Norton, 1962.

James, Henry. Norton Critical Edition of *The Ambassadors.* Edited by S. P. Rosenbaum. New York: W. W. Norton, 1964.

———. *The Awkward Age.* 1899; reprint, Middlesex, England: Penguin, 1966.

———. Norton Critical Edition of *The Turn of the Screw.* Edited by Robert Kimbrough. New York: W. W. Norton, 1966.

Nabokov, Vladimir. *Pale Fire.* 1962; reprint, New York: Berkley Medallion, 1968.

Nin, Anaïs. *Collages.* Chicago: Swallow, 1964.

Sorrentino, Gilbert. *Splendide-Hotel.* New York: New Directions, 1973.

Stein, Gertrude. *Three Lives.* 1909; reprint, New York: Vintage Books, n.d.

Sukenick, Ronald. *98.6.* New York: Fiction Collective, 1975.

———. *Out.* Chicago: Swallow, 1973.

———. *uP.* New York: Delta Books, 1968.

Index